Emotional Life and the Politics of Welfare

Paul Hoggett
Professor of Politics and
Director of the Centre for Social and Economic Research
University of the West of England
Bristol

Foreword by

Fiona Williams
Professor of Social Policy
University of Leeds

Consultant Editor: Jo Campling

First published in Great Britain 2000 by
MACMILLAN PRESS LTD
Houndmills, Basingstoke, Hampshire RG21 6XS and London
Companies and representatives throughout the world

A catalogue record for this book is available from the British Library.

ISBN 0–333–76071–9

 First published in the United States of America 2000 by
ST. MARTIN'S PRESS, LLC,
Scholarly and Reference Division,
175 Fifth Avenue, New York, N.Y. 10010

ISBN 0–312–23530–5

Library of Congress Cataloging-in-Publication Data
Hoggett, Paul.
Emotional life and the politics of welfare / Paul Hoggett ; foreword by Fiona
Williams.
p.   cm.
Includes bibliographical references and index.
ISBN 0–312–23530–5
1. Welfare state—Psychological aspects. 2. Public welfare—Psychological aspects.
3. Emotions—Sociological aspects. 4. Social psychology. 5. Social policy. I. Title.

JC479 .H64   2000
361.6'5—dc21

00–038235

This book is printed on paper suitable for recycling and made from fully managed and sustained
forest sources.

10   9   8   7   6   5   4   3   2   1
09   08   07   06   05   04   03   02   01   00

Printed and bound in Great Britain by
Antony Rowe Ltd, Chippenham, Wiltshire

For John, James and Jenny

Contents

Foreword

Now is the time to re-imagine our welfare futures. The transformations currently taking place in welfare states in the west are as significant as those that followed the Second World War. In Britain, the aims, purposes and values of welfare reforms are central to the articulation of the 'Third Way', a new democratic programme that seeks to transcend both 'old' social democracy and neo-liberalism (upon whose parentage these new politics are predicated). The attempt to articulate a new (or not-so-new) social, moral and welfare order gives ideas about future welfare an enhanced currency.

If we are to use this new space to the full, we need the freedom to roam across disciplinary boundaries, over the terrain of our own and others' experiences, in and out the caves of our imaginations, unleashing our minds and vocabularies to the elements. What a paradox, then, at the very political moment when such intellectual roaming is so important that, for academics and practitioners, the constraints against this have never seemed greater. Audits and assessments discipline us (in both senses) and time-regulate our productivity, driving our creativity into devising strategies to release ourselves from these bonds. Paul Hoggett's book is therefore a refreshing and invigorating intervention, which seizes the moment, and, as he puts it, 'mobilises fictions'. These fictions, or imaginings ('illusions which know themselves') are the stuff which connects our internal world of fear and need, of hate and envy, to the social world of relationships, groups, networks, communities and organisations.

The mobilisation of these fictions emerges from three important themes that underpin the book. The first, which transgresses the disciplinary divides, is that we have to pull together the internal world of the human subject on a continuum of understanding with the social world in which that subject exists. This pushes social and political theory beyond the point that it has so far reached. That is, it demands not simply that we examine the relationship between agency and structure, but that we examine that which constitutes agency. Our agency – our capacity and motivation for action – needs to be understood in terms of our intersubjectivity.

ix

Developing from the Object-Relations school of psychoanalysis and drawing on Klein, Bion and Winnicott, among others, Hoggett argues that at the core of ourselves is fear and self-alienation which is received and fed back to us by the social world – by our families, friends, colleagues – in ways which make us less or more able to deal with it. The capacity of that outside world to contain our internal fears, and by the same token, our own capacities to contain the fears of others, marks the quality of our social relations within society.

That which characterises the quality of social relations of gender, race, generation, between providers and users of welfare, within and between communities, is a second theme of the book. His analysis of the 'good enough conditions' for the containment of fear lead him to examine care, (inter)dependency, mutuality and solidarity as its key constituents. In doing this, he resurrects Titmuss's concept of the gift relationship but unlocks it from the bureaucratic-professional setting in which Titmuss placed it. This elaboration of care, interdependence and solidarity provides a welcome relief from the contemporary obsession with paid work and enlightened self-interest as the motor of society's moral regeneration. It also reminds us, as Nikolas Rose has pointed out, that it is on the terrain of ethics that our future political battles will be fought.

These conditions, Hoggett argues, also make possible the acceptance of difference within communities, and this relationship between difference and universalism marks out the third theme. The capacity of communities to hold their differences, while neither essentialising nor inferiorising some, is the crucial prerequisite for the development of locally run and locally organised welfare services. The final chapter follows this through and attempts to sketch out the key features of a welfare society that is universalist in principle and diverse in practice.

Hoggett's visions of a welfare society pick up those threads from the political struggles over welfare of the 1960s, 1970s and 1980s which were rendered invisible and invalid following the ascendancy of the New Right. While learning from the mistakes of this time, he captures its spirit through an insistence upon emancipatory politics organised in emancipatory ways. Such recall is important. The focus today upon global markets and quasi-markets and upon modernisation and managers threatens to consign any pre-1990s movements to the dustbin of the old and unreconstructed. In fact, these earlier local experiments in welfare services – from women's refuges, to community mental health services, to telephone help-lines, to self-help housing schemes – now constitute the basis of some of the best practices in welfare. They emerged from and sustained a political analysis which questioned the false universalism of the welfare state and the social relations through which it was delivered. What that analysis lacked was an understanding of the human subject, which could connect interiority to emancipatory goals. Finding this inner voice is what Paul Hoggett's book so ably helps us to do. We must use it to develop further these imaginings.

FIONA WILLIAMS
Professor of Social Policy
University of Leeds

Acknowledgements

Like most of my writing, this book has taken a full decade to accumulate. Two of the chapters are based on work I have published elsewhere. Chapter 4 is based on the article 'A place for experience: a psychoanalytic perspective on boundary, identity and culture', which first appeared in *Environment & Planning D: Society & Space*, 1992, 10, pp. 345–56 (Pion Limited, London). Chapter 8 was given as a paper at the International Centennial Conference on the work of W.R. Bion, in Turin in 1997 and appeared in the edited volume of conference papers *Bion's Legacy to Groups*, by Parthenope Bion, Franco Borgogno and Silvio Merciai (Karnac Books, 1998). For Chapter 5 I owe a great debt to Lyn Harrison and particularly to Syd Jeffers, two of my former colleagues at SAUS, University of Bristol. Anne-Marie Cummins, Elisha Davar, Robert French, Liz Lloyd, Chris Miller and Fiona Williams have offered really helpful feedback on all or parts of the text and Jo Campling and Nicola Bion have offered advice and encouragement for getting the book published. Thanks also to Sue Ollis and Sandra Stanleigh for helping me with some of the messiest bits of typing and to Angela Brooks and Karen Cox for help with text layout and just generally for being fun to be with.

Inspiration for the book originally came from students on the Masters in Policy Studies programme at SAUS who first gave me the confidence to believe that the emotional life of individuals and groups might have some relevance to understanding struggles within the welfare state. Over the last decade the book has benefited from collaborative work with many people. I'd particularly like to thank Danny Burns, Linda Martin, Caroline New and Simon Thompson. Other sources of insight, support and encouragement have come from David Armstrong, the Bristol Forum for Bosnia, John Clarke, Bob Gosling, Robin Hambleton, Gordon Lawrence and the Bion Reading Group, Julian Lousada, the Psychosocial Studies Research Group at UWE, the Red-Green Study Group, Erica Stern, Eileen Smith, Tara Weeramanthri, Bob Young and, in a less tangible but more enduring way, from Kate Barrows.

1
Unreasonable Subjects

Towards a generative welfare

Some fundamental questions are being asked of the welfare state in many European societies at the moment. From the political right, the magnitude of welfare spending and the balance between public and private provision has been consistently questioned since the impact of neo-liberalism in the early 1980s. From the so-called 'radical centre' the independence of social policy from economic policy has been questioned as attempts have been made to replace the idea of welfare as a means of redistribution with one which sees the value of welfare limited primarily to its contribution to wealth creation, that is, as something whose primary purpose is to construct a subject who is 'fit for labour'. Neither of these perspectives seems to offer an expansive vision of welfare, both assume that the 'onward march of welfare' has been halted. This is cause for much concern because, to the extent that the idea of common welfare draws attention to the intrinsic dignity and value of a society's citizens irrespective of their economic function, a welfare society can represent a different kind of social order, one in which decommodifying effects are maximised (Esping-Anderson, 1990). Thus while much intellectual effort has gone in to the defence of welfare, and rightly so, some voices have recently been heard calling for a new vision for welfare, a fundamental rethinking of the values and strategies on which welfare is based (Jordan, 1987; Doyal & Gough, 1991; Giddens, 1994; Leonard, 1997; Williams, 1998, 2000).

Central to this rethinking has been the rise of the new social movements based around so-called 'identity politics' and green politics. Suddenly a crowd of new terms – difference, diversity, respect, reflexivity, risk, hybridity, productivism, etc. – jostle for our attention alongside older ones such as equality, universality and solidarity. Nancy Fraser (1995) understands this development in terms of the rise of what she calls the new 'politics of recognition' alongside the old 'politics of redistribution'. Fraser (1995) uses the term 'recognition politics' to refer to the new struggles to valorise group identities and ways of living based around gender, ethnicity, different abilities and so on. While recognising the interpenetration of redistribution and recognition she insists upon the value of seeing the difference between economic and cultural injustice. While the remedy for economic injustice is some form of economic transformation involving a restructuring of capital-labour relations, the remedy for cultural injustice is some sort of cultural change:

> This could involve upwardly revaluing disrespected identities and the cultural products of maligned groups. It could also involve recognising and positively valorising cultural diversity. More radically still, it could involve the wholesale transformation of societal patterns of representation, interpretation and communication in ways that would change everybody's sense of self. (p. 73)

Fraser's analysis is an exciting one and has been taken up by Fiona Williams in her attempt to develop a new set of principles for welfare (Williams, 1998, 2000). But I have found Fraser's use of terms to be restricting, indeed much of the politics that I have identified with most over the last thirty years found no reflection there. The problem can be traced to the way in which Fraser chooses the generic term 'redistribution' to refer to the concerns of social democratic and socialist traditions in western thought. For, while Fraser makes it clear that under this heading she subsumes economic marginalisation, deprivation and exploitation, by choosing the term 'redistribution' she inevitably draws attention to the egalitarian impulse within these traditions while de-emphasising what I think of as the 'generative' impulse. By using the concept of generativity I am drawing attention to the idea of unrealised human powers and therefore the search for human relationships and social arrangements which can release and develop these powers. I have in mind a concept of individual and social development in which development is seen as the realisation of our aesthetic, moral, spiritual and practical capacities.

Like many radicals in the 1960s and 1970s in Britain I was repelled by Labourism not just because of its reformism but because of the way in which it construed socialism in a restricted way as the pursuit of equality. In contrast, Marxist and anarchist traditions focused on the issue of power and specifically struggles at the point of production around the social relations of production, i.e. capital and labour. Questions concerning peoples' position in the labour market and the distribution of the social product and attendant issues of poverty and social inequality were secondary to the struggle for power waged by the labour movement against the owners of capital and the controllers of the state apparatus. These traditions were concerned with the exploitation, commodification and alienation of human powers. Class struggle was seen as the struggle to release human powers from the chains of capital and the state. It was the transformation of social relations that was sought in order to bring about a society where peoples' aesthetic, moral and practical powers could flower free from exploitation. Fraser gives due recognition to this through her idea of the difference between affirmative and transformative political strategies but by casting both old and new forms of twentieth-century politics simply in terms of struggles for justice a great deal of what has been imagined by Marxists, anarchists, libertarian socialists, feminists and, more recently, by much of the Green movement can find no place. We don't just seek justice, we seek new kinds of freedoms and new forms of social relations.

The generative impulse within many twentieth-century political struggles has found expression in the work of a variety of recent writers. For example, it is present in much of Andre Gorz's (1985) work, particularly in his distinction between the heteronomous and autonomous spheres of life. More recently the generative impulse has found expression in the work of eco-socialists. Van Parijs and his colleagues (Van Der Veen & Van Parijs, 1987; Van Parijs, 1993) have provided a theoretical foundation for the Basic or Citizens' Income which stresses the generative possibilities inherent in what they call the conditions of 'weak abundance' (Van Parijs, 1993, p. 223) of late twentieth-century capitalism. It is as if we in the west are suspended somewhere between scarcity and post-scarcity society in which, for the majority there is now just enough to make the pursuit of freedom as pertinent as the quest for survival in everyday lives. In a partial and contradictory way the majority are increasingly becoming the 'leisure class' as the material conditions underpinning the work ethic are chipped away. Paradoxically we seem to be heading towards a socially polarised form of post-materialist society in which elements of the old and new orders exist side by side (Taylor-Gooby, 1999).

The concept of autonomy as a basic human need also surfaces in Doyal & Gough's (1991) recent contribution to British social policy. They define autonomy in terms of 'freedom of agency' (p. 67) and see it linked to three key variables: the degree of understanding a person has of herself and her culture, her cognitive and emotional capacities and 'the objective opportunities enabling her to act' (p. 60). When Doyal & Gough cite Raz (1986) approvingly, 'autonomous persons are those who can shape their life and determine its course', they are not very far away from Giddens and his concept of 'individuation'. Giddens links this term to its opposite, 'tradition-alisation' (1994). For Giddens modernity has had a fundamentally de-traditionalising effect upon peoples' lives in western societies, 'where everything that used to be natural (or traditional) now has in some sense to be chosen or decided about' (p. 90). Giddens argues that we require a new concept of welfare (what he calls 'positive welfare') for a de-traditionalised society in which the needs for 'security, self-respect and self-actualization' (p. 191) have become paramount.

Interestingly enough, Giddens (1994) also deploys the concept of 'generativity' extensively and it is worth taking a few moments to distinguish my own usage of this term from his. In his *Beyond Left & Right* Giddens (1994) introduces a series of novel concepts to facilitate our rethinking of welfare. First of all Giddens argues that one of the consequences of globalisation and modernity is that we now, collectively, face a number of challenges – ethical, ecological, technological – which defy traditonal 'left/right' political strategies. 'Life politics, and the disputes and struggles connected with it, are about how we should live in a world where everything that used to be natural (or traditional) now has in some sense to be chosen, or decided about' (Giddens, 1994, p. 91). For Giddens, life politics is about 'how we should live' and it is epitomised by the politics of the personal and by ecological concerns. Secondly, and drawing extensively upon alternative models of development from the 'Third World', Giddens introduces the concept of 'generative politics'. As he puts it, 'generative politics is a politics which seeks to allow individuals and groups to make things happen, rather than have things happen to them' (p. 15). This is a highly ambiguous phrase, one which could be praised by both the traditional left (self-management) and the traditional right (self-help). My sense is that this is as Giddens means it, that this is his way of transcending left and right. Unfortunately I feel he provides us more with a fudge than a transcendence. For example, in his chapter on 'generative politics and positive welfare' it becomes clear, both in the context of developing countries and advanced welfare states like Britain's, that behind the radical rhetoric of generative politics Giddens concurs with the traditional critique of the so-called 'dependency culture'. One can see why he has become Tony Blair's advisor, for here is the theoretical camouflage for the new spin-speak – 'not hand outs but hand ups', 'helping people to help themselves', etc. What is missing is any sense of power, domination, oppression, capitalism, imperialism, racism, etc. which might help us understand why poor people are as they are. In twenty years Giddens has moved from a kind of neo-Marxism to a period of questioning structuralism and objectivism to a situation where any idea of structure has disappeared altogether. Not surprisingly, in many places Giddens's 'analysis is in fact deeply voluntaristic. In a number of places he quite explicitly appears to reduce the complex problems of powerlessness to peoples' mind-sets, as if poverty and oppression would disappear by fiat if only everyone learnt to think differently (pp. 181, 191). There is no sense of the other, the antagonist, the opponent, here; rich and poor, capitalist and worker, male and female, black and white, presumably just have to come together 'in terms of mutual collaboration to overcome collective "bads"' (p. 191) because the accumulating contradictions of modernity (p. 193) demand it.

Giddens's analysis is strong on values, weak on means. His observations on the limited ethical horizons which guided the traditional left are spot on, as is his endeavour to link notions of positive welfare to broader conceptions of the good life and psychological well-being. But, eschewing any grand theories, his analysis at times seems lightweight, veering towards the humanistic self-actualising psychology of Maslow and American management-speak. Some of this by now sounds so tired, 'a person able to translate potential threats into rewarding challenges' (p. 192) – again one can hear Blair practising in the background. As Ian Craib (1992) so rightly observed, Giddens has ended up offering something which lacks depth. It's all too easy, we neither face external enemies nor are we enemies to ourselves.

Struggles for recognition and development

While the struggle for human and social development clearly over-laps with struggles for redistribution and recognition I feel there is something to be gained by not equating development with the latter. In what follows I will examine the concept of recognition through the work of Axel Honneth (1995), probably its most powerful con-temporary exponent, in order to trace the links between recognition and development. At the heart of discourses of recognition is the concept of identity and struggles around identity. Honneth out-lines three different sources of recognition the first of which primarily concerns our individual identity, the second and third of which refer more to our group identity. In social policy, David Taylor (1998) has recently made a similar distinction in drawing attention to the difference between 'ontological identity' (a deep psychologi-cal sense of self) and 'categorical identity' (membership of a group who identify themselves in the same way). In Chapter 5 of this book I will illustrate this distinction through the example of Mo, a nineteen-year-old Bengali Cockney.

Honneth suggests that the foundation of our individual identity is derived from the recognition we receive in our most intimate relations. The experience of reliable care and love in the family enables the child to develop what Honneth (p. 107) calls 'self-confidence'. Far from this being linked in any way with a brash or arrogant sense of worth, Honneth sees self-confidence in terms of security in one's sense of being. Here and elsewhere he draws heavily on the work of D.W. Winnicott, the paediatrician and psychoana-lyst. For Winnicott (1971), the establishment of a secure sense of being has developmental primacy over capacities relating to 'doing' and 'being done to'. Winnicott sees 'being' not as a solitary state but as a fundamentally social one, it is equivalent to the develop-ment of a sense of a benign and reliable human environment which is not just 'out there' but which is also inside oneself. This is what we mean by intersubjectivity, the sense of being with others even when we are alone. Well-being, then, is equivalent to being well with others. It draws our attention to the quality of the human relationships in which we are immersed. Just as good social rela-tions are indispensable to our well-being, so being well is indispensable to our agency in life. Thus, drawing on Winnicott, Honneth sees the 'capacity to be alone' as equivalent to 'the degree of basic indi-vidual self-confidence indispensable for participation in public life'

(p. 107). Very often, people who experience breakdown lose this capacity to be alone, instead what they experience is the most terrible solitude; it is as if they live in exile both from an internal community, a place of connection to others in their mind, and from the actual external world upon which they depend to survive (Glass, 1989; Hoggett, 1993).

From this basic foundation, 'this fundamental level of emotional confidence' (p. 107), the human subject is able to engage in two further struggles for recognition. The struggle for 'self-respect' revolves around our most abstract rather than intimate relations. It refers to the recognition of one's legal personhood by the universalised other that is the state. Here recognition is expressed through rights rather than love. Honneth (pp. 115ff.) draws on Marshall's (1963) concept of citizenship to argue that 'one is now respected with regard not only to the abstract capacity to orient oneself *vis-à-vis* moral norms, but also to the concrete human feature that one deserves the social standard of living necessary for this' (p. 117). Finally, Honneth refers to the struggle for self-esteem, something which is derived from the recognition of one's traits and abilities by the 'communities of value' to which one belongs. Self-esteem is contingent not only on recognition by one's group but also upon recognition of the value of one's group by society as a whole.

Returning now to Fraser's argument, although the fit is not perfect, identity-group politics is clearly linked to Honneth's notion of self-esteem whereas the politics of redistribution is much more closely linked to self-respect. As Fraser notes, for Honneth the struggle for recognition is the primary motor of political life underlying struggles around distribution and group identity. Fraser acknowledges the overlap between these two forms of struggle. Within social policy, for example, this is expressed in the struggle of groups such as people with learning difficulties both for basic citizenship rights and for the cultural revaluation of themselves as a group.

But what of the first and, according to Honneth, the primary form of recognition which provides the foundation for our well-being, for this seems to coincide neither with struggles around distribution nor identity-group politics? Clearly the question of the basic bodily integrity of the individual, i.e. the status of our physical being, is a political issue as it finds expression in struggles around cultural practices involving the bodily disfigurement of the young, around rape, child abuse, the use of torture, corporal punishment and so on (Williams, 1998). But, other than this vitally important area, are we to conclude that the struggle to provide a firm foundation for our individual identity is one which lies entirely outside of politics, i.e. as something which belongs properly to the sphere of the psychological rather than the political?

One of the main aims of this book is to offer the alternative perspective. Far from being something with no political consequences I will argue that the struggle for well-being and the development of human powers has a great deal to tell us about the realisation of agency and the unfolding of the generative impulse both at the level of the individual in 'coming to voice' (Chapter 6) and of the group in its use of creative illusion as a mobilising device (Chapter 7). The construction of ontological identity also has much to tell us about some of the dynamic processes underlying the development of group identities. Boundaries are vital to both forms of identity, and Chapter 4 examines the vagaries of boundary construction processes, particularly when the individual or group is besieged by fear. Individual development requires a form of understanding from the other which Winnicott terms 'unintrusive'. The child seeks recognition in its own right, in its own separateness and difference, rather than an imperialistic understanding which seeks to assimilate it into the other's schema. Several of the chapters in this book, but particularly Chapter 3, explore the nature of understanding and specifically the relationship between similarity, difference and understanding.

The last two chapters of this book more explicitly take on the task of sketching what a model of generative welfare might look like. They focus more at the level of principles and practices than policies and programmes largely because I have little experience of the latter and would inevitably say a lot that was naïve. In a strange sort of way you can see echoes of a generative approach in Labour's 'third way' policies and the idea that welfare should empower people rather than just help them survive. But this is empowerment for exploitation. Workfare is a deeply corrupted idea of the reduced human possibilities available to the structurally unemployed in a polarised society.

I would like to think that throughout this book there lies an implicit or quietly spoken perspective from which individual well-being and human development are seen as a metaphor for the generative impulse and those social conditions which make its unfolding possible. I prefer the notion of 'development' to autonomy as used by Doyal & Gough (1991) for, although they are aware of and seek to answer both forms of criticism (p. 64ff.), the concept of autonomy to my mind remains too closely associated to western capitalist discourses of independence and rationality. In contrast the very idea of human development presupposes a self engaged in interdependent relations with others. Human powers are therefore realised through others. When I speak of the 'generative impulse' what I therefore have in mind is the idea of the realisation of human powers – our moral, aesthetic, spiritual and practical possibilities – a theme one can trace back in western thought to Kant and later, to Marx and Freud, and more recently to some of the work of Habermas (1972).

A grounded subject

Although I deal extensively in this book with the group and group identity, my primary focus is the struggle that is individual development and how we might learn about the political from the personal. So when I speak of the 'subject' I do so in a slightly unfashionable way – as a concrete, embodied individual being engaged in here-and-now relations. Indeed, it is precisely this kind of subject which has been largely absent from much recent social and political theory. This might seem like a rather odd assertion given that the theme of identity has been crucial to many contemporary sociological debates about gender, sexuality, ethnicity and race. In recent years these debates have found a new resonance in British social policy as a number of writers have begun to examine the implications of post-modernism for the way in which we think about welfare (Carter, 1998; Hilyard & Watson, 1996; Kirkpatrick, 1996; Taylor, 1998; Taylor-Gooby, 1994). But there is a sense in which I have found the contemporary sociological interest in subjectivity quite frustrating, and this no doubt has something to do with my own background. Before I came to academic life I worked in a community mental health centre and ever since then I have been preoccupied with making sense of the joy and sorrow of what it means to be human in these closing decades of the twentieth century. To listen to someone talking to me about the voices in her head or to share with someone her despair about the way in which she tends to destroy the intimate relations she most values seems a far cry from the rather abstract debates about the subject which seem to dominate the academic world. With a few notable exceptions, and the writing of bell hooks (1989) springs to mind immediately, these debates seem unable to connect to raw human experience, particularly to emotional experiences such as anger, love or hatred.

Standing above many of these debates, watching over them, is the figure of Foucault (Gribbins, 1998). To Foucault we owe the debt of a way seeing where power is ubiquitous. Power is the medium of all human interaction. Suddenly discursive practices are everywhere constituting the gendered or racialised nature of our subjectivity. Much of this perspective is one I accept. One only has to read some of Freud's original case studies to see the power of Foucault's examination of the history of sexuality. One only has to look critically at the interaction between doctor and patient or housing officer and tenant to see the way in which these subject positions – patient, tenant – are constituted by the discursive practices of contemporary welfare professionalism. Yet something is eerily familiar with such accounts and something is also missing.

What is familiar is the tendency to provide an 'over-socialised' account of human behaviour (Shilling, 1997) which, like the Marxism that preceded it, provides no space with which to grasp the recalcitrance of the subject. For example, in their strong form both Marxism and Foucauldianism criticise the concept of human nature for being both normative and essentialist. But it strikes me that these positions are not free from ontology themselves. In their own way each makes similar assumptions about the nature of being. In particular, they both construe humanity in a peculiar and idiosyncratic way as if it were the only thing on earth with no grain or structure. If this is not quite the *tabula rasa* upon which society can inscribe what it will, then it is pretty close. It is as if the laws of nature apply only to the non-human world. This is a fundamentally conceited view which puts humanity somehow separate from and above nature, not of nature.

To repeat, I do not wish to deny that power is the medium in which all human interaction occurs. The personal is to some extent political. But I also wish to assert that there are aspects of our nature which are not only irreducible to the social but which give form and substance to the social itself. For example, and to put it inevitably crudely, societies are shaped by fear as well as giving shape to fears.

This brings me to the missing element within much postmodernist writing. While in the 1970s it was fashionable to speak of ideology and consciousness, in the 1980s and 1990s 'discourse' has definitely become the 'in' word. The name may have changed but the problem remains – how is it possible to understand any of the main issues of today simply in terms of systems of thought, meaning or representation? Can we understand racism in this way, or the nature of masculinity, or the place that ideas of 'community' have in the popular imagination? I would say not. I would say that our encounters with racism, masculinity and community are saturated with emotion.

What is really surprising, then, is how rationalistic the social sciences still are even though they developed in a century which has passed under the continuing shadow of Freud and even though it sometimes seems as if much of everyday life in this closing decade is in the grip of a therapeutic culture. But what do I mean by 'rationalistic' for, after all, reason and rationality are among the slipperiest terms we have? Indeed Freud regarded himself as a supreme rationalist referring only slightly ironically to 'our God reason' (Freud, 1927, p. 89).

First of all I have in mind an approach to the world which is preoccupied with thought and language, with the meanings people give to their behaviour and the behaviour of others, to signifying systems and discursive formations. All this existing alongside an absence of attention to emotion, sentiments, psychosomatic reactions, gut feelings, flows of affect, between people, within and between groups.

Secondly, I have in mind a preoccupation with intentionality, purpose, strategy, performativity, people as planners and shapers of their lives, creators of their own scripts, plucky troopers capable of agency in any kind of situation. All this existing alongside an absence of attention to self destructiveness, our ignorance of our own motives and those of others, the kind of stupidity which is born out of fear, the power of chance, accident, helplessness and vulnerability in all of our lives but also the creative contribution of spontaneity and impulse to cultural and political life. All of which is to say, in direct contrast to Doyal & Gough (1991, p. 65), that we normally act or fail to act, for better or worse, without fully knowing why. We act impulsively and spontaneously, and some of the most heroic and benign actions occur in this way as well as some of the most barbaric. And this is why it is apposite to speak of the *struggle* for human development. For the generative impulse not only faces inhibition or attack from the other but, as we shall see in Chapter 8, it is located within a subject which is often its own worst enemy. A realist account of human agency must squarely face the impact of fear, envy and other emotions upon our capacities to imagine, challenge, resist or lead.

I am therefore trying to draw attention to a contemporary rationalism which devalues emotion and affect and appears to deny the power of what is unthought and unthinkable in our lives. To give an example of what I mean: the idea that it is normal for parents (probably all parents) to hate their children and social workers and nurses to hate their clients and patients. To take this a bit further I am saying that there seems to be an unwillingness within the social sciences (though interestingly enough not within literature) to take the subject seriously. The most obvious consequence of this is a failure to come to terms with the negative emotions – hatred, murderousness, contempt and envy – and what (following the psychoanalyst Wilfred Bion (1967)) we might think of as our negative capacities. These refer to our capacities to prefer stupidity and mindlessness to painful awareness and to those dispositions within us which are anti-life, which seek to avoid human complexity and contradictoriness by choosing shallowness. Less obviously, for the same reasons we also lack a firm appreciation of all that is life-giving and life-enhancing in the human subject. As we shall see in Chapter 11, it is as if for some writers generosity or solidarity could be reduced to some kind of economic calculus of costs and benefits.

Bringing the subject back in to social science, bringing this loving/hating being back in to the way in which we think about families, community life, politics and the state, is equivalent to a plea for psychological realism. This is not just to suggest that most social scientists should go off and have a cold shower, though at times when Freud speaks of 'eduction to reality' (Freud, 1927, p. 81) it does seem that this is what psychoanalysis has in mind through its systematic attempt to rid us of the illusions that we have about ourselves. Bringing the subject back in can also serve to remind us of the good things that we are capable of. What I have in mind therefore is the need to develop a political culture which is both realist and visionary, one which retains a pessimism about the destructive acts we are capable of but also a passionate conviction that better forms of society are possible. And not just a better society, but that it is possible to create families, schools and welfare organisations which foster the development of human powers even within a global order which is deeply perverse and unjust. Holding this contradiction between realism and idealism in mind, one I've always thought of in terms of Gramsci's famous dictum 'pessimism of the intellect, optimism of the will', seems to be a central task for any renewed project of social transformation.

Why psychoanalysis?

There is a variety of possible psychologies which could be drawn upon to illuminate the subject in social science – attribution theory and others from social psychology, self theory from humanistic psychology, socio-biology, phenomenology and existentialism to name a few. But anyone concerned to understand the nature of powerful passions in everyday life and the public sphere is inevitably drawn towards psychodynamic approaches. The concept 'psychodynamic' is an inclusive term which simultaneously draws our attention to the psyche and to notions of tension and disequilibrium.

One of the great paradoxes of the social sciences in Britain lies in the way in which academia has recently looked across the sea to France in an attempt to incorporate a more psychodynamic account of the subject. This is surprising when one considers that one of the unique features of Britain since the 1930s has been the way in which its cultural life acted as midwife and parent to what has proved to be the two most powerful post-war traditions within the world psychoanalytic movement – the Kleinian and Object Relations schools (Kohon, 1986; Rustin, 1988). Moreover, the first of these is the only school within the psychoanalytic movement in which women have played an absolutely vital role in its development (Mitchell, 1986; Sayers, 1991). Rustin (1991) suggests that the answer to this paradox may be that the very strength of the British traditions, an empiricism which has meant that theory has been built upon the most detailed observations of infant development and the therapeutic encounter, has been ignored in preference to the intellectualism of Lacanian psychoanalysis.

This book draws avowedly upon the work of Klein and followers such as Bick, Bion, Rosenfeld and Meltzer (Anderson, 1992; Bleandonu, 1994; Segal, 1973; Symington, 1986; Spillius, 1988 a & b) and also upon the work of Winnicott, one of the foremost figures within Object Relations (Davis & Wallbridge, 1981; Kohon, 1986). There are a number of ideas which are fundamental to both traditions, as well as some differences, which are worth outlining here to provide an accessible introduction for the unfamiliar reader.

Is destructiveness part of our nature?

Although they vary in their interpretation of phenomena such as anger and hate, both Kleinian and Object-Relations traditions perceive a strong element of destructiveness within the human subject. This destructiveness may be directed at either self or other and is not simply a product of the environment. For Winnicott (1947, 1950) an element of destructiveness lies within the love impulse itself. The infant's love is ruthless; only with development does this primitive love acquire the capacity for concern for the other. But where Winnicott differs from Klein is in his insistence that this early destructiveness lacks intentionality. If the infant treats his mother as 'scum, an unpaid servant, a slave' (1947, p. 201) this is because the infant does not yet know his mother, because there are at this stage no 'others' in his world. In contrast Klein attributes hateful and destructive intent, albeit unconscious, to the infant from the very beginning. The Kleinian subject is wracked by conflictual impulses (Klein, 1935) which, depending upon the inner strength of the subject, may become projected on to an external world which as a consequence becomes peopled by vengeful, persecutory, idealised and/or adored others. For both thinkers the environment plays its part in either modifying and containing or fueling the destructiveness of the human subject. Both would also regard the idea of an environment which did not inevitably fail us in some way as myopic. Indeed it is because the environment fails us that we develop, otherwise we would never emerge from the symbiotic cocoon of infancy. Learning occurs primarily when the world fails to meet our expectations. From such shocks and surprises our aggression can be harnessed in a critical and deconstructive appraisal of our own preconceptions.

This is why it is appropriate to speak of the struggle of development. It is not just the frustrating and at times hostile other that we face but our own inner fears and destructive capacities. And others are vital to the outcome of this struggle because of their capacity to love and respect us in spite of ourselves.

What does this mean for rethinking welfare? For one thing it means that we should have no illusions about what people are capable of. All of us are capable of a ruthless attitude towards those on whom we depend, including the front-line workers and professionals who people the welfare state. We have almost become accustomed to neo-liberal rhetorics which constitute public-sector workers as an enemy within, a fifth column sapping the moral fibre of the British people. The ideology of consumerism gets to work on this ruthlessness, pitting the potentially tyrannical sovereign consumer against the service provider. Even within social policy one senses that at times the legitimate desire to empower service users connects with a one-sided perspective which sees public-sector workers solely as agents of control, bearers of discourses of domination, blindly pursuing their own interests under the guise of serving others. What seems much harder is to keep in mind the idea that workers and users are bound to each other in a relationship of conflictual interdependence. A relationship in which each has rights and legitimate expectations which may at times necessarily clash.

The psychological realism that I am arguing for would also imply that any project to transform welfare would have to recognise our fear of difference and our need to distance ourselves from the mad, bad, dangerous, profane and dirty parts of our own subjectivity (split off and externalised in asylums, hostels, residential homes, sink estates and so on). As I note in Chapter 2, it is not that I think such fears are immutable. As Irene Marion Young (1997) argues, difference can be a source of pleasure and wonderment as well as the lynchpin of the paranoid self. But we are still at the early stages of imagining the kind of social arrangements which provide the conditions for non-paranoid forms of sociability and a project to rethink and transform welfare must place this task at the centre of its ambition. As the Rustins once put it, what we need is a concept of welfare which represents 'the social architecture of a more benign world' (Rustin & Rustin, 1984).

Is there agency beyond resistance and opposition?

Foucault's vision of the ubiquitous and determining nature of power relations sometimes seems to leave little space for agency except as a form of contestation and struggle (Foucault, 1982). Moreover, if I understand him right, Honneth (1995) also traces the motor of historical struggles to the anger aroused by the refusal or denial of recognition and the exclusion, insult and hurt which is a consequence. This is why he speaks of 'the moral grammar of social conflicts'. It is anger that drives the struggle for social justice and not just abstract, intellectual appeals to concepts of right as some liberal political philosophers seem to imply.

But Honneth draws from Winnicott one-sidedly. For, while

Winnicott recognises the vital role aggression plays in the child's struggle to assert its difference, his concept of agency also includes a set of more vitalistic and creative impulses than aggression alone. This vitalism can be traced to Freud's final formulation of drive theory and specifically his concept of Eros, a life force. In Winnicott's work this theme finds expression in his theories of play and transitional phenomena (1971). For when Winnicott speaks of creativity he is not only concerned with a particular piece of behaviour but with a creative relation to life and reality, one which he contrasts with one of compliance 'where the world and its details are recognised but only as something to be fitted in with or demanding adaptation' (1971, p. 65). I will examine Winnicott's unique theory of play in much greater detail in Chapter 7. What is important is that he provides us with a deeply relational and embodied account of the emergence of the capacity for imagination, play, improvisation and experimentation – i.e. creative aspects of human agency which, far from being called forth by the experience of antagonism and opposition, are constituted by and in turn constitute a process of giving. It is this link between generativity and generosity that I try and develop in the final chapter of this book.

Imagined relations

Earlier I criticised the concept of 'autonomy' developed by Doyal & Gough (1991) for its rationalism and individualism. I also mentioned that they attempted to rebut both of these criticisms (pp. 65–6). Referring to the accusation of rationalism they argue that the model of choice and decision-making they advocate 'presupposes that individuals are potentially in charge of their lives provided that the physical, educational, emotional and social variables can be got right' (p. 65). This is a widely held view within much of the social sciences and social policy and therefore there is a responsibility on those, such as myself, who question such rationalism to explain a position which in many respects seems counter-intuitive.

A starting point is the importance both Kleinian and Object-Relations schools attach to the notion of 'object-relations' and specifically to the idea of 'internal objects'. Object relations draws our attention to the way in which the subject is always 'in relations with' the human environment. This, then, is a thoroughly social view of the subject. But why 'objects' and not people, and what is an internal object? For Freud an individual's 'objects' were anything that was a focus for their passions. This could refer to another person but Freud was at pains to point out that the object was the most contingent and fluid element of passion, thus objects could include works of art, fetishes, indeed anything which was endowed with meaning and feeling. Object relations therefore draws our attention to the nature of these relationships. Thus, for example, I am engaged in an object relation in the very process of writing. At times this book project feels like a troublesome and recalcitrant opponent, or a cherished baby I am giving birth to, or it may feel other and alien, persecuting me, mocking my abilities. Thus while I may be engaged in real relationships with real people many of my relations are also strongly imaginary. Kleinian and Object-Relations traditions assume the existence of an internal reality existing alongside, but not reducible to, our external world. For some people this internal world is far more powerful than the external one. We say that they are mad, but if we add that perhaps, more properly, they suffer from a surfeit of imagination we draw attention to the way in which this internal world is both the source of creativity as well as destructiveness.

The internal world is populated by internal objects. This is not as simple as saying that we have got a representation of our mum and dad inside our heads. When I dream that I am being persecuted by a cloud of flying insects or when I treat resilient and capable colleagues as if they are in need of my protection then both these insects and colleagues are different products of my imagination. To say that they are some of my internal objects is to say that they exist 'inside me', they are part of my psychic reality which is no less real than external reality – remember, it is this psychical reality that can drive people to murder and suicide. Freud was first drawn towards an encounter with internal objects in Mourning and Melancholia (Freud, 1917), his study of depression. The characteristic feature of the inner torment experienced by someone in a black depression is a constant and virulent stream of self-reproach – a critical, carping and damning inner voice. Freud had the genius to realise that this voice had somehow been internalised, in a distorted and twisted way, and set itself up inside the person as an internal tormentor (Butler, 1998). This internal object therefore was not just an internal representation, not just an idea, for it had agency, it persecuted and attacked the individual. This was the discovery that became the kernel of the idea that found fruition in the concept of 'object relations' – that we are not just engaged in an external drama with friends and family but in an internal drama also, and that the external and internal are not separate from each other but constantly interpenetrating and coalescing.

> In the early 1950s Paula Heimann, a member of the British Psycho-Analytical Society, posed a simple question that became crucial to the practice of psychoanalysis in what has come to be called the 'British School' of psychoanalysis (see Kohon, 1986). When listening to the patient's free associations . . . she asked: 'Who is speaking?' We can say that up to that moment it had always been assumed that the speaker was the patient who had formed a therapuetic alliance with the analyst, and therefore that he was a neutral or working speaker who was reporting inner states of mind. . . . But Heimann knew that at any one moment in a session a patient could be speaking in the voice of the mother, or the mood of the father, or some fragmented voice of a child self either lived or withheld from life. (Bollas, 1987)

It is in this way that Christopher Bollas introduces his book *The Shadow of the Object: Psychoanalysis of the Unthought Known* (Bollas, 1987). No clearer exposition could be given that what we call the self in fact contains a number of characters who speak in different tongues. Some of these will have forced themselves upon us, some may be preserved because they have been lost, some may be our own construction. The self emerges through the weaving together of human fragments which are shaped and given new meaning within our internal world. As I try to illustrate in Chapter 9, the idea of the rational individual engaged in strategic action and always in control of the choices he or she makes is based on the assumption of a unitary self. But if we accept the idea that each of us is inhabited by a multiplicity of different characters who speak through us and act through us at different moments in time then the paradoxes and contradicitions of human behaviour which are so richly imagined in literature, poetry and drama can be understood, indeed celebrated, as part of the richness of what it means to be human.

This view of the self may sound as if it is congruent with those post-structuralist arguments which insist upon the decentredness of the self and pronounce utmost scepticism towards any attempt to reinstate an autonomous subject. As we shall see in the following chapter this is also the perspective of the Lacanians for whom the ego is an alienated construction, a consoling delusion. But this is not the perspective of Kleinian or Object-Relations schools of psychoanalysis. Despite the fact that Kleinian theory more than any other draws our attention to the powerful splitting processes at work within the psyche, both schools are equally insistent on the presence of equally powerful processes of integration at work within the mind and, by implication, within society as well. At the heart of this perspective, within Kleinian work in particular, lies a struggle between two sets of forces, life and anti-life (i.e. Eros and Thanatos, the forces that Freud outlines in his later work).

Once Freud introduces this, his last formulation on the nature of the drives (Freud, 1920, 1923), the basis for transcending the old dichotomy between reason and passion, the ego and the id, comes into view. This is not a simple dualism which has been established. These two forces encompass all of life, both inner and outer. In terms of Freud's structural theory they are not just of the id, but of the ego and super-ego as well. Eros and Thanatos do not stand opposite each other as irreconcilable opponents, rather they need and interpenetrate each other. Splitting, aggressivity, destructiveness and disintegration can be in the service of life, indeed it is where we get much of our liveliness from. Without the capacity to pull things apart, push at the limits, knock things down and leap into chaos there can be no creativity, all of these capacities can be nourished by love. But if this is all there is then we have madness. We must be able to put things back together, repair what we have torn apart, build anew. But again, if this is all we have, if there is no disturbance, then there is tropism, stasis, sleep. In other words, even such apparently constructive capacities can be driven by a hate for life and liveliness. Development therefore rests on the possibility of this continuous movement, from stability to disorder and back again, from the exhilarating illusion of understanding to persecuting doubt and back again. For the Kleinians these are the two fundamental states of mind (which Klein terms the depressive and paranoid-schizoid positions) around which human development hinges. The life force is the energy released from the holding together of integration and disintegration. The individual or group which can contain this explosive tension is propelled towards development.

Agency within the fractured self

Psychoanalysis is also founded upon the assumption that there are limits to that in our lives which can be thought about. To insist that there are some things which are too difficult to bear is to simply say that these things will remain unconscious. At one level the so-called mystery of the unconscious is no more than this. But who or what is it that cannot bear such things? For Freud it was the ego, an elusive concept which ultimately escaped his attempt to confine it to all that was conscious. Freud's key insight however was that if the ego was anything it was a particular kind of agency, its distinctiveness lay in what it did rather than in what it was. Again, simply and inevitably crudely put, we can say that the ego is that which learns (or fails to learn) from experience. In Freud's immortal phrase, 'where *it (raw, unbearable emotional experience)* was, there I *(containing, meaning giving)* shall be' (my additions in italics). In contrast we can concur with Bollas (1987, pp. 8–9) when he suggests that the self, as opposed to the ego, has content and therefore character. As he puts it, it is 'the history of our internal relations' the fragmentary nature of which becomes articulated as if it were a coherent story.

But it is the ego which articulates and organises these fragments. And this 'I' is not structured by language and cultural codes. This 'I' asserts agency in the first hours of life by spitting out the breast, even at this point in development it is capable of refusal, of negative agency (Robinson, 1984, p. 169). The 'I' that spits things out or takes them in (food, ideas) through processes of introjection and projection is not structured by language. In a similar vein Benjamin (1994, p. 235) points out the subtle but crucial distinction between a (post-structuralist) perspective which simply sees the subject as split and one which can also grasp that there must be a subject, an 'I', that does the splitting (e.g. love from hate, me from not me). From the first perspective agency is chimerical, from the second perspective the possibility of agency, even within a divided subject, is real. It is this that Freud refers us to through his notion of ego, which, unlike the self, is not simply the product of language and culture.

To summarise, Kleinian and Object-Relations perspectives see human development in terms of the articulation of a fragmented gestalt. Although we speak with many voices and take up many different positions in regard both to self and others we nonetheless have the capacity not just to bear but to learn to take pleasure from these shifting versions of the self. As Bollas notes, that we know we are one despite the multiplicity of selves that inhabit us, is to say 'that all of us live within the realm of illusion' (Bollas, 1987, p. 9). But illusion is not delusion, as we shall see in Chapter 7. Illusion is at the very heart of our creativity, it signifies a playful attitude both to ourselves and the world in which we live. A self which is overly identified with one or two 'this-is-me' stories must repudiate so much which is 'other' to itself that it must inevitably come to reside in a world composed largely of its own projections. This is delusion.

Moreover, if we can become free of the need to take our selves too seriously then we are also more free to become passionate about the world that surrounds us and its aesthetic and ethical dimensions. Such life projects are less likely to be the simple externalisation of internal difficulties, their compulsive or manic quality will be less dominant, the need to be one-eyed and totalising about them mitigated.

2
Strangers to Ourselves?

A recurring theme of this book is that people's well-being ultimately depends upon the quality of the social relationships in which they are immersed. Unfortunately the modern welfare state is partly the creation of the kind of society which buys economic progress at the cost of the quality of its social relations. Or, putting it another way, improving the quality of social relations within society is the key to preventing the kind of social problems that Spicker (1995) and others argue social policies address.

The quality of social relations can be looked at from several perspectives. It concerns social relations within families whatever their form, it concerns relations between generations and sexes, the local social relations of communities however defined, the social relations of the welfare state and crucially the relations between professional service providers and service user and, last but not least, the social relations of work. The quality of these relations varies according to a number of dimensions, for example, the degree to which domination or solidarity, violence or love, is a characteristic of them.

Western political thought has tended to polarise around two opposing views regarding the nature of our social relations. One view, the pessimistic one, sees the poverty of social relations and the violence, misunderstanding and disrespect which are such a feature of them as a reflection of our social being. In other words, it is a part of the human condition that we are fundamentally estranged both from ourselves and others. In contrast, the optimistic view says, no, the poverty of our social relations is a reflection of the kind of society we live in. It is a socially created poverty, an effect of unequal power relations. Thus we find that the idea of self-estrangement is one of the most consistently recurring themes in modern political and social thought – from Hegel and the Young Hegelians, through Marx, to Weber and Simmel and the neo-Freudians, to the existentialists, to Lacan and the post-structuralists. Throughout the two hundred years in which the concept has been discussed, fought over, revised, dismissed and restored one senses an underlying question to which different writers provide differing replies. Put simply, and inevitably crudely, the question has been this – is estrangement an aspect of our nature as human beings or has society created this? Clearly the argument could run and run. Indeed one senses sometimes that it may not have moved on that much, that each generation may introduce the arguments of the last as if they were newly invented. In this chapter I want to suggest that both camps are right, that estrangement is both socially produced and also inherent to our contradictory status as beings who are both natural and human, of nature and beyond nature. In other words I will argue that dispositions such as fear and hatred are a part of our nature and are not just social creations. A truly radical politics is one which would recognise such dispositions in each one of us but which would also be able to imagine the kind of social arrangements which could inhibit the worst and bring out the best in us.

Perspectives on human estrangement

I am using the term 'estrangement' to signify a variety of related issues. Perhaps first and foremost the idea that we are strangers to ourselves, lacking any kind of centre or inherent nature we are lost souls seeking consolation in myths and stories about ourselves and the world in which we live. Linked to this, the idea that we exist as isolated units, each separated from the other by a space filled by fear and distrust, the other constituted as opponent and antagonist rather than as friend or fellow. Thirdly, that certain vital genera-tive human powers and capacities – sociability, imagination, the capacity to engage ethically with the world – have been lost or have remained underdeveloped leading to a lop-sided civilisation where technique has outstripped values and where the good life is construed in narrowly materialist terms.

Social theory provides us with several different accounts of the term. In what follows I propose to examine three accounts, the last of which will be pursued in some detail. The first account con-strues the problem in terms of loss. Crudely speaking one could say that this account assumes the form of a lament regarding modernisation and what is held to be its destructive effect upon family, community, intimacy and identity. The second account construes self-estrangement primarily in terms of the theft of human powers through the particular forms of domination associated with the emergence of capitalism. Each of these accounts assumes that in some way the loss of human powers and qualities is socially produced and, as such, each account therefore constitutes a form of social criticism.

The third account insists that self-estrangement is part of the human condition itself – we are strangers to ourselves and to our fellow beings, beings with whom we are locked into a continuing struggle for recognition. Of course the problem with this perspective is that it can so easily disarm us. What is the point in believing in the possibility of social transformation if the flawed world in which we live is simply an expression of our own flawed nature? Indeed, from the perspective of some forms of post-modernism there are no ethical positions which are not in themselves shot through with bad faith and traces of human weakness. In contrast I will argue that the project of social transformation is congruent with a view of humanity as fundamentally flawed, indeed that such a view provides the only adequately realist basis for such a project. For whilst we may be flawed we are also capable of development as thoughtful and feelingful beings given an environment which can facilitate such human possibilities.

Narratives of loss

I now return to the first of these narratives, the story of loss. As I noted this has often assumed the form of a lament about progress, about the onward march of history in which industrialisation, modernity or some other seemingly inexorable process is held responsible for the loss of human capacities and qualities. The accounts are innumerable and many overlap or rework previous accounts but in a different form. Some of the main varieties would include, urbanisation and the loss of community (Tonnies, 1887); mass production and the loss of human skill (Blauner, 1964); bureaucratisation and the loss of wonderment (Weber, 1922); technocracy and the loss of personal competencies (Lasch, 1985); mass society and the loss of intimacy (Wirth, 1964); late or post-modernity and the loss of stable identity (Jameson, 1983).

As each account has emerged so, before long, has a critique. These appear to have followed one of two basic tactics. Either an attempt is made to show that such accounts of loss are guilty of idealising the past or, it is suggested, they demonstrate a blindness, or one-sidedness, towards the present by stressing only what has been lost not what has been gained from progress. The first approach has characterised critiques of community (Stacey, 1969), a recent example of the second can be found in Giddens's (1991, pp. 191–3) critique of the link that has been made between modernisation and personal powerlessness.

But of course such critiques can themselves be criticised. The task of analysis is not simply to 'expose' the idealised, ambiguous and politicised nature of the concept of community but to come to terms with the enduring presence of the term in everyday speech, the many ways in which it is subject to contestation, the real effects of the outcome of struggles over such competing definitions and to understand the reasons why the concept of community so easily becomes the container of those collective sentiments which contribute to its idealisation (Hoggett, 1997; Day & Murdoch, 1993). Similarly, whilst Giddens is right to stress the way in which globalisation has made available new resources for human action his concern to avoid 'objectivist' accounts of structure and constraint means that reference to the new forms of domination present in globalisation processes is almost entirely missing from his account. Thus the apparent 'hard-headedness' of many sociological critiques of narratives of loss often conceals an abandonment of radicalism.

Marx and the theft of human powers

I have suggested that many of the narratives of alienation which have emerged in social theory over the last century are in fact narratives of loss. But Marxism contains a different account of alienation, one which gives emphasis to processes of theft and parasitism rather than loss. Marxism emerged through a critique of the 'the Young Hegelians' (Arthur, 1970) who saw alienation as the consequence of reification, that is the inversion of the subject-predicate relationship whereby humanity becomes the slave of its own creations. Humanity creates God and then prostrates itself before its own fetish (Marx & Engels, 1970, p. 72). For the Young Hegelians God, the State, and other fetishes derive their power, their hold over humanity, by virtue of their being myths into which we have projected our own powers. For the Young Hegelians the task of critique was a philosophical/psychological one, i.e. to reveal to humanity its self-alienation, the appropriation of its power by the products of its own imagination. Characterising this perspective as 'the German Ideology' Marx and Engels (1970) sought to attack what they saw as the idealism of this position, one which logically led to the assumption that if only humanity would stop believing in the existence of God then the power of religion would evaporate.

Marxism shared the idea of an external agency, created by the subject, which then deprives the subject of its own human powers. But for Marx this agency is not an idea such as God or the Holy Family but the product of alienated human labour itself, i.e. capital. Under capitalism labour's product, capital, confronts the subject as an alien power, as another person's property. Labour is external to the worker, it does not develop his physical and mental capacities 'but mortifies his body and ruins his mind . . . the worker therefore only feels himself outside his work, and in his work feels outside himself' (Marx, 1970, p. 110). In his *Theses on Feuerbach* Marx insists that neither the problem nor the solution lies in a method of thinking, 'the philosophers have only interpreted the world, in various ways; the point is to change it' (Marx & Engels, 1970, p. 123).

Historical materialism arose from the confluence of the critique of Young Hegelianism and the appropriation of political economy. As Meszaros (1970) notes it was by virtue of this bringing together of differences (i.e. of two bodies of thought which previously had stood unconnected to each other) that Marx was able to take 'a great step forward' in the *Paris Manuscripts* of 1844 by recognising that the key to all alienation – religious, juridicial, moral, artistic, political, etc. – is 'alienated labour' (Meszaros, p. 233), the product of a particular mode of production, capitalism.

I do not wish to dwell here upon the totalising claims of this last statement, i.e. the attempt to attribute a huge variety of complex social ills to a single causal factor. Nor is this the place to give a detailed account of Marx's theory of alienation, for this has been done by countless other writers (Ollman, 1971; Meszaros, 1970). The issue I wish to draw attention to however is that whilst in one sense Marxism transcended Young Hegelianism it did so one-sidedly. Whereas the Young Hegelians drew attention to humanity's self-alienation and therefore problematised the subject, Marxism located alienation entirely outside of the subject, in a single Other, i.e.

capitalism, thereby denying the possibility of self-alienation. So the transcendence was incomplete; because Marxism stood as antithesis to the idealism of the Young Hegelians its materialism failed to include the subject itself as a unique material form. For Marxism the human subject was shapeless and structureless. In its worst manifestations Marxism construed the subject as an infinitely malleable material to be shaped by whatever social arrangements could be engineered. It was as if the human subject was the only natural phenomenon with no grain of its own, with no negativity or recalcitrance (Hoggett, 1992) or as if the laws of nature were meant to apply only to the non-human world (Whitebook, 1994).

The French (re)turn 1: Sartre and Laing

But of course the human subject with its own internal structures and dynamic, its own needs and passions, its own strengths and failings, can not so easily be dismissed. Not surprisingly therefore the problematic developed by the Young Hegelians returns, this time in a different form, in the twentieth century, i.e. as existentialism. Meszaros registers this return of Hegel, 'the modern irrationalistic re-edition of the Hegelian idea' (p. 242), as the idea of the alienation of modern man. Sartre and others, strongly influenced by Kojeve's reading of Hegel given at the Ecole des Hautes Etudes between 1933 and 1939, saw alienation as inherent to the condition of humanity. It was not only Sartre who was influenced by the return of Hegel via Kojeve but also Lacan (see Wilden's (1968) introduction to Lacan's *The Language of the Self*). And of course from Lacan the thread leads towards the post-modernist movement of today. Rather than mourning the loss of human powers some within this movement argue that alienation should be accepted, celebrated even – artists should affirm their subordination to the machine or to money through their art, oppressed groups should affirm their status as the oppressed by parading their identity as queers, and so on. Again the trick is not new, Sartre's (1952) analysis of Genet followed a similar route and, for a while, in the 1960s Laing had sought to elevate the status of the schizophrenic by arguing that schizophrenia was perhaps the only sane response to a crazy world (Sedgewick, 1982, p. 94).

The return of the Hegelian concept of alienation is manifest in one of its most vivid forms in the pages of a number of books and articles produced by Laing in the early 1960s. Unlike many of those across the channel Laing's work was rooted in empirical detail and therefore provides the most accessible way of examining the concept of self-alienation as it has recently returned (Collier, 1977, p. 95).

Laing will be remembered not for his turn to mysticism in the late 1960s (Laing, 1970) nor for his attempts to extend the psycho-analytic framework of Melanie Klein into a genuinely transpersonal social psychology (Laing, 1961, 1966) but rather for the way in which he implied that the infernal drama of the schizophrenic's family was the metaphor for all families and Hegel's 'dialectic of recognition' was the foundation of all social encounters with another person. The schizophrenic family is engaged in a game designed to send one of its members crazy. The key move is the double-bind in which one or more members of the family are subject to contradic-tory injunctions or 'binds' so that if they obey one they break the other. The members subject to such double-binds are therefore con-stantly subject to a process of disconfirmation. Mrs Doublebind and her son meet on the psychiatric ward. As the son moves towards her to embrace her she freezes leaving a glassy smile upon her face. The son recoils from hugging her. Mrs Doublebind says 'there you are Johnny, your mummy loves you so much but you still can't bring yourself to love her as she loves you.' In this game there is no stable position from which Johnny can view his world ('she loves me, she loves me not . . .') nor himself ('I'm a lovely child, I'm a despicable child . . .'). As Laing and his collaborators began to develop their picture of the double-bind family (Laing & Esterson, 1964) so the role of the various family members within the game could be brought into view. As Sedgewick (1982) graphi-cally put it, 'the Doublebind menage is a blood-besmirched arena for internecine assaults and insults, a telephone network of crossed lines, scrambled messages and hung-up receivers' (p. 83). In this sense the family was merely an extension of the everyday warfare that all individuals were assumed to be engaged in.

In Sartre's hands (exemplified by Part Three of *Being and Nothing-ness*) 'the dialectic of recognition' referred to an endless series of moves and counter moves through which warring monads sought to objectify each other. An endless process of psychological invali-dation, disconfirmation, attribution, denial, engulfment, collusion and counterfeit. For Sartre it was impossible to relate to another without making that other an object for oneself and hence fixing them, petrifying them in the sense of turning them to stone. Con-versely, it was impossible to be related to by another without being objectified by them. The other in its 'radical alterity' (i.e. insisting on its reality and separateness as a being with its own needs, feelings and preoccupations) therefore presents itself as the loss of my own possibilities, as the negation of my own freedom. As the receiver of the other's look, as the object of his attention, one is constantly in the process of being turned into a being-for-the-other. Interpersonal relations become a kind of judo in which each tries to fix the other whilst avoiding being fixed by the other. In the hands of writers like Franz Fannon (1967) the dialectic of objectification could become a dynamic element of a historically grounded account of racial oppression through which it became possible to see how 'to be black' was to be constituted by the white gaze. But for many others, including Laing for a while, this dialectic between self and other, master and slave, was the foundation from which the very possibility of intersubjectivity was attacked. In a classic statement Laing (1962) denies the possibility of human reciprocity, rather he sees the ties that bind people (in a way which was shocking at that time) as a strategy for enforcing personal indebtedness,

> my need is to be needed by another. My love is a thirst, not to satisfy my love, but a thirst to be loved. My solitude is not for another, but for another to want me . . . and, similarly, the other wants to be wanted by me, longs to be longed for by me. Two alienated loves, two self-perpetuating solitudes, an inextricable and timeless misunderstanding – tragic and comic – the soil of endless recrimination.

This is a perspective worthy of the most rabid free market cartographer of the interpersonal sphere. In this psychological law of the jungle all human virtue is turned into its opposite – my concern for you is merely a kind of psychic investment, a means of placing you hopelessly in debt to me; my love for you is merely an indication of the lack or gap at the heart of my own being, I love you not from my strength but from my weakness.

What emerges from the view of life propounded by Sartre and Laing is the idea that because we are strangers to ourselves we search tirelessly to find a trace, an image or imprint of ourselves in the gaze of the other – if I cannot recognise myself then at least I shall be held in the firm gaze of the other; if I cannot love myself then at least I shall be loved by another. My subjectivity is therefore always outside myself, located in another.

At the heart of this account of the struggle for recognition lies a particular construction of the human subject, one dominated by the idea that it is the self (or in Lacan's hands, the ego) which is at the root of our alienation. For Sartre the basic problem of humanity lies in our inability to face our own freedom, that is, our own possibilities, and the responsibility that this entails:

> We should like to preserve from the original intuition what it reveals to us as our independence and our responsibility but we tone down all the original nihilation in it; moreover we are always ready to take refuge in a belief in determinism if this freedom weighs upon us or if we need an excuse. Thus we flee from anguish by attempting to apprehend ourselves from without as an Other or as *a thing* [original emphasis] (Sartre, 1966, p. 82).

According to Sartre, the constitution of the self is essential to this flight for the motivation lying behind its construction is to make oneself just such a thing, something with all the solidity and facticity of a non-human object such as an inkstand. Then I can be sure that I exist as something beyond the nothingness of mere possibilities. The self, then, 'is a fiction eminently reassuring since freedom has been driven down into the heart of an opaque being' (p. 81). Here the links between the Young Hegelians and the French appropriation of Hegel via Kojeve becomes quite explicit for, as Sartre adds, 'it is a matter of envisaging the self as a little God which inhabits me and which possesses my freedom as a metaphysical virtue' (ibid.). As we might say, humanity creates the autonomous self and then prostrates itself before its own fetish.

For the (alienated) self the other person is both threat and promise. On the one hand the other offers the possibility of recognition, that this self that I am might be seen by the other with all the certainty with which they might look upon an inkstand. I am seen therefore I am. On the other hand this other apprehends me as the possibility through which she might be recognised. In Laing's (1961) hands this struggle for recognition is pictured in terms of a dialectic of confirmation and disconfirmation. If I see myself as a little known and misunderstood person I will seek to be the object of another's puzzlement and mystery. To be the object of another's understanding will be threatening. If the other is a hapless victim of fate to whom the Gods have been unkind and for whom life is a constant misfortune, then she will seek to become the object of my sympathy. To be the object of my contempt would be threatening – it would imply that she had some responsibility for her pitiful condition. My constant concern is to force the other back into his/her being an-object-for-me, to fix the other into a position from which he/she will have a particular mode of consciousness of my self. Ultimate bliss is the accomplishment of what Laing (1961, p. 108) calls a 'collusive pairing', a mutually confirmatory relationship in which each self finds the recognition it requires from the other. This has implications for the psychotherapeutic task, as Laing argues (in a way which strikingly parallels Lacan), 'it is in terms of the basic frustration of the self's search for a collusive complement . . . that Freud's dictum that analysis should be conducted under conditions of maximum frustration takes on its most cogent meaning' (Laing, 1961, p. 123).

For Laing, and Lacan, the self is a fundamentally alienated construct, a misrepresentation through and through, a lie that we tell about ourselves, a form of consolation. Lacan traces the development of this structure to 'the mirror stage' (Lacan, 1977). The mirror is a metaphor for the process whereby the infant grasps itself as something whole and unitary, a psychological Gestalt. Lacan dwells for sometime upon the experience of young children and other animal species before the mirror. Clearly his theory of the mirror-stage is designed to provide a real foundation for Freud's original theory of narcissism (Freud, 1914) – the fascination with the image, the reflected self – which projects an imaginary wholeness beyond the fragmented, chaotic bodily experiences of early life. For Lacan the subject becomes captured within this reflection which 'symbolizes the ego's mental permanence and at the same time prefigures its alienating fate' (Lacan, 1977, pp. 2–3). According to Benvenuto and Kennedy (1986) the ego for Lacan is thus formed on the basis of an imaginary relationship of the subject with her own body, 'the ego has the illusion of autonomy, but it is only an illusion, and the subject moves from fragmentation and insufficiency to illusory unity' (Benvenuto & Kennedy, p. 56). Note the pejorative use of the term 'illusion' here, an issue I will return to both later in this chapter and in Chapter 7.

For Lacan, therefore, the ego is above all else a mechanism of defence. It is founded upon mesconnaissance (consciously or unconsciously wilful misperception) and as a lie the ego can only apprehend the world by misrepresenting it. The ego's relationship to the other simply gives expression to its own narcissistic formation.

The other is not apprehended in its own right, as something separate and different, but through 'the grid of the narcissistic relation' (Lacan, 1988, p. 167). From this perspective the other is always self-referential, a subjective object, an object of domination.

Lacan has had a considerable impact on certain forms of postmodernist thinking. As a consequence the very idea of identity has become suspect in some quarters. Whether considered in the ontological sense, as sense of self, or in terms of our group identities (i.e. as gay, Bangladeshi, etc.) it has become fashionable to emphasise the mutability of identity rather than its fixity. But this is not just a descriptive judgement, it has also become a normative one. It is as if our identities *should* be constantly shifting and changing, as if we should never really believe in them because ultimately they are a source of consolation and terrorism, a delusion that perhaps all but a handful of supermen (and women) cannot do without.

The French (re)turn 2: feminism and the critique of the autonomous subject

It is intriguing to note the way in which many of the refrains of the existentialist and Lacanian appropriations of Hegel have been taken up by some elements within contemporary feminism. Specifically we could say that this movement has sought to investigate the earthly kernel behind the new God of twentieth-century society – the autonomous self. Butler (1990) provides a lucid summary and critique of the way in which a variety of feminist writers, from Gilligan to Mitchell and Rose, have sought to demonstrate how the autonomous subject is in fact a thoroughly gendered construction, 'a masculine cultural prerogative from which women have been excluded' (Butler, 1990, p. 326). For Butler the notion of the individual self is not just an alienating illusion but one based upon exclusion and repression, 'autonomy is the logical consequence of a disavowed dependency' (Butler, 1992, p. 12). From this perspective the dialectic of recognition, the agonistic relationship between self and other whereby each seeks to assimilate the other into itself, are indicative of the intimate embrace between the subject and domination. The racialised or engendered subject is formed through domination, indeed there can be no subject without domination. The struggle against hierarchy and exclusion is therefore synonymous with the struggle against the tyranny of the idea of the autonomous (male, occidental) subject.

But, I would suggest, a critique which simply attempts to bring a Sartrian or Lacanian Hegelianism down to earth by historicising it and grounding it in actual gendered relations of power is insufficient. Indeed, as Butler (1990) and Benjamin (1994) in their different ways indicate, it is a critique which could well lead feminism as a form of transformative practice to an impasse.

The first problem lies in the acceptance of an essentially narcissistic conception of the subject in which the other exists primarily as a bundle of projections. If things really are that bad, if patriarchal relations have become so deeply embedded and so destructive of human solidarity that we are doomed to antagonistic social relations until patriarchal structures are overcome, then as human subjects struggling in the here and now the prospects of our making common cause are pretty grim. From this reference point, feminism appears to lack a position from which otherness can ever be recognised and accepted as something which is not inherently alien and the site of violence. As Whitebook (1994) argues, this is a paranoid position, one which views the other with basic mistrust, i.e. as a potential persecutor. Paradoxically, given the role it might be thought that the mother can play, this perspective seems to deny the possibility of another who might be good to me.

If difference is to be recognised, the possibility of intersubjectivity, that is, of forms of exchange between separate beings who are not simply bundles of defensively organised projections, must be theoretically provided for (Benjamin, 1994, p. 231). As Benjamin (1994, pp. 240–1) points out, some feminist accounts are unable to transcend a basically intrapsychic perspective – one which can only conceive of the subject 'relating through identifications to the subjectively conceived object' (p. 236). Benjamin's use of Winnicott is highly appropriate here for of all psychoanalysts it is Winnicott who is most careful to draw the distinction between object relating and object usage (see Chapter 6 of Winnicott's seminal book *Playing and Reality*, (Winnicott, 1971). The point that Winnicott is making is that if real human exchange is to occur the other must have the capacity both to accept the projections which are aggressively directed towards her and to survive them. As he notes, it is as if the subject is able to say to the other 'you have value for me because of your survival of my destruction of you' (p. 90). Because of this survival the possibility exists for the other to be placed outside the area of omnipotent control, 'in these ways the object develops its own autonomy and life, and (if it survives) contributes-in to the subject, according to its own properties' (ibid.). In a crucial passage Winnicott adds 'from now on ... projective mechanisms assist in the act of noticing what is there, but they are not the reason why the object is there. In my opinion this is a departure from theory which tends to a conception of external reality only in terms of the individual's projective mechanisms' (ibid.). Benjamin (1994, p. 237) adds that the other who survives can be seen in its alterity – its recalcitrance to my wishes can be accepted, its status as another with its own needs and desires who is able to have a decisive impact on myself can be recognised.

It is worth dwelling on this for a little longer for the idea of the other's survival for me may be puzzling. A couple of examples should help. Imagine an infant and its mother. The paradox is that for the infant to be able to grow up the mother must be strong enough to cope with its aggressive liveliness. If the mother is too fragile and insecure she may not be able to withstand the infant's de-mand for separateness. We would say she identifies too closely with her child, she cannot allow it to be something other than an ex-tension of herself and her own unrealised possibilities. Thus she colludes with that part of the infant that does not want to grow up. The same applies to any kind of helping relationship, between teacher and pupil, nurse and patient, and so on. The helper has to be strong enough to survive the ambivalence, i.e. the gratitude and the resentment, that the other must be allowed to experience if he is to move from dependency to interdependence. Or put yet another way, we all need to bite the hands that feed us and we all need the other to survive this if we are to move on.

There are also important political implications to this position. The emergence of modern social movements based upon gendered, sexualised and racialised identities is precisely a vindication of the idea of a subject capable of surviving the Other's psychological violence. It is as if this subject can say, 'I am not as you see me, I have survived your attacks, I force you to take back into yourself what you have dis-owned and thrust inside me, I insist you re-evaluate yourself.' Moreover the encounter with differences based upon gender, sexual-ity, ethnicity, disability or whatever is inherently conflictual. Differ-ences can only be negotiated, reconciled or transcended through a conflictual process of engagement involving the breakdown of rela-tionship and its repair, 'the experience of repair allows one to see destruction's creative, differentiating function, placing the other in a space outside coercive reconciliation' (Benjamin, 1994, pp. 241–2). Or, put more simply, democracy is about conflict. The task is to create a democratic and pluralist culture within civil society which can enable such conflict to be contained and worked through without being either suppressed or allowed to explode civil society into fragments.

Subjectivity and the synthetic impulse

My argument over the last few pages has been that certain post-modernist inspired feminist attacks on the autonomous subject are in danger of leaving no space for intersubjectivity and agency and therefore no space for the possibility of social transformation. Like the Young Hegelians, what we are left with is a denuded form of practice restricted, as Sivanadan (1990) once put it, to changing the word rather than changing the world. In a parallel fashion post-modernist criticisms of identity sometimes appear to leave no space for collective agency. By privileging difference over identity, by counterposing the 'reality' of the former to the illusoriness of the latter, the basis for unity in struggle is rendered permanently suspect.

While such post-modernist positions like to look as if they were able to eschew any essentialism, scratch beneath the surface and one quickly finds a whole set of psychological assumptions are being made. Moreover much of this is bad psychology, that is, it is guilty of confusing a number of basic terms such as illusion and delusion, the unity of the self with its coherence, etc.

We have already noted how both Laing and Lacan consider the self/ego to be a lie, a lie we tell both to ourselves and to others. But let us note in passing some assumptions which are being made here, and not too explicitly. First of all, particularly with Lacan and many of the post-structuralists who followed, there is the assumption that the idea of the ego is tied inextricably to the idea of there being some 'centre' to the psyche. Secondly, note the way in which this ego is assumed primarily to possess some kind of thing-like qualities – it can be seen, it can be positioned, it can be developed and adjusted like any other kind of narrative which can be shaped by its author. This does not seem to be an agency which 'does'; rather it seems to be something one 'has'. Of course the point is that narratives can't do anything. They can't test reality, they can't make judgements, they can't love or hate, they cannot enquire or pose questions, they cannot give meaning to experience or create symbolic means of expression. Narratives are the consequence of all such actions, they are the aftermath of our encounters in life.

For the post-structuralists these stories we tell about ourselves, this-is-who-we-are type stories, are necessarily lies and delusions designed to give decentered nomads the consolation of coherence. But the point is that this is not all there is to the subject, for the most vital element of subjectivity, agency, is still missing.

We need to untangle some concepts which all too easily become lumped together – specifically the subject, the ego and the self. Following Benjamin (1994) and Bollas (1987) I suggest that the subject comprises both 'I' and 'me', both ego and self. The latter is a construction of the former but it is the 'I' that constructs. That is why Bollas (1987) refers to the ego as the 'organising idiom'. It is not constructed through language but is part of what, following Winnicott, Bollas calls our 'inherited potential'. Moreover the ego is first and foremost a body ego (Freud 1923), an idea subsequently developed by Bion through his idea of the mind as an analogue of the digestive system (Robinson 1984). According to Meltzer, 'Bion says if you do not digest your experiences you will poison and destroy your mind' (Meltzer, 1978, p. 50). Paradoxically, therefore, the roots of human agency lie in our bodily and biological inheritance, in our first nature, not in language or culture.

Is the self therefore a delusional system? I think the answer is yes and no. Again Winnicott is helpful to us here. In his classical paper *Transitional Objects and Transitional Phenomena* (1951) Winnicott discriminates between illusion and delusion by hypothesising the existence of an intermediate area of experience occupying the space between the inability and developing ability to recognise and accept reality, a reality which includes death and separation. He adds,

> I am therefore studying the substance of illusion, that which is allowed to the infant, and which in adult life is inherent in art and religion, and yet becomes the hallmark of madness when an adult puts too powerful a claim on the credulity of others, forcing them to acknowledge a sharing of illusion that is not their own. *We can share a respect for illusory experience, and if we wish we may collect together and form a group on the basis of the similarity of our illusory experiences. This is the natural root of grouping among human beings* (1951, p. 3) [my italics]

This intermediate area of experience is the illusional or transitional space between that which is purely subjective and that which is objectively perceived. As Winnicott puts it, in order to grow up and become a subject the parents' task is to gradually disillusion the infant, for only in this way will it realise the existence of the others on whom it depends. This is almost an unbearable realisation which arouses not just intense anxiety but hatred for the other also. Thus, as Winnicott notes, 'the task of reality acceptance is never completed' (p. 13). The transitional space, the space of artistic and political production where reality is both accepted and denied, is therefore ringed by intimations of tragedy. But also hope, for ultimately, as Butler (1998) remarks, it is our love for those on whom we depend which enables us to endure such disillusionment.

It is in this transitional space therefore where another and much more intimate form of production occurs, the production of the narratives of the self. When we take these narratives too seriously, when we force our claims for their veracity upon the other, then the struggle for recognition becomes tinged by fear and violence. But if we 'can manage to enjoy this personal intermediate area without making claims' (Winnicott, 1951 p. 14) then we can also enjoy the play of interaction with other selves. The self, located within the boundary of the skin, is therefore the most sophisticated and vital illusion we are capable of. Without this illusion we would have no way of containing our contents. As Chapter 4 illustrates we would literally spill out into or be invaded by the world in which we live.

Returning to the theme of identity, it is only by recognising the distinction between ego and self that we can begin to isolate the agency which lies at the heart of subjectivity. When Taylor suggests that there must be something 'at the core of each individual which unifies the fragmentation of experience' (Taylor, 1998, p. 335), I would reply that it is the ego which performs precisely this function. In health, each of us has a unique sense of our own identity (our 'ontological identity' according to Taylor). Moreover, the more self-awareness we have (that is, the more reflexive we can be about our own feelings) the more able we are to sustain this identity despite the contradictions, inconsistencies, inner conflicts and silences that we know it is based upon. As Taylor (op. cit., p. 340) notes, a coherent identity can be sustained despite an inner disunity. The same applies for an identity we share with others ('categorical identity'). As we shall see in Chapter 7, both self-identity and group identity are creative fictions. To believe that such fictions are necessarily alienated delusions is to disavow the very possibility of imaginative agency. This indeed is a recipe for despair.

Recapitulation: accounting for alienation

So far we have considered three kinds of account of alienation. The first is really a form of lament for human powers which are thought to have been lost through the modernising process. As we have seen this is an account constantly subject to dispute both for its tendency to idealise the past and for its one-sidedness towards the present. The second attributes responsibility for human alienation to the Other, specifically to the system of domination of capitalism/patriarchy through which human powers are appropriated in the labour process/division of labour and re-presented in the fetishisation of the commodity/self and the universal medium of reified exchange, i.e. money/recognition. The third account construes alienation as self-alienation, that is as something inherent to the human condition, a timeless insufficiency in our being. But there is a fourth account, one to be glimpsed at times in the work of Laing and explicit in the tradition of theory and practice that Laing and many of his colleagues were immersed in during the late 1950s during their stay at the Tavistock Clinic in London. This tradition, based upon the work of the Kleinian and the Object-Relations schools of psychoanalysis remains dominant within the world psychoanalytic movement today. Within this tradition human alienation is seen as a psycho-social phenomenon. We are all to some extent strangers to ourselves and yet the social environment, starting with the family in which we live, has the capacity to make a difference, that is, to some extent to return us to ourselves. This tradition eschews the tendency at work within the other three accounts to locate the problem either entirely within the subject or in the external world, in other words it refuses to engage in the split and antagonistic discourses of idealism and solipsism on the one hand or materialism and objectivism on the other.

The debt that Laing owed to Klein in particular is graphically displayed in his early writings (Laing 1960). While he disputes some of the key tennets of Kleinian theory such as the possibility of 'unconscious phantasy' much of what is written in the *Divided Self, Self and Others* and other early texts is clearly informed as much by Kleinian theory as by existentialism. The concepts of splitting, engulfment and projective idenitification saturate the pages of these texts. These concepts refer to psychical processes which constitute the primitive grammar of the internal world according to Klein, and specifically to the 'state of mind' (Ogden, 1986) Klein referred to as 'the paranoid-schizoid position'.

What is strikingly absent from Laing's account however is any reference to the other primary state of mind which Klein held was a basic quality of human existence, that is, the 'depressive position'. For if the first position refers to the subject in its divided state – a fragmentary, exploded cacophony of colliding elements – the second position refers to the capacity for reintegration, for the return of the disowned and the repudiated and for the development of the capacity for concern. It should not however be thought that Klein's account is one of alienation overcome, of the return of the individual to a lost state of grace. For Klein the first position is never fully overcome. As Bion put it, the psychotic and the non-psychotic elements of the personality continue to co-exist (Bion 1957), madness is the foundation of sanity. The achievement of development is to establish this primitive state of mind as a dynamic configuration which informs life without destroying it.

In what follows I will try to provide an accessible introduction to this fourth account of estrangement. It is one which insists that the human subject cannot be understood except through its location within an encompassing intersubjectivity. It also insists that the 'social' can equally act as a site for the alienation and for the development of our psychological capacities.

Projective identification

Klein's concept of projective identification (Klein, 1952) is without doubt one of the essential conceptual discoveries of the psychoanalytic movement (Bott Spillius, 1988a, p. 81). It has become key both to understanding normal and common features of human development and the pathologies thereof. Projective identification is a pre-verbal mode of human communication, one we resort to as individual or collective subjects whenever we face experiences in life that we cannot adequately give words to. Projective identification is the first form of communication available to us. Speaking of human development Ogden (1979) notes, 'projective identification is a means by which the infant can feel that he is understood by making his mother feel what he is feeling' (p. 363). In a later essay Ogden (1992, p. 25) suggests that it is a form of direct communication unmediated by interpreting subjects, it is predominantly a communication between the unconscious of one person and that of another. If the other lacks the capacity to receive and contain what is offered then this temporary state of alienation, of placing an aspect of our subjectivity outside ourselves, may become a permanent state of estrangement. For example, the parent may take the infant in his or her arms but the embrace is rigid and cold, the child is held physically but not emotionally; as a result the infant is fed physically but not psychically. Rather than receiving something back which can reduce its fear of its own bad feelings what it gets back is the coldness and emotional deadness of the other. In terms of its object relations, the baby internalises an object 'which assists it to un-think, to mis-understand, to elaborate lies and hallucinations for the purpose of evading rather than modifying frustration and distress' (Meltzer, 1978, p. 51). Something foreign develops in the baby's internal world.

Bion (1962) suggests that we might think of the process of projective identification in terms of the relationship between the container and the contained. The contained refers to those elements (typically unbearable feelings and phantasies) of one's subjectivity which become located, mapped upon or placed within the other – i.e. another person, group or social collectivity. That which contains (voluntarily or involuntarily) these elements Bion refers to as the container. Imagine a social group in which a member for some reason becomes the consistent container for others' projections. They become filled up with undigested emotional matter that others continually thrust into them, this is the scenario for the schizophrenic's family that Laing observed.

Such processes of unmediated communication occur all the time both within the family, the social group, the organisation and the wider society. The more the individual or group feels itself to be endangered or endangering, the more violent will be the processes of projective identification into the other. And what self is forced to disown the other is forced to internalise; a double alienation. The recipient of such projections becomes 'controlled from within', forced to play a part in the other's unconscious phantasy. As Ogden (1979) notes, 'there is a pressure exerted via the interpersonal interaction such that the recipient experiences pressure to think, feel and behave in a manner congruent with the projection' (p. 358). It was this kind of process that Fannon (1967) detected at work in racism, in this case a form of violent cultural projection ('I was burdened down by tom-toms, cannibalism, intellectual deficiency, fetishism, racial defects . . .'). As Anthias (1990) notes only where practices of exclusion (which are the hallmark of all ethnic phenomena) are accompanied by processes of inferiorisation against the ethnically constituted difference can we talk about racism (pp. 22–3).

In such instances there occurs a racialisation of ethnically constituted difference. What the black has to carry is what the white cannot own. Such forms of violent projective identification are therefore the medium through which self-alienation on the one hand, and oppression on the other, occur.

The Kleinian theory of projective identification is therefore an account of the way in which we alienate ourselves by disowning experiences which are unbearable. But it also provides an account of the way in which the other has the capacity to return us to ourselves. It therefore enables us to grasp the benign possibilities of the social environment.

Containing the capacity for thought

In Chapter 7 we will examine the predicament of a child which finds itself trapped in a violent situation that no-one can think about. We will see that in such instances the one who is forced to contain the violent emotions of others may respond by falling ill. A distress which cannot be thought about is mapped onto the body, a kind of 'internal action' in which the body itself is forced to become the container for poisonous emotional elements (Britton, 1992, p. 106). In both cases action is involuntary and unreflexive; in neither case does it lead to development, rather its effect is always destructive.

For Bion the essential task of life is the development of the capacity to contain one's own experience by being able to think about it. Crucially for Bion this is a function of the social environment. If all goes well the infant will take into itself not only nourishing thought but the capacity for containing such thoughts, a capacity at first performed for it by those that nurtured it. Although we have come a long way from the early years of the psychoanalytic movement this capacity to contain experience clearly parallels Freud's concept of the ego. Indeed just as Freud (1923) insisted that at first the ego is a bodily ego 'not merely a surface entity, but itself the projection of a surface', so, following Bion, Esther Bick (1968) suggested that at first the internalised container is experienced concretely as skin. The skin then is the first boundary. As we shall see in Chapter 4 this is the reason why individuals who experience chronic difficulty in containing experience so often manifest this through the configuration of their skin or body.

Ultimately, as the capacity to contain experience develops, the person's way of being in the world will shift from a mode in which splitting and projective identification is dominant to one in which it is subordinate to a way of being in which processes of reintegration and symbolisation are dominant. From this position, that is, Klein's *depressive position*, the tensions and contradictions of life can be held onto rather than used as the signal to tear things apart. That which is new or different is related to as if it were nourishing rather than threatening, the tendency towards idealisation on the one hand and denigration on the other can be held in check so that one's own lack is not visited upon the other. From this position we are able, as Young (1997) puts it, to transcend our own experience. Understanding the other can be experienced 'as sometimes getting out of ourselves and learning something new' (Young, p. 354), this can be likened to 'wonder, of an openness to the newness and mystery of the other person' (p. 357). But the ability to sustain this kind of attitude towards the world is constantly prone to internal and external attack (Hoggett, 1992). The social world makes a difference, and not just during the early periods of infant development when we are most dependent upon the other. It is hard to hold onto your own mind when all about you seem to be going crazy. Conversely the individual or group which is capable of sustaining the depressive position can make for a better world around them. The role of institutions is therefore crucial and it is to this that we shall now turn.

Cultures of development in welfare organisations

For development to occur there must be emotional contact with the other. This sounds like empathy but what I have in mind is something rather different. The idea of containment suggests a subject who is able to allow another's state of mind to be evoked in her. The prototype of this relationship is the infant and the nurturing other. Through projective identification the infant is able to evoke in the other states of mind which the infant cannot think about let alone give words to. This is, in one sense, the opposite of empathy if we think of empathy in terms of placing oneself in the other's shoes. What Bion has in mind is rather a subject who has the capacity to make herself available for the other so that the other can put something of himself which is overwhelming or unbearable into that person – his fear, his despair, his hatred and so on. As Young (1996, 1997) notes, the danger with empathy is that in placing oneself inside the other one projects something of oneself into him. Empathy can so easily become an intrusive, even oppressive, act through which the subject, in her desire to 'get inside the other' and experience the world in the way in which she imagines the other experiences it, actually makes herself unavailable to the other. In this sense empathy can be the enemy of receptiveness.

Let us imagine some examples. Think of the patient who fears he is dying but cannot give words to this experience out of shame or embarrassment. Think of the parent who is in despair about the behaviour of a child, or the disabled service user who feels so full of rage about a service which simply doesn't seem to understand how she feels. To make oneself available to such experiences, to be someone that the other feels they have finally 'got through to', means to be available to the other to evoke these unbearable experiences without seeking to smooth them over or make them better. In this sense, if containment is to occur, the individual worker, the group or institution must be available to be touched, moved, galvanised and disturbed by the other's experience.

Without emotional contact there can be no development, neither for the patient, client or pupil nor for the nurse, social worker or teacher, nor for the institutions to which they belong. This relationship between container and contained Bion (1970) terms 'symbiotic', meaning an encounter which is beneficial to both parties. In a by now classic study of the organisation of nursing at a large London teaching hospital in the late 1950s Menzies (1960) described an organisation geared to the avoidance of real emotional contact between nurses and patients. Rather than a culture constructed around the need to support staff who bear the anxieties which the work inevitably aroused, what she encountered was a socially structured defence system which by splitting up nursing tasks, depersonalising patients, promoting professional detachment, diffusing responsibility and removing all elements of staff discretion attempted to eradicate all elements of non-physical care from nursing practice. Not only was this injurious to patients by, for example, having adverse effects on factors such as recovery rates, it was also detrimental to the organisation, leading to low morale, excessive staff turnover and a high drop-out rate of those nurse trainees considered to be the most emotionally mature.

Without emotional contact between the users of welfare services and the group that provides for them there can be no developmental culture. A school which fails to understand the emotional reality of its pupils or a social work department which does all in its power to defend itself against the emotional reality of its clients avoids the potential explosiveness of real emotional contact but at the cost of the opportunity of development. One of the more perverse effects of the impact of the new managerialism upon the welfare state is what I have referred to as 'the new formalisation' (Hoggett, 1996). A culture of audit, quality assurance, performance monitoring and evaluation has descended upon the British public services in the 1990s. Teachers and nurses complain that they now spend as much time reporting on what they have done or plan to do as actually doing it. Taken to its extreme it is as if the time-consuming processes of completing assessments or detailed activity logs, writing up work plans or monitoring reports and reviews has become a simulacrum for real contact. It has also become a kind of resistor, a device for inhibiting the passage of disturbing social currents and affects into the sphere of government.

Considered now in terms of inter-group relations rather than in terms of the interpersonal encounter, how is it possible for the users of a service to speak forcibly of their experience as a group in a way whereby the other has to take notice? This poses fundamental questions both about the way in which silenced groups come to voice (Chapter 7) and about the conditions which facilitate democratic dialogue in contemporary society. This is the theme of the next chapter.

3
Conflict, Difference and Dialogue

Imagine the following situations. The elected management committee of a community association in a multi-racial urban area meets to develop a strategy for the use of its new community centre. A group of tenants on a housing estate meet to see if they can revive the tenants association which collapsed two years ago. A multi-disciplinary team of professional workers within the public sector meet with a variety of representatives of a local area to review strategy for promoting economic regeneration. A group of managers meet with a number of black and female staff to discuss perceived failures in the organisation's equal-opportunities policy. The elected political leaders of a declining maritime city embark upon a massive programme of consultation with neighbourhood and other communities to develop a programme for root and branch reform of the city's administration. Using parliament and the media a coalition government initiates a 'great debate' on the future of abortion and other aspects of women's rights in a strongly Catholic society.

All of these are real examples of politics in action. In different ways they all pose the same issue – to what extent is it possible to promote real dialogue between groups whose identities and interests are different? More specifically, in a world where the powerless are increasingly fragmented into different movements and communities, how can they prevent such differences from becoming sources of division and how can they use such differences to enrich their struggle against dominant classes and elites? Are there ways in which people can speak across the boundaries of gender, class, race, sexuality, ethnicity, emotional distress and disability so that their voices are listened to? Or is the quest to democratise everyday life a fruitless one, will patterns of dominance always undermine the effort to speak truthfully and to listen openly? These are vital questions both for those who seek merely to understand public life in all its complexity and for those who seek to change it. The question we are concerned with here is the possibility of human communication. This is to be understood not simply as the transfer of information or facts but as a form of human exchange in which our potential for self-understanding is enhanced and hence the capacity for the self-organisation of life can be developed in opposition to the regulation of the market or the state. But anyone who has participated in the kinds of situation described above knows how difficult it is to achieve such a dialogue. And the difficulty is no less great for those who are already united in common cause. The women's movement, for example, has in the last thirty years moved through an initial phase of undifferentiation to a phase in which the particular identities of women in terms of class, race, sexuality and so on threatened to overwhelm the common identity of gender. The problem of working in common cause within difference emerged as one of the key issues facing this movement in the 1990s (Albrecht & Brewer, 1990).

What is it then that stands opposed to the possibility of social dialogue? In this chapter I will examine two interlinked obstacles. First, there is the distorting effect of power on communication. Secondly, differences in and of themselves can arouse anxiety, as a consequence we are ambivalent towards the otherness of the stranger and lack steadfastness in our desire to engage in dialogue with it. I will argue that while neither of these obstacles sets absolute limits to dialogue much more care needs to be given to the kinds of political and institutional practices capable of modifying the distorting effects of power and containing the fear of otherness.

Communication without power?

One avenue for approaching the possibility of dialogue has been developed by Habermas (1970, 1983) through his notion of 'communicative action' exemplified by the 'ideal speech' situation. For Habermas communicative action is action oriented toward mutual understanding (McCarthy, 1991). Communicative action can be contrasted to strategic and manipulative forms of interaction and that whole range of interaction 'in which these and other elements are combined in a variety of ways to constitute the "organised artful practices of everyday life", "relations in public", "games people play", and the like' (McCarthy, 1991, p. 132). I do not wish to enter the extensive debates that this perspective, sometimes referred to as 'communicative ethics', has provoked (Benhabib & Dallmayr, 1990). I find it useful to think of communicative ethics in terms of the belief that people do have both the desire and the capacity to understand and be understood by others – a simple enough idea you might think but, as we shall see, one fraught with difficulties. Later, in Chapter 8, I will explore the opposing possibility (i.e. that 'not-understanding' and misunderstanding are to be preferred to understanding) but here I want to assume the perspective offered by communicative ethics has some, albeit partial, validity and will therefore examine what kind of social and political practices undermine or facilitate the possibility of dialogue. I will do this by building upon the work of Benhabib (1990, 1992), a sympathetic critic of Habermas, who offers a modified version of communicative ethics, one which seems more open to the tension between the necessity for dialogue and the power of difference that often confronts us.

Benhabib (1992) describes a number of preconditions which must exist if communicative action is to occur. For example there must exist in principal the possibility of actors reaching a 'reasonable agreement' (though not a consensus) which can be arrived at under conditions corresponding to a fair debate, that is a debate conducted according to mutually agreed procedural rules. Benhabib (1992) points out that such rules in fact presuppose the existence of 'a moral idea that we ought to respect each other as beings whose standpoint is worthy of equal consideration (the principle of universal moral respect) and that furthermore.... We ought to treat each other as concrete human beings whose capacity to express this standpoint we ought to enhance by creating, whenever possible, social practices embodying the discursive ideal (the principle of egalitarian reciprocity) (p. 31). The first principle is roughly equivalent to the traditional saying 'do unto others as you would have others do unto you' (p. 32) and is founded upon the norm of reciprocity which, as we shall see in Chapter 10, is argued by some to be universal in its applicability. The second principle is outlined most clearly in Benhabib's earlier essay where, speaking of the ideal speech situation, she suggests, 'within such conversations each has the same symmetrical rights to various speech acts, to initiate new topics, to ask for reflections about the presuppositions of the conversation, etc.' (1990, p. 337).

Clearly the boundary between these two principles is sometimes blurred and I will return at a later point to explore them in more detail. For the time being I simply wish to indicate, if my understanding of this perspective is accurate, that the idea of ideal speech suggests that in principle there are in existence universal rational and moral grounds which can provide the foundation for a degree of mutual understanding.

As I understand it the perspective of communicative ethics is an idealised one in two senses. First, in the sense of it being an 'ideal type' towards which real instances will only ever be an approximation. Second in the sense of it being an ideal towards which political and social practice should aspire. Clegg (1989), summarising the position of Habermas, suggests,

> In principle, according to Habermas (1984), it is always possible to settle any difference in agreement if the parties to the disputation are mindful to do so and if the appropriate conditions exist. He argues ... that the search for consensus is inherent to community expressed through language, because such a speech-community can be built only on trust, not power. Where power is present, communication is 'systematically distorted' (pp. 93–4).

So is it possible to construct spaces for social dialogue in which an ethic of trust and inquiry takes precedence over the play of power? As we shall see, there are no simple answers to this question. To help us think through some of the issues it is time to move from the realm of theory to look at a few practical examples of attempts to create dialogue within work organisations and political systems.

A space for dialogue within organisations?

In the late 1960s a tradition of organisational intervention emerged concerned to promote what it termed Organisational Development (OD) (Argyris & Schon, 1974; French & Bell, 1978). If it can be agreed that the continuous process of revising and remaking reality, i.e. of interrogating traditional practices, is of one of the fundamental principles of modernity then contemporary managerialism stands very much as the exemplar of this principle (Hoggett, 1997). OD, and its more contemporary variants concerned with 'The Learning Organisation' (Pedler, Burgoyne & Boydell, 1991), can be seen as a specific 'intervention technology' which emerged to address the problem of organisational inertia. This problem was becoming acute as traditional bureaucratic forms proved unable to cope with the pace of change in political, technological and consumer environments in the late twentieth century. If organisations were to become more adaptive and flexible, if they were to become permanently innovative, then the manner in which organisations learnt or failed to learn would have to become a focus both for study and intervention.

One of the most influential figures within this OD movement was Chris Argyris (Argyris & Schon, 1974; Argyris, 1976). Drawing upon the work of Gregory Bateson (1973) (work which incidently also had an important impact upon Laing and others investigating schizophrenia within family systems) Argyris suggested the existence of two models of learning (single and double loop learning) within organisations. For Argyris the problem of inertia could be traced to the way in which power was exercised in organisations. He attempted to tackle squarely the issue that had exercised the minds of management theorists for decades – the seeming impossibility of generating bottom-up flows of information within organisations. Argyris was exercised by the phenomenon we will examine in detail in Chapter 7, that when power assumes the form of dominance it has a silencing effect. For those concerned to enhance organisational effectiveness this posed a problem, for if an organisation was to learn, adapt and innovate it had to devise means of learning from its experience. But this requirement was undermined within a company culture which stated 'do not confront company policies and objectives, especially those that top management is excited about' (Argyris, 1977). As Argyris notes this then placed employees in a double-bind for one set of (implicit) rules stated 'hide errors' whereas another set (typically more explicit) stated 'reveal errors'. Argyris therefore drew attention to the way in which value and belief systems within organisations operated at two levels, at the level of explicit rhetoric and at the level of implicit practice. Typically actors would follow the rules which were implicit to the practice of the organisation – 'well the company might say X but you quickly learn that what it really believes in is Y'. If learning was to occur in such organisations then the blocks to communication which occurred around the organisation's boundaries (i.e. between different organisational levels or between different functional groupings) because of the play of power had to be addressed.

OD practitioners (Schein & Greiner, 1977) developed a variety of techniques for intervening in organisations to overcome such blocks to communication including role-swapping, the development of 'shadow structures' and various participative techniques for pursuing problem solving and forward planning (techniques which today find an echo in the techniques of 'continuous improvement' and 'employee empowerment' which are central to Total Quality Management). But perhaps the most familiar technique, one which has virtually acquired the same symbolic status as the psychoanalyst's couch, corresponded to the workshop method. As Argyris put it, 'the strategy is to get a group of people (usually away from the office) to sit down and level with each other. The sessions are managed by an expert in group dynamics and problem solving. The president gives his or her blessing and assures people that no one will be hurt if he or she speaks the truth' (p. 121). For a period of time in the States in the 1970s and then in Britain and Europe in the 1980s such 'development workshops' (e.g. team development weekends and awaydays) were a familiar, if esoteric, feature of the organisational landscape. Nor was this attempt to create 'ideal speech' situations within the unpromising environment of the modern business organisation the kind of catastrophe one might otherwise be inclined to suspect. Some bosses did listen, the learning capacity of some organisations was enhanced and, as mentioned before, the principle of open communication has now been adapted towards the more task-centred organisational learning technology of TQM.

Nevertheless by the mid-1980s the interest in OD, which at one time had been so great that the 'OD movement' took on the characteristics of one of those rather exotic social movements which occasionally sweep the management world (Soeters, 1986), was beginning to wane. The key problem was not so much that company presidents were firing staff for being open but the conditions of openness which had been generated in workshops were not being generalised within the company as a whole. Hence participants had the experience of a 'high' which could not be sustained 'back in the organisation'. Furthermore it became apparent that the kinds of organisations which employed OD interventions were those that were in some way already predisposed towards developing more open forms of communication – where OD practitioners attempted to intervene in organisations which were resistant to participative methods the results were often disastrous. The more acute practitioners began to reappraise the extent to which such interventions were feasible within what one critic called 'power cultures' (Reason, 1984). Such cultures existed in organisations in which small elites governed via the use of manipulation, threat and misinformation, i.e. where there was no attempt to seek legitimacy for the authority which was being asserted. In these settings power was used to suppress and distort communication. It might be argued that this is what most business organisations are like, a mixture of what Etzioni (1961) described long ago as the coercive and calculative rather than moral basis of organisational attachment. But this is in itself a gross over-simplification. The 'groupism' of the Japanese corporation (Dore, 1989), the high-commitment workplace of many advanced-technology organisations (Lowe & Oliver, 1991) and even the complex negotiated order of the traditional public institution defy categorisation simply in terms of crude and simply structured power cultures.

In a subsequent section we will examine the play of power within public institutions but first we should pause to reflect upon two issues raised by the OD experience. First of all we need to consider the possibility that leaders with formal authority may seek to use the power which accompanies this authority to promote dialogue rather than undermine it. Secondly, we should remember that while forms of dialogue may be developed in particular sites and spaces they will tend to be encircled by power cultures in which strategic and manipulative forms of behaviour dominate.

Power in the service of dialogue

Power is not one-dimensional, it can have positive or negative effects. We need to remind ourselves of this sometimes, so used are we to experiencing power as something destructive and disabling. We need to revise the problem of 'ideal speech'. Power may have distorting effects but a person may also use her power to empower another. In other words, power may be exercised to build trust and assemble the preconditions for dialogue. If power has the capacity to systematically distort communication then it may also have the capacity to systematically facilitate communication. These would clearly be two very different forms of power, a subject we will return to later. The possibility that power might be used to facilitate open communication seems essential to the very idea of 'making things public' by making them 'accessible to debate, reflection, action and moral-political transformation' (Benhabib, 1992 p. 113). No better contemporary exponent of this philosophy can be found than Vaclav Havel.

The philosopher-president reflected upon his experience of being in a position of formal authority in his collection of essays *Summer Meditations* (Havel, 1992). Havel insists that it is largely up to politicians which social forces they choose to empower and which they seek to suppress, 'whether they rely on the good in each citizen, or the bad' (p. 4). Havel speaks of the politicians' 'moral responsibility', indeed of the idea that politics should itself be the practice of morality. He constantly refers to the need to hold in the imagination an idea of the general good, a responsibility 'to and for the whole'. He is aware that many might think him naïve, for democratic politics has become so dominated by the manoeuvre and half-truths of political parties (what Havel calls the 'dictatorship of partisanship' (p. 53)) that it seems far removed from the ideal of open speech. Yet Havel insists that it is possible for leadership to be moral. Speaking of one of his critics within his own government he argues

> The idea that the world might actually be changed by the force of truth, the power of a truthful word, the strength of a free spirit, conscience, and responsibility – with no guns, no lust for power, no political wheeling and dealing – was quite beyond the horizon of his understanding (p. 5).

There is a long but firm line from the abstractions of Habermas to the personal convictions and practices of central Europe's divided republic. But what Havel makes clear through his meditations upon 'being in power' is the character, the texture and the taste of a culture that would be democratic. And in a similar way Havel 'knows' its opposite, knows it intuitively,

> As in everything else, I must start with myself. . . . I am frequently advised to be more 'tactical', not to say everything right away, to dissimulate gently, not to fear wooing more than my nature commands, or to distance myself from someone against my real will in the matter. In the interests of strengthening my hand, I am advised at times to assent to someone's ambition for power, to flatter someone merely because it pleases him, or to reject someone even though it goes against my convictions, because he does not enjoy favour with others (p. 7).

Here, then, is a way of being which is antithetical to open speech. It is the cult of power, the culture of power in which every word, silence, expression and action becomes part of the currency of territorial advantage. If Havel is the exemplar of open speech then Machiavelli's 'The Prince' is the exemplar of the power culture. Clegg (1989, p. 202) is careful to acknowledge his own indebtedness to Machiavelli and points out how Foucault and others have also explicitly acknowledged the Machiavellian antecedents of their arguments. From Machiavelli we draw an altogether different picture of social systems as sites where factions organise, alliances are formed, agendas are hidden, deals are struck, vulnerabilities exploited and strengths flattered. The Italian Marxist Antonio Gramsci (1977), whose most famous essay 'The Modern Prince' clearly demonstrates the debt he too owed to Machiavelli, notes that the modern partisan is constantly aware of the balance of forces. 'Reality' at any given moment is always a dynamic reality, a temporary equilibrium into which the partisan seeks to intervene to create a new balance of forces, one which corresponds to his or her will. To survive and prosper in a power culture the prerequisite is to become a skillful political operator, both a tactition and a strategist.

The language of power

Clegg (1989, p. 142) argues, if we see that 'all interaction involves the use of power' then organisations, families, social movements, governments, etc. are simply sites for the play of power. An example may help here.

In the early 1980s I witnessed one of the most glorious failures in the recent history of British urban government (Hoggett, Lawrence & Fudge, 1984). The London Borough of Hackney, which was and still is one of the most deprived localities in the whole of the UK, had been taken over by a new group of politicians, a group containing many community, feminist and other activists committed to a wildly radical programme to transform the government of the borough along the lines of Red Bologna (a city several of them had visited). As their proposal for transformation was developed (the 'Hackney Redprint' proposed radical schemes for introducing both industrial and tenant democracy) it was fascinating to watch as the balance of forces within the Town Hall began to crystallise. On each side there was a coalition of different interest groups which had their own objectives for either supporting or opposing the changes being advocated. For example, those pushing for change included a number of powerful young senior managers who, although they were completely opposed ideologically to the Redprint, saw it as an opportunity to shake up Hackney's ossified bureaucracy and, as one of them put it, 'bring its management into the twentieth century'. Opponents of change included a powerful group within the white collar union, NALGO, known fondly as 'The Tankies' (i.e. a group of ultra-orthodox members of the Communist Party of Great Britain), most of Hackney's long-standing cadre of white, male managers and a group of senior managers within the housing department who were among the most progressive in the whole borough. The latter opposed the Redprint because it threatened to undo their own programme for reforming the local housing service which was already partially implemented. In a similar fashion the Hackney Labour Party was itself divided not just between old and new guard, for the new guard was divided between the libertarian and non-libertarian left. Finally the local government trade unions were also divided, the manual workers unions (many of whose workers lived in the borough and knew what lousy services it delivered) generally favoured the proposals for change while the white collar union NALGO virulently opposed it – eventually this led to the latter taking industrial action against an alliance of building workers and tenants in a dispute about the running of a local estate office (Puddephat, 1987).

In spite of the hectic factionalising that was going on the socialist politicians in charge of developing and implementing the Redprint attempted to use a set of methods for taking their ideas forward which were deeply democratic. A massive programme of open-ended public consultation was embarked upon using interactive small group methods, video work and so on. Similarly an attempt was made to consult with the workforce though this was continually blocked by the white collar unions. Slowly, but inexorably, the initiative began to sink beneath a sea of consultation for as the one side sought to extend the frontiers of open dialogue the other sought to organise and manoeuvre until, at last, the white collar unions struck forbidding their own members to carry out any duties related to the Redprint initiative. Because the forces for change had not been organised they lacked the strength to take on the white collar unions and the whole initiative was effectively paralysed for almost a year. By this time the political leadership had lost credibility and was replaced.

Like Havel, the young leaders of Hackney's council were seen by their opponents as naïve, their lack of pragmatism and 'political nous' leading to their undoing. The feminist notion that the means should prefigure the ends was seen as fine in theory but disastrous in practice.

With this example in mind I wish to sketch a picture of the welfare state as a site for the play of power in which factions, each with their own discrete objectives and drawn from different structural interest groups, form alliances with other factions around a common agenda in order to engage in a struggle for position in different arenas. The concept of structural interest group I derive from Alford (1975) and from the work of Kouzes and Mico (1979) on Domain Theory. Alford focuses primarily upon the struggle between two structural interest groups – the professional and managerial – within the US health sector. I wish to extend the concept slightly to refer to those social formations which have become institutionally embedded within the apparatus of the welfare state, and as such are national in scope rather than purely local phenomena. This leads me to suggest that the character of the welfare state is partly the outcome of a complex power game played by four primary players (i.e. structural interest groups) – professionals, managers/administrators, organised labour and competitive political parties. Following Alford we can assume the existence of a fifth player, 'the public' (local citizens, service users), whose rights are ritually invoked by the other players but who is rarely able to play an independent role. We can therefore think of power as the medium through which the struggle for position between these players occurs within the state. However the players themselves are not homogenous groups. As the preceding example indicates, although organised labour is partly institutionalised it also exists partially outside of this context, capable of taking 'unofficial' action and forming independent alliances with service users. The different professions are also engaged in struggles between themselves to extend the territory of the labour markets they control (Friedson, 1994).

From this perspective two kinds of change may occur. First order change (change within pattern) occurs when a shift in positions enables some players to become more dominant and others less so. For example, recent government reforms in the UK appear to have been aimed at strengthening the hand of managerialist interests while weakening some of the most powerful professional interests (e.g. Hospital Consultants, Headteachers) by incorporating them within the managerialist paradigm (Ball, 1993; Clarke and Newman, 1997; Hoggett, 1990). When a group of players obtain a dominant position they will attempt to change the rules to their own advantage (Clegg likens this to 'skewing' the table upon which the game is played (Clegg, 1989, p. 209)) thereby continually 'outflanking'

(Clegg, p. 220) their opponents. Just occasionally however someone (typically representing social forces excluded by the institutions
of welfare governance) comes along who threatens to challenge the
very nature of the game itself (i.e. the nature of the rules, the status and number of the players and the nature of the stakes which
are being played for). In such situations, as Hackney's young feminists and socialists found out, opposing structural interest groups
unite together to defeat those who dare question the nature of the
game itself. In the rare situations where such insurgents are successful, second order change will occur (i.e. change of pattern), this
is equivalent to a qualitative transformation in the local social relations of welfare. Such victories will typically be recouped either
as wider political forces move in to abort the development (see
Duncan & Goodwin (1988) on the abolition of the Greater London
Council) or as the traditional players recover their composure, regroup
and begin to recoup the losses incurred. This is often achieved by
'bending' the radicals' strategy to a more traditional agenda.

To return to Gramsci's notion of the balance of forces, at any
given moment in time a dynamic equilibrium will be constructed.
But this equilibrium is not equivalent to an equal balance of forces,
rather it relates to a status quo defined in terms of what some
players can get away with and what others are forced to accept. In
other words the equilibrium refers to a pattern of accepted dominance. We can think of this as a set of stable or recurring games in
which most players win something (but some win more than others)
and lose something (but some lose more than others). Thus although
at one level actors are engaged in unequal power relationships, i.e.
of dominance and submission, at another level they are engaged
in a complex process of collusion and collaboration. All actors have
a stake in how things are, including trade unions and subordinate
professional groups such as nurses. As the Hackney example illustrates, the forces at work draw upon both nationally organised,
and therefore structural, interest groups but also upon specifically
local interest groups – networks, cliques and factions built upon
ties of connection, tradition, etc. specific to that locale.

This way of picturing the institutions of the public sphere draws
our attention to the fact that although power within the local public
sphere is typically dispersed it can nevertheless coalesce quickly to
produce a concentrated force when the game itself is subject to
challenge. At these moments a dominant coalition forms as the
institutionalised interests combine together to defend themselves

against the new insurgents. This is equivalent to the creation of a temporary form of 'sovereign power' as a number of key players unite to form a kind of establishment (see Chapter 9) which fights to preserve the rules of the game. Innumerable examples of this form of struggle exist. In a previous article (Hoggett, 1984) I noted how, in the late 1960s and early 1970s, the anti-psychiatry movement constituted just such a form of insurgency. Such forms of insurgency are typically dealt with via processes of marginalisation and recoupment. To use this example, dissident professionals were either driven out of the state apparatus altogether or abandoned the struggle within the state to set up alternative practices outside it. Some of their ideas however underwent a process of recoupment and came to inform the routine problem solving activity of the traditional policy community but in a neutered form (e.g. the de-institutionalisation movement). Moreover sometimes the assertion of sovereign power will be supported by the direct intervention of the central state – it is worth remembering that in Britain in the 1980s some insurgent organisations were abolished, dissident local politicians surcharged and disqualified and a number of equalities-type practices and policies were outlawed (Burns, Hambleton & Hoggett, 1994).

Such attempts to change the pattern of welfare (as opposed to change within pattern), reveal a further dimension of the inertial nature of the welfare establishment. Here Giddens's (1984) framework is helpful, for the play of power within the welfare state can be seen as a form of routinisation. Even those in less powerful positions such as organised labour and the semi-professions have a psychological investment in maintaining a reality which, while it may be unfair, offers some material rewards and is at least orderly and predictable. Such forms of routinisation provide workers with a way of not thinking or feeling too much. As we saw in the previous chapter, routinisation provides a way of containing anxiety and other negative emotions aroused by working with the sick, the dying, the distressed, the bad and the mad.

Contrasting pictures of the public sphere

We appear to have two equally legitimate accounts of the public sphere. One emphasises the ethical basis of human behaviour and the possibility that even leaders may behave in an ethical way. Public life can be seen as the sphere in which needs and interests can be made accessible to debate, reflection, action and moral-political transformation. The other account insists that all interaction within the public sphere involves the use of power, and hence the purpose of communication is to conceal rather than to reveal. Interaction is about positional advantage – feelings are to be disguised, vulnerability to be hidden, agendas to be concealed. Underlying our notions of political democracy there is therefore a paradox, for, viewed from one direction, the public institutions which give expression to democracy appear to be saturated with a power culture which precludes open speech. Moreover some interests and voices, often those of the least powerful, appear to be excluded altogether.

But we have also uncovered some other possibilities. If all interaction involves the use of power then it is also clear that power may be used to enable as well as disable. Our collective experience of organisations and work teams reveals that within some social contexts the spirit of inquiry and the search for mutual understanding is strong whereas in others it is weak. Within the social space of the team, the organisation or even the locality, we know that it is feasible to create cultures which are more or less democratic, so that while we might note the malignant effects of *power cultures* we might also celebrate the benign effects of *cultures of dialogue*. But after twenty years of working in the local public institutions as activist, researcher and consultant I am now convinced that there are real limits to the extent to which politicians, managers, professionals and trade unionists will engender cultures of dialogue in the absence of pressure from outside, from the excluded public, to do so.

Civil society: the need for, and fear of, the Other

Drawing upon the work of Hannah Arendt, Benhabib (1992, p. 93) usefully contrasts two different models of the 'public space'. The dominant perspective corresponds to the 'agonistic' view, one with its antecedents in the image of the Greek *polis*, a competitive space 'in which one competes for recognition, precedence and acclaim'. This is the sphere of political society, of formal government, of public institutions. But there is another form of public space, the 'associational' one, one which emerges whenever people act in concert by engaging in struggle, creating their own communities and milieux or sharing dreams and experiences. For much of the time this is an excluded public – the object of consultation and co-option whose voice is ritually invoked but never actually heard by the structural interest groups which compete for territory within the institutionalised and agonistic public sphere (Alford, 1975). Tenants associations, rank and file trade union networks, women's groups, cultural associations, community organisations, campaign groups, all such organisations 'engage in concert' every day. This is the realm of participatory democracy, of non-party politics, of civil as opposed to political society. The associational model enables us to go beyond equating the public sphere with government and thereby enables us to redefine 'the public' to include sites where 'the usually excluded' act together in concert.

It would be understandable to view this realm as a more naturally and openly dialogic sphere than its more institutionalised counterpart. But this would be mistaken, for if public institutions are corrupted by the play of power the dialogic capacity of civil society seems to be undermined by a different phenomenon, the disintegrative impact of differences.

According to Benhabib (1992, p. 9), standing somewhere behind the image of the ideal speech community of Habermas lies the idea of the 'general interest'. The concept of the representative, as opposed to the delegate, assumes a relationship between a constituency of interests and needs on the one hand and the re-presentation of them in a different time and place by one entrusted to do so on this constituency's behalf. While there may be much that is wrong with representative democracy it is the only system to have been devised so far which gets close to representing a collection of interests as opposed to a particular interest (Burns, Hambleton & Hoggett, 1994). While the modern political party undoubtedly gives expression to some particular interests (e.g. class interests) more than others, unlike the vast majority of organisations of civil society it is not built upon the basis of a particular interest or identity. This difference can be seen vividly in Eastern Europe today where the difficulty of creating parties of the modern form is illustrated by hundreds of tiny pseudo-party organisations representing religious, peasant, ethnic or other interests. Because the organisations of civil society are built upon particular interests or identities they are in their nature sectional or particularistic (Spicker, 1993). For political society the recognition and acceptance of politics beyond the struggles of competitive parties is the key problem. 'Active citizens' are to be praised so long as they don't protest, shout, organise or fight among themselves. Civil society however is built around a myriad differences of which gender, age, culture, lifestyle and belief are but a few. It is the overcoming of such differences to create what Arendt describes as 'an enlarged mentality' or what we might call a more transcendent and critical consciousness which is the problem. In a fragmented society how can the babble of excluded voices speak in concert?

The question of difference cannot be grasped without visualising it at both the real and the 'imaginary' levels. At the real level of the concrete other I can be engaged in competition with a Bengali family for scarce public housing in my neighbourhood or in argument with older members of my community association about the way in which its social facilities are run. I may also know something of this other's life, about where she lives or works, misfortunes within her family which have been endured, the character of her children, and so on. She is a real person, with texture and form. But this person is not just someone who has different interests or preferences to me – she may also be black while I am white, or she may be old while I am young. To the extent that blackness or age assumes significance for me this person also exists as someone empty of particularity, as the Other, i.e. a generalised instance of all the others of that category – black people, elderly people, etc. A hierarchy of values becomes mapped upon such differences, a hierarchy which partially, but only partially, corresponds to the differential location of such groups within the division of labour, a division which places women, black people, elderly people and others at both a material and cultural disadvantage (Fraser, 1995).

But the meaning that the Other contains for me cannot just be understood in terms of the structuring of disadvantage within societies. We cannot understand the Otherness of the gay male for the heterosexual in this way, or the Otherness of the Downs Syndrome child for the child with no learning difficulties. For the Other is also a container for my own fear, her difference to me perturbs me at a deeper level, for her Otherness is a reminder to me of what I have repressed in the construction of my own identity – my sense of inferiority, my bisexuality, my fear of physical imperfection, my fear of aging and death. In this sense the Other exists as a container for that which I cannot bear, for that which the individual or collective body lacks the capacity to understand as a part of itself. This phenomenon, which I explore in greater detail in Chapter 4, implies that the Other has an emotional meaning for me, she exists as an object of my unconscious phantasy, she is the return of my repressed nature.

The working through of differences is therefore not simply a process of rational understanding in which I learn about what it is to experience things as another experiences them, it is also a process of re-integration whereby that which has been split off and denied or repressed is taken back in. Returning to the theme of the last chapter, it is my self-alienation partially overcome. In other words it is both a cognitive and emotional process in which I and my group engage intellectually and passionately. It is a process in which what the other offers I accept by allowing myself to be affected and enriched – for what he or she returns to me I once possessed but have now lost. In this way the self-understanding of the individual, the group or the movement grows and hence their autonomy is enhanced; this is the full meaning of Arendt's 'enlarged mentality'. But how are such differences to be worked through, how is it possible for self to engage in dialogue with Other?

Picture this conversation, a real one that was reported to me, in a community centre, between Lyn, a young, white feminist, and a much older woman, Alice, who has lived in the area all her life. Lyn has never been to the centre before, she is a trainee community worker and Alice, a key figure within the community association which runs the centre, is showing her around. Lyn innocently asks Alice whether the area has changed in all the years she has been there. Alice embarks upon a long and winding story of how the area has declined and in doing so eventually gets on to the topic of 'the Asians':

> The Asians have taken over all the shops . . . we used to have a lovely shopping centre on Chelsea Rd . . . there's one English shop on St. Mark's Rd, all the rest are Paki. . . . I know I shouldn't say that but I tend to . . .

Lyn could have objected vociferously to Alice's use of language and added that it was a clear manifestation of her racist outlook. On the other hand she could have thought these things without saying them to Alice's face. It would have been likely that Alice would soon have noticed that Lyn had become quiet and distanced and the conversation would soon have ended. Alternatively Lyn could say to Alice warmly but firmly, 'you're quite right Alice, you know that "Paki" is a term of abuse and I'd prefer you not to use it, that said, tell me more about the lack of shops selling the things you need around here'. In the first instance Alice's language acts as a sign to Lyn that the woman is irredeemable, a lost cause, a racist, someone to be argued with but not someone with whom one could have any kind of dialogue. In the second instance Lyn makes clear that she does not share Alice's perceptions nor is she happy with her style of speech but while stating her difference she persists with her belief that dialogue is possible and with a desire to understand the world as Alice sees it. In the second conversation Lyn recognises Alice's desire to be understood, whereas in the first this is refused.

In reality Alice worked effectively with many black people on the community association, some of whom she regarded as her friends. She also became strongly committed to the association's equal opportunities policy so long as that included a commitment to 'her community' by which she meant the older, long-established white residents in the area. By demonstrating a willingness to understand, Lyn has recognised Alice as a particular other with a history which is both specific to her own biography and shared with others. If all goes well Lyn will learn something of what it means to be old, a woman and working class and Alice may learn something of what it means to be young, a feminist and a member of the local Asian community. Both may learn something about the way in which different oppressions interact, of how it is possible to contain within oneself both the oppressor and the oppressed. As Pheterson (1990) says, 'it is important to note that internalised oppression and internalised domination interact not only between different persons but also intrapsychically within one person' (p. 45). Each may therefore learn something of the standpoint of the other.

Benhabib (p. 168) notes that this capacity for understanding, for exercising Arendt's 'enlarged capacity', should not be confused with empathy although it is related to it. She notes that empathetic individuals may lack this mentality for their empathetic nature may make it difficult for them to draw the boundaries between self and other sufficiently to allow difference to be maintained. Rather, in our cameo Lyn demonstrates an ability to combine what Khan (1974) calls 'compassionate empathy' and 'aggressive differentiation'. This desire to understand and therefore to provide the other with the opportunity of being understood is what I think Benhabib means by 'universal moral respect' – one of her normative preconditions for the existence of the ideal speech situation. To recognise difference and yet retain curiosity can provide the basis for a dialectic of understanding. As Benhabib notes, in her criticism of Habermas, there is no assumption here that such a dialectic will lead to consensus, rather, if all goes well, it will correspond to an 'open-ended process of moral argumentation (p. 169).

Alperin (1990) suggests that the process of adopting another's standpoint, of being able to see the world as they see and experience it, is crucial if the various fragments of civil society are to come together as a more coherent force. When people struggle on the basis of class, race or gender they sharpen their understanding of the relations of dominance which are specific to that oppression. While each develops a critical understanding it tends to be limited to particular aspects of the social system. Contrary to the classical Marxist view no single form of domination (i.e. of class) can be considered *a priori* to be the driving force in all contexts; rather, as Alperin notes,

> it is imperative for oppressed groups with different standpoints to form alliances in order to understand how different types of oppression interact. If different critical standpoints are more readily available to different oppressed groups through struggle, and if different types of oppression are interrelated, then it would follow that a thorough understanding of the complexity of social relations in any particular historical moment could be achieved most effectively through alliances between groups with different standpoints. (pp. 29–30)

Preconditions for dialogue

In this final section I wish to draw upon and develop Benhabib's two fundamental principles (of universal moral respect and egalitarian reciprocity) in order to outline some of the conditions which contribute to social dialogue in a hypothetical encounter between two parties.

There must exist a genuine spirit of inquiry, a desire to understand the other and be understood by the other.

This relates to the principle of universal moral respect. Psychoanalysis suggests that the spirit of inquiry will always be marked by a certain ambivalence. Resistance will be encountered at the point at which a genuine understanding of the other of necessity leads to a reappraisal of the self. Moreover there is a legitimate limit to how far the other, particularly the other without power, wishes to be 'known' and a point beyond which self's desire to understand becomes an intrusive and violent need to penetrate and 'lay bare'. But to say that the spirit of inquiry will never be pure is not to say that a genuineness of spirit cannot exist. The individual and collective subject is fractured and contradictory, I am simply insisting that there will always be a space within that subjectivity where the spirit of inquiry is strong. The task is to create cultures of inquiry which facilitate this spirit.

Experience must be capable of representation, both to self and to other.

Benhabib (1992, p. 8) describes communicative action as 'the model of a moral conversation in which the capacity to reverse perspectives, that is, the willingness to reason from another's point of view, and the sensitivity to hear their voice is paramount'. But for this to occur the other must have found their own voice in order to be heard in their own terms. As we shall see in Chapter 6 empowerment involves the capacity to represent (through language and other media) experience which was previously unrepresentable to self, i.e. a process of 'coming to voice'. Secondly, some forms of experience, those which can be described as traumatic, are virtually beyond representation. For example, only now are we beginning to find ways of hearing the voice of those who have been subject to violent sexual abuse in childhood. As Valerie Sinason (1994) has pointed out with regard to satanic abuse, the problem for some children is that even the most well meaning adults cannot bring themselves to hear what the child needs to speak of. Jewish victims of the holocaust and the peoples of Bosnia and Kosovo today face precisely this problem. Moreover traumatic experience may be cumulative (Khan, 1974) rather than specific to a particular set of incidents and, although this is speculative, it may be fruitful to consider the experience of, say, the black person growing up in a racist society in such terms.

There must be a common medium through which self and other can engage in dialogue.

In arguing that collective decisions must be taken through procedures which are radically open and fair to all Benhabib (1992, p. 9) notes that the voice of some groups 'may not be formulable in the accepted language of public discourse.' One is reminded here of public meetings organised by political parties or local authorities, the very language and style of which exclude a whole range of different groups, a theme we will return to in Chapter 6. Every meeting space will be bound by certain conventions many of which unreflexively express a class and gendered character. Young (1996) argues persuasively that the very models of deliberative democracy which have emerged in political theory privilege the cool, reasonable and disembodied voices of white middle-class men. Instead she insists that deliberative spaces must be ones which welcome the 'embodied and excited' voices of excluded groups and include greeting, rhetoric and storytelling as essential forms of communication.

In recent years many new ways of running meetings have been introduced as established conventions have been questioned and 'the meeting' itself becomes a site for experimentation. To give some examples – the informal neighbourhood forums of the London Borough of Islington (Burns, Hambleton & Hoggett, 1994); service user forums for people with physical disabilities, learning difficulties and mental health problems (Martin, 1994), the unstructured forums of the Exodus Collective (Clarke, 1999), the 'listening posts' organised by the London-based Organisation for the Promotion of Understanding in Society (OPUS); the 'spontaneous agendas' of grass roots coalitions fighting the Criminal Justice Act, the road building programmes and destructive farming methods (Brass & Koziell, 1999; Wall, 1999); the open local and regional meetings of the Anti-Poll Tax Campaign (Burns, 1992), and so on.

One specific issue which should be highlighted concerns the problem of racist and sexist language in public forums. The paradox must be accepted that if a common medium is to be established then rules of discursive constraint must apply. In other words there must exist a set of rules proscribing certain ways of speaking if usually excluded groups are to be able to enter social dialogue. If forms of discursive constraint can be negotiated rather than imposed then they are likely to be more effective but such is the interplay between different forms of disadvantage that establishing an agreed framework within groups whose members are drawn from different class and ethnic backgrounds and have different sexualities can be an extraordinarily complex matter (Harrison, Hoggett & Jeffers, 1995).

The limits to understanding must be understood.

The question is not whether consensus can be reached or agreement can be complete, rather the question is whether a 'good enough' understanding can be constructed for people to be able to act in concert. I would concur with Christopher Bollas in believing that the idea that we can understand one another is largely illusory. But, as he notes, this is not to counsel despair; because we do not comprehend one another we are free to invent one another. 'We create and re-create, form and break our "senses" or "understandings" of one another, secured from anxiety or despair by the illusion of understanding and yet freed by its impossibility to imagine one another' (Bollas, 1992, p. 186).

4
A Place for Experience

There is nothing to fear but fear itself

This phrase has such a universal application. At one extreme think of the experience of torture or of dissidence within a totalitarian regime. But think also of the infant learning to be alone, of the adolescent first falling in love, of the woman coming to terms with the anger she feels towards a friend who has let her down.

I am going to tell a story, spin a myth if you like. Picture a young child learning to swim. We know the paradox that the medium will support the child if only it could learn to trust it. There is an original medium, the amniotic sea, in which the embryo-of-a-child is held unproblematically. We might ponder that the essential task of human development is to rediscover such a medium to which we could entrust ourselves; but in this case it is a primary social medium, one which would support us in our going-on-being. The problem is that this social medium, unlike the original physical medium, can never be perfect. It might be 'good enough', but even then there is always a chance that it will fail us. Actual failure is experienced as catastrophe, a nameless anxiety that is felt as terror. In everyday langauge we speak of someone experiencing 'breakdown', it is akin to the experience of drowning, of falling through space, of the nameless dread.

Consider then that from the moment of birth this catastrophe is immanent, indwelling, within our subjectivity. You might say that it is the way in which the contradiction that we are, both natural and yet human (i.e. having a human nature), becomes registered as we are catapulted out from our original 'state of grace' onto the surgical sheets of the hospital where we are born.

The story I have told is by no means an original one, rather it is the one given to us by psychoanalysis, particularly the psychoanalysis of Klein, Winnicott and Bion which dominates much of contemporary practice. I want to focus upon the centrality of terror to this way of thinking about the world. Later on I will tell the other part of the story, the one that deals with our better nature. But for the time being let us think about terror. What these psychoanalysts suggest is that there is something indwelling within our subjectivity which could be likened to a basic fear. It is this that the moment of violence within the state connects to, and it connects long before the police come knocking at the door. It is this that the perversity of parents and teachers also connects to, a knowledge that somewhere this child is vulnerable. But it is also this basic fear which accounts for the way in which we keep ourselves in check, police our own experiences, deny our own possibilities. As Chapter 8 argues in more depth, we might think of an internal establishment which promises to protect us from catastrophe so long as we live within the boundaries that it prescribes for us.

So what is it we fear, what is this catastrophe that stalks us like a crazy dog? We cannot say because we cannot name it. But its there, right in our guts, and as soon as we find the means to do so we seek to represent it despite the fact that it cannot be represented. We construct an endless series of misrepresentations all of which share one essential quality, the quality of otherness, of being not-me. For this is how the establishment operates. It quietly goes about running its protection racket. So good citizens, rest easily in your beds, the forces of evil will be kept at bay so long as you are fearful and so long as you are loyal. This collusion could run and run, a parasitical relationship so perfect in its conception, a subject frozen or suspended in a state of subjugation.

This is the paranoid-schizoid position first outlined by Melanie Klein (1975). It is a state of pre-subjectivity, a primitive world of good and evil. A phantasmogoric world within which the synthetic movement of Eros, the life-force, struggles to bring together and connect the exploded fragments of our experience. It is a world lacking in dimensionality and perspective. There is only one way of seing things here – a world of good or bad, us or them, black or white. It is a world which is ordered in its fragmentariness, regimented in its chaos, safe in its fearfulness.

First fear, then threat

Because this fear springs from within us it has no name. The power of Klein's work lies in the dramatic picture she sketches of our attempts to escape from our own fear. The first movement in this bizarre polka is beautiful in its simplicity: 'I fear' becomes 'I am frightened of', the danger within becomes 'the danger without'. Now it can be named, albeit incorrectly; now it can be placed and located, albeit inappropriately. This act of omnipotent control Klein describes through the concept of projective identification – the psychical process through which a fear which cannot be contained is visited upon the external world where it fuses and blends with the real violence and poison of our social environment. You could say that from the moment we are capable of giving some kind of meaning to our surroundings we fear the worst in others – the fear that was immanent within ourselves becomes the danger immanent within the Other. The actual others that populate our lives, and particularly the figures that care for us when we are young, may either confirm or undermine such expectations through their behaviour. Its as if we assume our parents are guilty of failing us until they can establish their innocence.

It is crucial that we grasp fully the nature of this first movement of expulsion that Klein describes, for in the begining what we expel is our own fear (Bott Spillius, 1992). A state of internal fear therefore always precedes the experience of external threat. It is not the threat that is the subject of expulsion, rather, the threat is created by the act of expulsion – the alien exists as a consequence of my fear, indeed is constituted by my fear. As Sartre noted, it is the anti-semite who makes the Jew. Once the 'danger within' has been externalised in this way then the establishment can get to work, offering its protection, keeping the threat at bay, zapping intruders, policing the boundaries. This it does so well, and with such enthusiasm. The point to remember from this however is that our fear comes first, our violence and hatred comes after.

So here are the first few moves that Klein sketches – the expulsion of fear, the creation of threat, the mobilisation of defensive violence (we should all be clear by now that the real purpose of arms is to keep the peace). They constitute the starting point for a phenomenology of defensive object-relations, a game of move and counter-move, of expulsion, incorporation, colonisation, exile and incarceration.

To give this some concreteness I would like to cite a lengthy extract from a psychoanalytic case-study. In this instance the case material is provided by a Hungarian analyst, Judith Szekacs (1985):

> Helen, 26, a single woman suffering from anorexia nervosa, presented herself as someone unable to inhabit the spaces she possesses. At the first interview she looked very pale, skinny ... but what made the most striking effect was that everything that she was wearing – even her boots – was very loose, sizes bigger than she needed. ... She complained that she was unable to eat for several days and then she would have a fit of chocolate, biscuit and jam eating. ...
>
> She was unable to stop stuffing herself until she felt 'totally full up' – a very painful sensation of pressure in her body. ...
>
> Her bowels functioned in a similar way: she had no excretion for over a week and then, suddenly, in great pain she would produce a large amount of faeces. She had not had her period for more than half a year.
>
> Her fields of activity – both in fantasy and reality – were bound to the territory of the kitchen, bathroom and toilet. ...
>
> Not long after the shock caused when her first 'boyfriend' ridiculed her virginity in public, a total collapse of her inner regulatory functions came about, accompanied by the growing power of her parents' – especially her mother's – control. She had to be hospitalised a few months after her mother gave up her job in order 'to look after her daughter in trouble'.

Szekacs adds,

> Looking back at the time we started analysis I would say that her body functioned – except for those very short and intensive episodes of pleasure and pain – as a closed space which outer things could not enter and from which inner contents could not leave.
>
> Suspended or blocked body functions, closed openings and rigid boundaries, an almost total surrender to outer control, were the signs of an impaired ego functioning on an archaic level.

Controlling danger

Here then is a woman who is haunted by her early experiences within a family in which she still lives. She exists as a dwarfed and shrunken soul constantly afaid of intrusion by phantasised alien phenomena represented in the form of foods for which her desire is as intense as her terror, foods which no doubt stand for early good experience overwhelmed by a badness which she has found no means of adequately expelling. Her 'closed openings' are spasmodically inundated by desire and she floods or stuffs herself. She attempts to control 'the desired but feared' (which is now within) through a phantastic form of mastery – she refuses to let nature take its course, the 'closed openings' now imprison the alien force until the pain becomes unbearable. Crude and mechanical attempts to forcibly control her bowels substitute for the collapse of natural self-regulation.

So there would seem to be two basic strategies for controlling danger. One involves expulsion and exclusion, the other inclusion and incorporation. In the latter, the dangerous object (for example, an idea, a food, a person, or group) is controlled by taking it into the body of the self, the group or community in order to neutralise, encyst, engulf, or bury it (Cohen, 1985).

Consider a progressive housing department within an inner London local authority committed to a set of anti-racist policies but quite without the organisational capacity to contain such an explosive issue. A complex and sophisticated system of ethnic monitoring has been developed which shows clearly that black families receive the poorest quality of council-owned accommodation. Yet such findings co-exist uneasily with the dominant perspective of white tenants that black families are always given special treatment in this borough. The report summarising the findings of the ethnic monitoring is discussed exhaustively at housing allocations subcommittee. A plethora of recommendations, working groups and one-off meetings follow. And yet, despite all this industry, one thing never happens, the knowledge (of discrimination, albeit probably indirect and unintended) never leaves the boundaries of the organisation. No dialogue is ever initiated with the predominantly white tenants' associations in the borough. It was as if to bring this report out into the open would be too explosive. It is by such processes that political issues are rendered into technical matters. Within the closed, private world of the department, the danger is slowly buried under a pile of paper. The image that came to mind was of a piece of radioactive matter being encased in concrete.

Invasion and exile

I would now like to consider a further twist within such processes of exclusion and inclusion. So far we have been considering this dynamic from the perspective of the subject – i.e. the individual or group engaged in controlling phantasised alien forces. But what about the experience of the other who becomes the container or embodiment of these phantasies? According to psychoanalysis, as we have noted, control by exclusion is governed by the mechanism of projective identification. Herbert Rosenfeld, a key figure within the Kleinian tradition, describes projective identification as 'a violent and powerful expulsion of unbearable material' (Rosenfeld, 1987, p. 191). From the point of view of the other this is experienced as a kind of forcible intrusion of something dangerous and alien. If the other is strong enough such intrusions may be contained, worked on and rendered harmless. Often however this will not be the case and in such situations two options would seem possible. One may be captured by the invading force or, in psychoanalytic terms, trapped inside a bad internal object. Alternatively one can abandon one's internal space to the invading object and live a life of exile, forever outside of one's internal home. The processes of being projected into and captured by this invading force are vividly illustrated by the following extract from one of Rosenfeld's case studies:

> Clare was thirty-five years old at our first meeting in 1975. . . . Exhibiting great anxiety, she told me that things had been amiss between her husband and herself since her baby's birth and that she had lost her appetite and her ability to sleep. Her husband would come home from work at some point in the afternoon, tell her to put on a mini-skirt to excite him, and request her to make love immediately. There was a strong persecutory tone in her report, and her charges against the husband were very violent. In contrast to this was her description of the things her husband had obtained from her. She had agreed to his demands, which seemed to betray her need to share with him the illusion that she could do everything. She could learn how to play the piano for him; to play chess; to study mathematics, and above all put on weight. Her husband would bring home pastries and demand that she eat them; she had thus been able to put on 10 kilos.

Reflecting on this case Rosenfeld remarks that Clare was so completely identified with her husband 'that one feels that she is the husband' (p. 195) – in the process of analysis one of the essential tasks is always to discover 'who is speaking?' Just as her husband had lost himself inside an external object (Clare) so Clare had become captured by an internal bad object (her husband).

Think now of the operation of such processes at the group level. One is reminded of Fanon's dialectic of the coloniser and the colonised. In *Black Skins, White Masks* (Fanon, 1967) Fanon analyses the process through which the black becomes trapped within the white's imaginary construction of him. The alternative is internal exile, an intolerable experience of being lost to oneself. In a perceptive article Valerie Sinason (1989) reflected upon such dynamics in her therapeutic work with black and white children in east London. In 1975 she published a poem by the black poet Accabre Huntley who was then only seven. The poem dealt with the racist abuse she experienced at school and the inner resources she called upon in facing this abuse. Sinason reflected upon Huntley's poem thus, 'but when the teacher hit her "till I was dead in my heart" she could call upon the "Black mother" at home and in her own heart' (p. 218). Here, then, we have the inner strength through which colonisation may be resisted. A strength which is derived from the existence of a benign place within the self which finds both internal ('in her own heart') and external ('home') representation. This is Klein's 'good internal object' which, though subject to idealisation when fear is at its greatest, is primarily simply something good enough to keep alive an inner conviction that things can be different, indeed that people have in them the capacity to make a difference.

Boundary and space

The case study of Helen vividly illustrates the centrality of notions of boundary and space within contemporary psychoanalysis and, specifically, pathologies of boundary and space. As the reader may have guessed, part of my purpose is to suggest that this phenomenology of object-relating may provide a dynamic perspective for the analysis of socio-spatial processes, for example the character of defensive communities, strategies of social control, the construction of collective identities. But this is to anticipate.

Within this phenomenology two essential notions reappear

constantly – boundary and space. The first and most essential task of human development is to find a space for experience. An inner space in which our basic fear can be contained just sufficiently to modify the need to externalise it, to temper that need for the Other in which we can misrepresent our own nature. This first space is provided by the other who cares for us, the one who takes hold of our nameless distress and contains us within her embrace. And by holding the infant in this way, by rocking and calling to it beyond its distress, the child is provided with the first experience of a social medium which may in time become a good enough substitute for the original physical medium within which it was first held.

In Bion's (1962) terms, the parent acts as a container for experience which, to begin with, we have no means of giving form or shape to. The infant evacuates its distress, the parent makes it better and in modifying the experience in this way provides an auxilliary mental apparatus, an apparatus for thinking and making sense of experience: a thoughtful establishment. Bion has a very particular notion of 'containment' in mind, the original notion if you like, one which we have lost as we increasingly conflate the idea with that of control. For Bion, a container is simply a place in which you put things – in this case the fluid-like nature of experience which, failing containment, just slips through our fingers. But, like any container, it may be more or less adequate to its task – it may be too permeable (i.e. leaky), too rigid, too constricting or too loose. The essential characteristic of containment however is that it constitutes some kind of bounded multi-dimensional space within which both meaning and anxiety can be held and therefore worked upon. Furthermore the boundary may assume a number of forms – physical boundaries (territory, place) time boundaries, social boundaries (i.e. the boundaries of routines, rituals, and rules).

So the developing child moves from the original physical containment of the parental embrace to an endless series of displacements and substitutions each of which has the potential to be a place for experience – the place within one's skin, a quiet place for reverie within one's room, the places people mark out for themselves in the office or down the pub (Brian's seat), a place within one's mind or the mind of another, 'our place', and so on. Such boundaries are always more or less precarious, always subject to pathology, as the case of Helen so vividly illustrates. Just as the very first boundary, a skin surface, is a projection, an illusion sustained and supported by the others who care for us so all boundaries, marking off differences, are ultimately illusions – we cannot say whether we constructed them or whether they were already there. According to Winnicott (1985), without illusion there would be no culture, no humanity. We can see then how the act of containment constitutes the basis of the primary social medium which will support us in our humanness. But it will only do this if it proves trustworthy, able to withstand the worst fears we have of it.

Bion elaborates that nascent element within Klein's work which roots all human experience within the earliest framework of body, skin, mouth, anus, etc. He develops what might be called a corporeal epistemology which insists that the foundation of human knowledge lies in a primitive 'knowledge of the body'. Within Bion's schema of a corporeal epistemology incorporation and evacuation (the taking in and expulsion of substances from the body) become the prototype of judgement (i.e. acceptance and rejection of ideas), digestion becomes the prototype of thought, the skin the prototype of boundary, and so on. The radical implications of this lie in the psychoanalytic belief that such early experience leaves an indelible mark upon all subsequent human life. In this sense it is not just foundation but structure, or rather, a set of generative rules of structure which shape cultural experience in an unobtrusive but powerful way. In other words, societies may make what they will of this bodily inheritance of ours but only insofar as it constitutes an essential grain of the human material, a grain which informs the shape and form of what is culturally possible.

This is not a conflation of the social and the psychical rather it is an insistence that both contain their own endogenous generative rules, rules which create form. Within the form of the city or the spatial community we can discern both the promptings of the division of labour and the texture of the body. The spaces, territories and boundaries of the urban environment can be construed, from this perspective, as the result of the interpenetration of social and psychical structures and processes.

A space for subjectivity

Within the internal and external geography of boundary and space the idea of the good object should be central. I am speaking of a place for experience, a bounded space within which both meaning and anxiety can be contained. Such a place is therefore crucial for development, specifically for the development of a subject which can face its own fear without visiting this upon the other. This form of subjectivity, one which in Kleinian language corresponds to the attainment of the depressive position, refers to a self having the internal capacity to go beyond simply being the object of its own intolerable but possible knowledge and the violent intrusions of other's projections. Such a subject, which may be either individual or collective, has the capacity to emerge above the endless series of expulsions and invasions, occupations and flights we we have seen as characteristic of defensive object relations. It therefore has the capacity to go beyond being an object for itself and others towards being an agent capable of dreaming and imagination, of engaging in the transformation of the world in its own benign image.

The tragedy is that many people have the sense of the existence of just such a place for experience but feel forever trapped outside of it. Again Sinason (1989), reflecting upon her experience of working with fourteen-year-old Irish boy who was a keen supporter of the fascist organisation the National Front, illustrates this experience. The boy, Sean, at risk from parental abuse, lived with his mother and a baby brother of a different father. His fascistic tendencies were intensified when he moved with his family into dirty bed and break-fast accommodation where they shared a kitchen with a large Bengali family. Sean was driven to distraction by his mother who persisted in allowing her violent boyfriend to share their cramped accom-modation. Sinason suggested to Sean that he must feel all women were weak in allowing bad, violent things to happen. Sean replied,

> I can't be cross with my mum. That's what happens when you have a working-class Irish woman. That's what she goes and does. That's how a whole family end up in homeless accommodation full of Pakis. If that man touches me again I'll run to my grand-parents in Ireland. They are not like that in Ireland. (Sinason, 1989, pp. 221–2)

Reflecting on Sean's remarks Sinason notes,

> he had talked before about the poverty and violence of Ireland but right now he wanted to feel there was a country, a place inside him where he was biologically accepted and valued. He agreed. (p. 222)

In Klein's terms, Sean was trapped outside a good internal object.

Configurations of object-relationships

In a moment I would like to move away from the present focus upon the internal geography of the self to the geography of external spaces and boundaries. But before doing so it would be useful to summarise the phenomenology of object relationships that psychoanalysis provides us with. The beginings of such a phenomenology have already been sketched by Donald Meltzer (1986).

To recapitulate, 'objects' are elements of meaning which draw upon aspects of both self and other. They are always embodied in some thing – Ireland, my TV set, Pakis, my stomach, my son, blood, food. As such, objects may be good and life-giving or bad, alien and dangerous. Objects may be 'internal', that is, meanings which have been forced into us or ones which we have voluntarily internalised, or they may be 'external', i.e. meanings which we have forced into others or which exist, independently of our imaginary control, outside of the self.

From this it would seem possible to develop the following schema of psychosocial configurations of boundary and space:

1 A bad object may be outside the self ('I fear' becomes 'I am frightened of', defensive violence is then mobilised).
2 The self may be inside a bad external object (identification with an external alien force – the classic case of the victim's identification with the aggressor).
3 The bad object may be inside the self (either encysted and buried or as an occupying, colonising force).
4 The bad object may have occupied the inner space of the self, a self which has been effectively abandoned (internal exile).
5 The good object may be inside us (internal refuge – Accabre Huntley).
6 We may be adrift, outside a good internal object (Sean).
7 The good object exists outside of the self and we are able to identify with it (a shared ideal, benign cultural symbol, etc.).

I would suggest that such configurations are possibly the effect of generative rules of space and value common to both internal and external realities. Although I feel unable to give a considered examination of this issue here I feel convinced that by using this schema of possible configurations of boundary and space we could begin to develop a far more detailed and sophisticated analysis of, say, the way in which individuals and groups relate to the idea of 'community'. In other words, developing Anderson's (1983) concept of 'imagined community' we might begin to think of the status of 'community' as a psychical object – 'the community in the mind' – an object which might be good or bad, inside us or external to us, within which we are either trapped or from which we are exiled, and so on. In the rest of this chapter however I wish to wrestle with an easier task. I wish to return to the theme of the struggle to create a benign space, a space for experience, both in the life of the individual and the group. I also seek to explore the way in which external social processes connive to undermine this possibility.

Two dimensionality

All of the internal and external spaces that we have explored so far have a certain dimensionality to them. But recent work with autistic children suggests that their inner worlds lack much of the dimensionality even of the paranoid-schizoid position. They appear to cling to objects, typically hard, inanimate objects made of metal or stone, which have no meaning even in the phantasmogoric sense of danger and purity. Their mental world seems to lack places where any kind of experience or meaning can be put. As Meltzer (1975) notes, things seem to go in one ear and out the other. As such, autism appears to resemble a form of two dimensionality in which inner space is structured around 'flat planes' and empty spaces. Esther Bick (1968, 1986) drew attention to the way in which such two-dimensional forms correspond to a tragic attempt to simulate a bounded and meaningful place that the infant has had no actual experience of. As a result there is the construction of false or simulated skin boundaries to which the self becomes adhesively attached or identified. The child beholds such 'objects' with a kind of desperate fascination, and because such objects have no 'insides' the mechanisms of projection and introjection are replaced by forms of clinging to the objects' surface qualities.

This would appear to be the developmental prototype of the simulated two dimensional world that Baudrillard (1983) and others have explored. If this line of analysis is correct then we have to begin to think about the possibility of cultural autism. A world in which objects are emptied of their symbolic content and therefore lose their capacity to contain meaning. Objects which lack even that depth which would provide a place into which primitive emotion could be projected.

I have attempted elsewhere (Hoggett, 1992) to illustrate the development of forms of cultural autism within organisational life by focusing upon the way in which the new generation of post-bureaucratic companies, such as Hewlett Packard, seek to harness the potential of their workforce. Here we observe the creation of regimes of active organisational commitment which resemble simulated moral communities. There is no hidden depth here, rather everything is on the surface – the buddyness, the enthusiasm, the solidarity, the values (Sennett, 1998). The new regimes have not, as Peters and Waterman in their bestseller (1982) imply, abandoned the use of rational planning, rather the object of planning has shifted from systems and procedures (the 'formal' organisation) to human relations themselves. Indeed we can see the parallel between this movement towards the painstaking design of institutional interiors and the commodification of meaning and experience in current designs for leisure and retailing spaces. In work and leisure the accent is upon the construction of 'ambience' – something to do with the tone, the atmosphere, the 'feel' of the place.

Containing differences in groups

Subjectivity can only develop within an individual or social body ego capable of providing a place for experience, a place within which the self, its fear and hopefulness, can be contained rather than disowned and visited upon the other or dissipated into the simulated body of the organisation or leisure-plex. A benign space – reliable, thoughtful and bounded – which can allow the movement from self-as-object to self-as-subject, a self capable of containing difference and therefore capable of making a difference.

Just as the child requires a benign parental space in which to develop its own internal capacities so, as social beings, we seek benign socially bounded spaces through which our collective internal capacities can be developed. The original body of the nurturing figure finds elaboration in an endless series of external representations – the body of the family, the social network or group, the community, the organisation, the state. There is nothing essentially good or bad about any of these objects, the key point is that each has the capacity to act as a container of meaning and anxiety, each has the capacity to simulate such containment, and each also has the capacity to constitute a malignant rather than benign social body.

If the benign social body can be seen as both externalisation and source of our inner hopefulness then the malignant body can equally be seen as both externalisation and source of our own internal establishment. This is the realm of the 'reversed family' (Meltzer, 1986), the paranoid-defensive community, the reified and idealised organisation or political party, the totalitarian or post-totalitarian (Havel, 1987) state. We must never forget that there is always a victim and a collaborator inside us. Speaking of the state, Havel recognises how it oppresses us but adds, 'at the same time alientated humanity supports the system as its own involuntary masterplan, as a degenerate image of its own degeneration' (Havel, 1987, p. 54).

To contain difference and conflict or to expel it; to remain in touch with ourselves or to lose ourselves in the endless polka of flight, of expulsion, incorporation, colonisation, exile, entrapment and invasion; that is the question. Because psychoanalysis has been consistently concerned to reveal the crucial role that the good object (Klein), container (Bion) or 'facilitating environment' (Winnicott) plays in individual and group development it provides us with a resource for our hopefulness. It indicates how, from the outset of life, the development of bounded spaces and territories within the internal and external world can and does provide the means by which we learn from experience. This seems to be an important point to remember for it is becoming fashionable for social theorists to construe the group in all its guises (as nation, community, political party, etc.) primarily as a problem.

Sibley (1988) grapples with this issue. Drawing upon insights from social anthropology he demonstrates how processes of boundary formation are accompanied by processes of purification and rejection both within the life of the mind and the social environment. The phenomena he draws our attention to are in many ways similar to those associated with those bound up with Klein's notion of the paranoid-schizoid position – processes of splitting, idealisation and denigration through which the equations self-us-good and other-them-bad are constructed. But his analysis appears to dwell too much upon the destructive consequences of boundary formation, he fails to demonstrate how boundary formation is as crucial to learning and development as it is to the destruction of these vital qualities. The issue is revealed most clearly through the issue of 'difference' – to the idea, the individual or group which 'won't fit in'. From the paranoid-schizoid position such anomalies are indeed construed as persecutory impingements, as poisonous, bad objects, and therefore as the signal for the mobilisation of defensive forms of object-relating. But from the depressive position, the position of a fuller subjecthood, anomalies are construed quite differently – as novelty, enrichment, and as a locus for the extension of the self's possibilities, as the source of 'wonderment' (Young, 1997). From the first position 'unity without difference' is the only form of unity tolerable whereas from the second position 'unity with difference' is the only route towards development conceivable. From the depressive position ambiguity and uncertainty are not only tolerated but welcomed as 'the stuff of life', they are what makes life worth living.

There is a danger that boundaries and differences are going to become problematised by urban geographers and sociologists whereas surely the problem is not the propensity of groups and individuals to construct boundaries but the meanings that are ascribed to them once they have been constructed. To put it another way, in the context of 'community relations' the existence of differences is the not an analytical or social problem rather the problem is the racialisation (Omi & Winant, 1986) of such differences. To give an example, in London's East End in the early 1990s the Bengali community was subject to mounting harassment and violence from white working-class but also black Afro-Caribbean youth. In other words 'colour' was not the main line of difference; the white youth contained and, in part, embraced one line of difference in the process of erecting a barrier against another. It is the Bengalis who were 'the blacks' in the East End.

Social catastrophe

Now a number of contemporary analyses such as Dickens (1990), tend to register this distinction between subjective and pre-subjective states in terms of the distinction between the expressive and biotic orders. The latter is essentially concerned with the struggle for survival, the implication being that only when the conditions for satisfying basic human needs are met can the individual move on to consider 'higher', expressive requirements (i.e. the search for self, identity and creativity). But surely the point is that immiseration alone does not lead to amoralisation, this line of analysis seems to overlook the mediating role played by what we might call 'the social fabric'.

Rapid social and economic change has profound effects upon particular localities and communities. It corresponds to a prolonged period of uncertainty for individuals, families and social networks in which sudden, or gradual and remorseless, changes occur which challenge traditional patterns of loyalty, social identities and life careers. In many instances this stretches or punctures existing social fabrics to the point of collapse. A struggle for survival then ensues but, for most, this is primarily a struggle for collective psychological survival rather than physical survival.

I would argue that it is the threat to the social fabric of a given community (one which may or may not be spatially organised) which brings about, at the social level, the experience of catastrophic anxiety which inaugurates the dynamic of defensive object relations which I outlined in the earlier part of this chapter. My own research experience in the early 1990s within the borough of Tower Hamlets in London's East End illustrated such processes vividly (Jeffers, Hoggett & Harrison, 1996; Burns, Hambleton & Hoggett 1994). Tower Hamlets is an essentially bi-racial locality within which a rapidly expanding Bangladeshi community is concentrated in the western end of the borough (alongside the City) whereas a traditional white working-class community occupies the east. The whole area has been subject to the most massive social and economic change as the City inexorably encroaches upon Bangladeshi Spitalfields and the redevelopment of London Docklands encroaches into the East End from the south.

Racial tensions in the area were acute and led to a series of tit-for-tat stabbings and other assaults between white and Bangladeshi youth in early 1990. The white community represented its fear of invasion through a number of forms, but particularly the cockroach. The Liberal politicians who ran the local council between 1986 and 1994 embarked upon a massive modernisation programme of the council estates which dominated the landscape of this area. An unforseen consequence of the introduction of double glazing and central heating was a major cockroach infestation – the warm temperatures and maze of ducts and pipes provided the perfect habitat for them. The evidence that the infestation had structural and physical causes cut no ice with white tenants for whom the cockroach signified a complex knot of resentment, fear and hatred. As we shall see in more detail in the next chapter the deepening of defensive and paranoid anxieties in both communities encouraged the development of introverted indentites – Muslim fundamentalism on the one hand and a kind of white East London ethnocentrism on the other.

The resentment the whites felt towards the Bangladeshi community was made poignant by the fact that the latter community had many characteristics – extended and intensive kinship networks, a respect for tradition and male seniority, a capacity for entrepreneurialism and social advancement – which the white working class in the area had lost. In his harassment of the Bengali community we can see how local white was engaged in an envious attack upon a Bengali who represented his lost powers, in Zizek's (1992) words, one who had stolen his enjoyment. For the white tenant this Other was small in stature, multiplying fast, unclean and resilient hence, no doubt, the symbolism of the cockroach.

The culture of uncertainty

The case we have just been considering captures in an extreme form the experience of social uncertainty which I have argued elsewhere (Hoggett, 1989) is characteristic of all periods of structural crisis within capitalism. During such periods all existing social and economic solutions are put in doubt, all of our certainties – moral, economic, political and aesthetic – become shaken. This was no less true during the last period of structural crisis between the two world wars than it is today. In the essay referred to above I sought to examine one particular manifestation of the way in which such periods of crisis become registered at the level of everyday life, specifically through the idea of cynicism as a diffuse but fundamental cultural phenomenon.

Others, particularly Jameson (1984), have developed a similar form of analysis but have suggested that such cultural experiences may be an expression of the new forms of life corresponding to the emerging form of late twentieth-century capitalism rather than to the period of structural crisis preceding such economic renewal. For Jameson the cynicism and relativism of post-modernism is a symbol of our present incapacity to map 'the great global multinational and decentered communicational network in which we find ourselves caught' (p. 83). For Jameson the newly emerging form of capitalism appears to be organised in a way which threatens the basic human need to locate itself spatially and cognitively in a world which is still meaningful.

Such a line of analysis indicates another way in which the developmental task of securing an internal place for experience may be subject to attack from outside as well as from inside. Again, to cite Jameson, 'this latest mutation in space – postmodern hyperspace – has finally succeeded in transcending the capacities of the individual human body to locate itself, to organise its immediate surroundings perceptually and cognitively to map its position in a mappable external world' (pp. 83–4). If, to use Bion's model, the process of human and group development hinges upon the existence of a reliable, consistent and flexible container for experience then we seem to be heading towards an era in which the social body looks increasingly like being unable to perform this function.

As the stability of identity and the reliability of experience become endangered any form of oppositional movement within culture and politics faces the task of making a space for experience central to its project. The possibility begins to open up for a politics which at last takes the subject seriously – not just as the complex precipitate of external social processes (as is frequently implied through the notion 'the personal is political') but as the irreducible determinant of social and political processes themselves ('the political is personal').

Within contemporary social science there are already signs of such a rehabilitation of the subject (Giddens, 1984; Dickens, 1990). This is to be welcomed, but one also senses an over-reliance upon the rationalistic and rather superficial subject of Goffman's (1971) self theory and Rom Harre's (1979) realist phenomenology. The danger is that social science becomes the champion of a skin-deep subject for a skin-deep society. Given the systematic attack upon the integrity of experience in contemporary society (Tseelon, 1992) it becomes all the more important to find a place for experience in critical social analysis. This goes further than the need for good ethnographic study for it raises the issue of the writer's own experience and the capacity to be reflexive about it. We all have our experience of cities, motorways, shopping malls, neighbourhoods and homes. We all know of fear, uncertainty, desire and envy. Yet somehow this never becomes visible in the dry words of academic argument. I remember reading, with great interest, Shields's article on the West Edmonton Shopping Mall (Shields, 1989) yet only once (p. 154) did he appear to come out from beneath the figures and references to speak in his own voice of his own experience. Why can't we social scientists let ourselves go and become a bit poetic? So here goes, see what you make of it.

It is my experience that nothing ever happens in the country. The city has become the locus of promise, if the country exists it is as a kind of anti-matter. Viewed from the motorway small settlements seem to be suspended outside of the energy stream. People exist here but not life. Life, liveliness is in the city, or rather, the image of the city. What do these country people do? How do they pass their time? Time passes in the country whereas in the city time is precious, it is intolerable, and so it is filled. The time-emptied country, the time-filled city. Every moment is sacred – to be planned, filled, punctuated, evented. A frenzied refusal of time and the absence that it is. But in the country what do they do?

The city beckons us like a vortex. It promises eternal life, that certain moment, that chance encounter. The city is a refusal of time. An impossible gesture, a fabrication woven so beautifully that we are all sucked willingly and helplessly into its texture. Somehow the frustration of it merely serves to increase our belief in its promise.

Here all power lies. Ideas may be generated outside the city but they cannot be realised. They cannot be sold, portrayed, televised or fought for anywhere but in the city. Without the city they hang uselessly. Within the city they find realisation as a flicker – but no more than this, still like gnats in the evening sun.

OK, so I write as a member of the urban intelligentsia living in a period which, because of telecommunications, is possibly the last in which the city will assume such power. So my experience is specific to time and place, as is everyone's. But why should critical social analysis have so little space for experience? I offer it simply as food for thought, something that might stir, connect or provoke. Anyway I have an expert to back me up. According to Baudrillard 'all events are epitomized in the towns' (Baudrillard, 1984, p. 129). So there.

As I see it the issue is not just what we write about but, as importantly, how we write about it. Even when we write about exciting things we academics tend to write in a style which is impersonal, distanced and ultimately boring. There is no passion any more, no space for experience or feeling. Everything has to be so measured, so hedged with justification. As a result it becomes increasingly difficult to cross boundaries – we all work away in our little boxes and talk to our own small gangs. As Sibley (1988) citing Olsson (1984) notes, 'to sin is to trespass'.

5

Building Castles in the Sand: Racial and Ethnic Identities in Civil Society

Many analyses of racial and ethnic formations focus upon their expression at the national or supra-national level. In this chapter I will focus upon what might be called the 'local dynamics of race'. Drawing upon research involving small area studies in Bristol, Leicester and the London Borough of Tower Hamlets (Harrison, Hoggett & Jeffers, 1995; Jeffers, Hoggett & Harrison, 1996) I will trace the fluid and contested boundaries through which ethnicised and racialised identities are both internally generated and externally imposed.

This chapter seeks to examine what Anthias (1990) describes as the discursive and intersubjective dimensions of race within small spatial areas such as neighbourhoods. By 'discursive' I mean the categories, concepts and vocabulary through which racial and ethnic formations are sustained. By 'intersubjective' I mean the actual, concrete patterns of interaction (including emotional interaction) occurring between individuals and within local groups and social networks. I will examine how such dynamics are expressed within the local associations of civil society – in this case community associations, cricket leagues, tenants' groups, etc. Are such organisations simply sites in which wider dynamics are reproduced or can they make a difference of their own?

Race and ethnicity: problems with definitions

The question 'what is race?' tends to resemble the infamous rhetorical question 'what is art?' in that it has generated fraught, earnest but often frustrating debates that polarise disputants into a number of camps. For example, today there are those who take issue with the grammar and vocabulary of 'race' and put quotation marks around the term to highlight its dangerous and unstable nature. There are also others who tend to see race as a fairly straightforward but awkward fact of life the social significance of which is demeaned by the use of quotation marks. Without resorting to the use of quotation marks I nevertheless wish to highlight the problematic nature of things ethnic and racial and specifically the many different local forms that such social identities may assume.

The paradox which must be held on to is that while such identities may appear to be dynamic and fluid there are grounds to believe that identity is also relatively fixed and enduring. Identities are not just the product of voluntarily chosen identifications. They are often also the outcome of our stubborn but hopeless search for certainty and the need to manage a relationship to a past which contains many experiences which are dangerous to think about. Identities are also the outcome of enforced introjections. Individuals and groups are often forced to swallow definitions of themselves because they lack the symbolic and emotional resources to refuse such definitions.

To say that an aspect of something may be relatively fixed is not to imply that herein lies its supposed essence or nature. An identity remains something that one has rather than something that one is. Anthias (1990) tries to outline some of the distinctions which she argues can and cannot be drawn between race, ethnicity, class and other social categories. Anthias argues that race can only be considered an analytically valid category by including it within the more heterogeneous category of ethnos. What distinguishes race from ethnicity is not so much processes of inclusion and exclusion (processes which are also the hallmark of ethnic phenomenon) but the fusing of these with processes of inferiorisation based upon assumed biological or physiognomical differences. Such assumptions are typically tacit, they constitute the quiet background to the more noisy and articulated racisms which find public expression within political society at national or local levels. Anthias recognises that such racisms are the product of the interplay between different social divisions within the context of historically produced social relations, divisions in which class may be primary but which also include gender and generation.

Identity, ethnicity, race

Mo is a nineteen-year-old clerical officer working in an estate office in Tower Hamlets. He speaks broad Cockney, wears enormous trainers and uses a Batman telephone. But Mo is also short for Mohammed. Mo is a Bengali Cockney. Local white tenants were initially thrown when Mo started work in the office. Those who first spoke to him on the phone assumed that he was 'one of us'; when they visited the office and met Mo they were surprised. As Mo put it, 'many of them refer to me as if I was a half-caste'; the fact that he is a Cockney and also a Bengali defies the categories that local whites have developed when thinking about themselves.

This cameo illustrates a number of crucial issues concerning the nature of identity, considered both in its individual and its collective sense. For Bengali youth in Tower Hamlets identity is constructed from a number of sources – from the broad, ethnic identity of sharing a common culture (Bengal), from the narrower national realisation of this culture (Bangladesh), from religion (which for most Tower Hamlets Bengalis is Muslim), from contemporary local identities of place (East Ender/Cockney), from the common experience of youth and from one's own personal biography – experiences at home, work, and school, and so on. Every young Bengali draws in a different way upon each of these sources and yet each also draws upon them in common. Mo is probably different from many of his contemporaries. He has a job, he exudes an air of confidence, he is immensely street-wise; physically he looks big, strong and muscular. The latter counts a lot within the dominant culture of the East End. He is 'one of us' yet also 'one of them' – a 'fuckin' Paki.' To use an analogy, Mo is like a rocket which has been launched but in flying is constantly pulled 'down to earth', back to his place. His identity is constantly in tension between an expansive, outward, form of self-propulsion and a set of forces which seek to push him back in upon himself, back in upon a defended, introverted, redoubt.

According to Benedict Anderson (1983) all communities are imagined. They are imagined 'because the members of even the smallest nation will never know most of their fellow-members, meet them, or even hear of them, yet in the minds of each lives the image of their communion' (p. 15). Although national communities and the ethnicities they give expression to are the primary focus of Anderson's study, he is clear that his analysis applies equally to all constructions of 'community'. As he notes, 'in fact, all communities larger than primordial villages of face-to-face contact (and perhaps even these) are imagined. Communities are to be distinguished, not by their falsity/genuineness, but by the style in which they are imagined' (p. 15). With this brief phrase Anderson seems to have sidestepped a knot that geographical and urban analysis has tended to get tied up in for many years, i.e. the search to establish criteria against which one might judge whether or not a 'community' can be said to exist.

For all the poverty, the destruction of social fabrics, the anomie, the absence of neighbourliness, the lack of clubs, associations and networks which in many respects now characterises the white working class of the East End there remains a strong sense of belonging to a community – East Enders, Cockneys, people like us'. Moreover, this is a community which continues to act in distinctive ways. It sought political representation through a local political elite (the Tower Hamlets Liberal Party) which was probably one of the most distinctively populist groupings in British politics in the early 1990s – one shunned by its own national party establishment and loathed by what is construed as 'the race relations industry' (Burns, Hambleton & Hoggett, 1994). It is a community within which a long tradition of racism and vigilantism (Husbands, 1982) has re-emerged this time in terms of racial attacks upon the Bengali 'incomers' rather than the Jews. But it is also a community of paradox, where local Afro-Caribbean youth could be found joining the first protest demonstration called by largely white locals after the stabbing of a white boy by Bengali boys at the Morpeth School in 1990; where active supporters of the local struggles of hospital and print workers could be found, as tenants, virulently attacking attempts by local housing officers to develop effective racial harassment policies, and so on.

The nature of social identity

What does all of this tell us about the nature of social identities? For one thing, it tells us that while there may be a continuity within identity there is also a fluidity and contingency. One's identity may be a collage of experiences from the past – some remembered, some forgotten; some idealised, some spoiled – but it is also constantly moulded by the present, by the social encounter in which one finds oneself, by the roles one has to occupy. In Bristol a black woman living in Easton may at times forget her status as the Other, the non-white; but should she travel to middle class Clifton, to the white outer-city estate of Hartcliffe, or to the seaside at Weston then her 'blackness' will return. An old white, working-class, Labour-voting man in Poplar may feel a unity of the dispossessed when both he and his Bengali neighbour have their TV reception destroyed by the shadow of Canary Wharf, but as a tenant the Bengali remains just another one of 'those Pakis who've brought down the area'.

The Bengalis in Tower Hamlets have constructed a number of collective identities, some secular and nationalist, others religious and transcendent (Eade, 1990) but they have also been forced to confront the imposed identity of 'the Paki' and the practices of discrimination and exclusion which accompany this. As we saw in Chapter 4, this Other – inferior, dirty, small and primitive – con-stantly intrudes upon them, forcing itself upon the individual and collective psyche putting them 'in their place' (both psychologi-cally and spatially back into the ghetto of Spitafields). But the same kind of processes operate for other identities beside race. When Alice, a member of the residual elderly white community of Easton in Bristol, sat through another endless discussion of aspects of its Equal Opportunities policy, what she was reminded of was her class, that she was not 'educated' like many of the younger members with their newfangled ideas. So, paradoxically, the elaboration of the EO policy tended to put her in her place, reminded her of her difference. Alice was fortunate to be involved in an initiative where many of the participants were very sensitive to the complex inter-play of different forms of disadvantage. Their support and her spirit were sufficient for her not to withdraw into silence. She spoke her mind, while being careful of the language she used. But in the absence of this kind of facilitating environment, the experience of inferiorisation, of being put back in your place (an experience which is so much an integral feature of racism), leads directly to with-drawal and silence.

All identities involve the construction of boundaries which regis-ter similarity and difference – the very process of understanding 'what we share in common' simultaneously involves an understanding of how 'we' differ from others. But this does not mean that the individual or group which is different is necessarily viewed nega-tively or reacted to in a paranoid fashion. In Leicester the Belgrave Cricket League offered a common group identity to many white and Asian players. Moreover to be a part of the cricketing community in Leicester it was not important to define oneself in opposition to another group, indeed many of the cricketers within the Belgrave

Cricket League are also soccer players or hockey players by September. What was important to the white and Asian players is that they were all cricketers in the summer. To this extent they all belonged to a particular subculture, the specificity of which can be understood when contrasted with amateur football in the same city or amateur cricket in a different region. Amateur football in Leicester is quite different. Here although Asian, Afro-Caribbean and white clubs participate in common leagues there is no shared sense of a common sub-culture. Rather the nature of the encounter between the different ethnically based clubs is quite different, involving a history of violence on and off the pitch (Hoggett and Bishop, 1985). Again, in Yorkshire the cricketing subculture is quite different from Leicester, the degree of segregation between white and Asian clubs is much greater – for many white Yorkshiremen the idea of a Yorkshire Asian cricketer is as impossible to contain as the idea of a Bengali Cockney housing officer is to some white tenants in Stepney.

Such examples enable us to understand something about differences. Within the Belgrave Cricket League Ethnic differences were clearly recognised; most of the clubs tended to be all-white or all-Asian, but such differences appeared to carry little significance because of the strength of the common identity all members of this subculture shared. In other words, within this highly specific context ethnic 'difference' carried little emotional meaning. Perhaps the main reason for the lack of significance given to difference here lies in the interdependence between the two groups, white and Asian, for, as the white players acknowledged, the cricket league would not exist if it were not for the Asian participation. But the survival of other local leisure activities has not depended upon ethnic minority participation – as a result the organisation of football in the same city is highly racialised, as is cricket in other regions.

Mo's experience of being perceived as half-caste reflects the way in which for white East Enders 'Bengali' and 'Cockney' are mutually exclusive categories. Mo could not be both, and if he was a Cockney then he could not be a Bengali. For the white working class community of Tower Hamlets, a community which in many ways feels besieged, overlooked and left behind, its traditions and culture barely existent, defining itself against the Other, the Bengali, becomes one of the few sustainable sources of identity that it has left. To say that an ethnic or subcultural identity has become defined primarily in terms of difference rather than commonality is to describe the way in which a group develops a consciousness of itself in terms of what it is not, rather than in terms of what it is. In such cases the construction of 'me' or 'us' necessarily accompanies, indeed to some extent follows from, the construction of an Other, i.e. a 'them' which is both feared and despised.

Suttles's concept of 'the defended community' (Suttles, 1972) is clearly relevant to understanding the reaction of residual, spatially concentrated white communities such as that to be found in Tower Hamlets and, in a milder form, one can see similar processes of boundary construction at work within the ageing white community in Easton. What is striking about many of these residualised communities is the mediating impact of generational differences. Throughout Tower Hamlets the organised tenants movement tends to be represented by older men and women, many of them retired. In Easton and the adjoining neighbourhood community of Barton Hill, again one finds that it is the older members of the white community who play a key role in its representation. A number of factors appear to contribute to this. Older people have more time to become involved in community activity. Because they have re-sided in the area for so long they develop a more natural identification with their neighbourhood, an identification no doubt reinforced through an understanding that they are likely to remain in the area until they die. But the process of ageing itself no doubt has an impact. The inexorable processes of physical and bodily deterio-ration bound up with becoming old tend to give rise to a set of experiences which cannot be thought of and are projected outwards from the internal to the external world. In this way unconscious thoughts of 'internal decay' are hidden behind the conviction that one is living in an area in decline. This process seems to be fairly ubiquitous, it is not limited to inner city areas which have been subject to processes of in-migration but tends to be experienced by elderly people wherever they live – in rural villages, small town, etc. The point we are making is that where older people have become spatially concentrated within residualised working class communi-ties, then the meaning of neighbourhood and community within such areas can become highly racialised as the fledgling black com-munity becomes the visible symbol of this group's complex experience of deterioration.

To adequately understand the dynamics of multi-ethnic communi-ties, the particular nature of the collective identities involved must be explored, including those dominant collective identities within the local white population. No two localities will be alike; different traditions, subcultures and patterns of interaction will emerge. Moreover, it follows that our understanding of white racism must be one which is sufficiently sophisticated to allow for the fact that this sentiment will assume different forms of organisation and articulation in different local social systems as Husband's analysis of racism and vigilantism in London's East End clearly demonstrates (Husbands, 1982). In a sense the analysis I offer here parallels that adopted by Wallman (1986) and, I hope, complements her study of ethnicity in Battersea and Bow which drew attention to the effect of local context on the marking and meaning of ethnic difference. The main difference being that whereas I focus upon the inter-subjective and discursive, Wallman offers an analysis of the structural ecology of the boundary process and specifically the influence of local resource systems such as employment, housing and leisure.

Essentialised identities

Keeping Anderson's remark in mind, that communities are to be distinguished by the style in which they are imagined, it would seem possible to pick out at least one axis around which such imagining occurs. I have in mind here the possibility that any identity consists of both a projection into the past and a projection into the future. Where differences emerge is around the nature of these projections and the relative emphasis given to the past as opposed to the future. Stuart Hall (1990) makes the point that the recovery of the past constitutes an essential 'resource of resistance' for all groups who have been subject to the colonising process. It enables them to confront the way in which their history has been misrepresented by the dominant regimes of the West. As Hall notes, it is not that this history can ever in actuality be rediscovered but it can be re-told, re-presented through literature, politics, music and cinema. But within some communities at some points in time the phantasy of actual rediscovery is immensely powerful and finds expression in a quest to recover an essence, a truth about one's cultural and religious self – African-ness, Jewishness, Islam.

This idealised phantasy paradoxically condemns such a community to an impossible task – to live in the past but in the present. For in reality 'the present' insists that this community negotiates with it, comes to terms with it, defines itself through it. Key is the strength of the 'phantasy of rediscovery' (i.e. of an essential identity from the past) for the stronger this phantasy, the more the community harbouring it appears to resemble a closed-system and the more impermeable will be its boundaries (compare Wallman, 1986, p. 231). My impression is that there seems to be a link between this style of imagined community and the extent to which the group in question feels endangered. It would be tempting to consider this in terms of models of voluntary ethnic segregation as discussed by Chisholm (1990), in other words as a stage that all minorities go through in their progress towards full cultural assimilation. I would reject this idea not only because the assimilationist model seems increasingly incongruent when set against the actuality of increasing cultural pluralism within all Western countries, but also because the minority communities themselves appear to be highly differentiated between different localities – Liverpool's black community has probably the longest experience of exclusion and hostility of any within the UK and yet it has not sought refuge in an idealised historical past.

The phantasy of rediscovery of the past seems to lead inevitably to the construction of essentialised forms of ethnic identity. In other words while, as Anthias notes, all ethnic constructions 'are based on a historical notion of origin or fate, whether mythical or real' (p. 20) in some cases this imaginative construction lacks the 'as if' quality which, as we shall see in Chapter 7, necessarily distinguishes the creative illusion from the delusion, and thus the symbolic life of the group becomes concrete and deadening (Rodrigue, 1956; Winnicott, 1974). The boundaries of such groups lack softness and permeability. The skin of the group-body becomes taut and stretched, a kind of artificial membrane stitched together over an injured flesh with a thread of rigid conventions concerning dress, manners, worship, gender-specific role behaviour, and so on – a 'second skin' as Bick once called it (Bick, 1968, 1986). A repeated complaint made by white tenants in Tower Hamlets was that the Bengalis did not want to mix. This was not just a rationalisation for their own hostility – many longstanding progressive community and political activists and church leaders in the area admitted to a similar perception. It is important to understand therefore that 'difference' is not simply a threat to the indigenous community in an area, it can be equally threatening to a minority community where their construction of ethnicity is becoming elaborately pure and essentialised.

In an area like Tower Hamlets we therefore need to think beyond the idea of cultural diversity towards the possibility that a locality may contain a set of differences which are, in some way and for some time, incommensurable. Where 'difference' denotes danger and contamination for both communities the possibility of mutual contact becomes remote. In such instances there may be few if any other sub-cultural identities through which such differences can be transcended.

A recent study of inter-ethnic conflict in Northern Ireland (Hamilton, McCourtney, Anderson & Finn, 1990) examined the notions of seg-regation, polarisation and integration as ways of characterising community relations. My experience of Tower Hamlets suggested that the concept of 'cohabitation' could be usefully added to this list. Certainly the degree of segregation between the white and Bengali populations within the educational system in this borough was virtually complete and there were strong pressures to establish similar forms of segregation within the sphere of public housing. Where community initiatives, such as the Bancroft Tenant Management Cooperative (one of the largest in the UK), were successful in tem-porarily countering this trend towards segregation and polarisation, it would appear that the most realistic policy goal which was achiev-able consisted in peaceful cohabitation within a shared space. In this sense the success of the Bancroft initiative lay in the way in which it enabled the white and Bengali tenants to live together peacefully on the estate. However, integration between the two communities did not appear to be anywhere on the agenda, not on the Bancroft or anywhere else in Tower Hamlets for that matter. It is interesting to speculate whether the intensely racialised boundary between the white and Bengali community has facilitated the in-corporation of the small Black Afro-Caribbean population into the surrounding white working class culture of the East End – as I noted in the previous chapter, it was as if it were the Bengalis who had become the 'real' Others in this area (Jeffers, Harrison & Hoggett, 1996).

Collective identities and intersubjective dynamics

So far I have considered the dynamics of racial, ethnic and other identities at the level of the locality, area or neighbourhood. But how do these broader processes of identity formation and inter-action became refracted through the life of particular organisations – a cricket league, a community association, and so on? Can such organisations provide environments in which processes of racialisa-tion are reversed and where people can work through their differ-ences, or are these organisations helpless pawns through which broader conflicts and misunderstandings are simply re-enacted and reproduced?

A starting point in this investigation is to look at the processes of communication to be found within each of the initiatives. I will begin with a brief cameo focusing upon three older members of a Community Association in Bristol who we shall call Ron, Jim and Alice. These individuals also belong to the 'Evergreens', a self-help club which had been a key part of the Community Association almost since its inception in the early 1980s. In the past, members of the Evergreens had been less than welcoming to members of local ethnic minority groups and this had eventually led to a major confrontation with some of the younger, white and radical Community Association members. In terms of the power struggle within the association the Evergreens and their allies were defeated. For a while Ron had resigned from active involvement in the council of the CA but during the course of our case study we were able to watch as both he and Jim slowly renewed their involvement in the association. What was striking was the way in which both men were able to adjust their language and behaviour to meet the 'rules' which now prevailed within the community association. Reflecting on Jim's behaviour at one council meeting I noted, 'Jim's fluency with the new "EO-speak" was striking, indeed at times his apparent conversion to feminism represented through the praise he heaped upon the City Council's Women's Committee raised a few eyebrows among those present.' So was it just 'put on'? Underneath was he just prejudiced as he had been in the past, before the bust-up?

It is difficult to answer these kinds of questions without complying with the logic behind them, a logic which implies that racism is a matter of all or nothing – either you are or you aren't. Certainly in one sense Jim and Ron probably retained many racist attitudes but they kept them to themselves, they had developed an appreciation of distinguishing between the private and the public spheres. Even within the intimacy and confidentiality of the research interview neither let anything slip. Compare this with the extract of the interview with Alice which I have already cited in Chapter 3. Alice was also from the Evergreens and a key member of the CA, talking in an interview about the changes she had seen in the area she said:

> The Asians have taken over all the shops. We used to have a lovely shopping centre on Chelsea Rd. There's one English shop

on St. Mark's Rd, all the rest are Paki. I know I shouldn't say that but I tend to.

Alice's comment, 'I know I shouldn't say that', strikingly revealed her awareness of the distinction between private and public speech. In private her deeply held feelings about the changes that had occurred to her community and the meaning which she attributed to these changes remained unchanged. But this did not mean that nothing had changed. As we saw in Chapter 3 Alice worked effectively with many black people within the community association, several of whom she now regarded as her friends. So changes in her way of thinking, her patterns of association and friendship, and her behaviour occurred, despite the fact that in her private speech she still drew automatically at times upon the unreflexive, taken-for-granted racialised category of 'the Paki'.

We need to be able to hold in our minds a conception of change which allows for the actual complexity of intersubjective processes. The simple counterposition racist/non-racist is far too crude to express the actual complexity of consciousness and identity. The consciousness of a group or individual needs to be thought of more as a collage of different elements, thoughts and sentiments, rather than as some kind of seamless and uniform mass. We might think of the relationship between these elements in terms of Figure 5.1. We suggest that change processes occur primarily at the level of overt public speech and behaviour. Interaction at this level necessarily facilitates the development of new public identities and new forms of attachment. In this sense Alice, Jim and Ron had all changed, they were active members of the council of the 'new' community association and in that sense were different to, and were perceived to be different by, other members of the Evergreens who had withdrawn from active involvement. This involvement drew them into new patterns of behaviour and association. For example, the Chair of the CA remarked upon her surprise and delight when one evening she spotted Jim and Ron leaving the community centre and wandering across to the Plough, a West Indian pub on the corner opposite. A couple of years ago 'they wouldn't have been seen dead in there' as she put it. No doubt the trip to the pub was made easier by the fact that the landlord was himself an active member of the council of the CA and therefore someone Jim and Ron knew well. So we can see how new involvements lead to new patterns of association which lead to new behaviour and so on. And of course at a certain

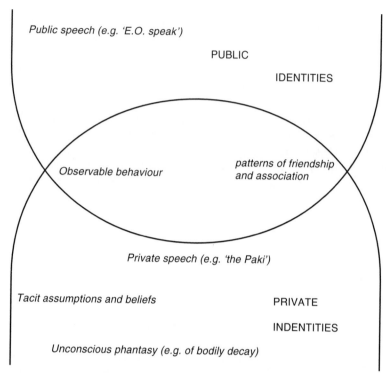

Figure 5.1   Consciousness as a college of elements

point in time the new public identities taken on come into increasing conflict and tension with the older private identities and the attitudes and sentiments that sustain them.

I am not saying that deep-seated change is inevitable – contradictory identities can be sustained for a long time. Moreover, our public identities tend to be more fragile and contingent and therefore more easily reversed should they encounter rebuff or challenge. So there is no necessary reason why the experience of 'playing together' or 'struggling together' means that people will 'stay together'. What is clear, however, from our case studies is that there are a number of factors which can make a difference to this process, factors which can enable people to move beyond the social and psychological barriers which become constructed within racialised spatial communities and institutions.

Racial and ethnic discourses are constantly undergoing processes of elaboration, contestation and renegotiation within the institutions, associations and public spaces of local civil society. Such discursive practices are fused with micro-political projects which, as Anthias notes, need not be formulated on the premise of class formation but on the basis of struggles over citizenship, territory, culture or access to communal resources. The local sites within which such struggles occur constitute spaces which vary in their capacity to contain difference. While this capacity will be influenced by contextual factors such as the degree of interdependence of competing groups it can also be influenced by the actions and choices of actors engaged in such sites. For example, interaction within such sites may be governed by agreed rules of discourse which facilitate communication (see Chapter 3). In a number of our case studies equal opportunity policies functioned in this way. In other words they represented forms of agreed discursive constraint (i.e. language which was overtly oppressive to others was forbidden) which encouraged actors to distinguish between private and public speech. Our experience suggests that local organisations can facilitate communication across boundaries (and in that sense approach the ideal of a 'discursive community' (Benhabib, 1992)), where they are able to sustain a creative balance between the need to articulate issues in public and respect for individual and group privacy.

Containment of difference

In sustaining this kind of balance the respect for privacy seems crucial. Another of our case studies had interpreted their equal opportunities strategy in quite a different way. All attitudes and feelings, particularly those regarded as potentially oppressive, were regarded as legitimate matters for group discussion and as a result meetings were intensely charged and often highly personalised affairs. But if we are to hold on to the idea that communication involves some kind of processes of exchange, of give and take, then paradoxically in this group it seemed that whereas everything had to be discussed nothing could actually be communicated. To understand this paradox the psychoanalytic concept of 'containment' (Bion, 1962; Hinshelwood, 1987) is very helpful. As I have illustrated in previous chapters, 'containment' refers to the function that groups and organisations can perform in providing a place in which potentially explosive thoughts and feelings can be contained and worked through. According to Hinshelwood (pp. 164, 218) if an organisation is unable to perform this function then a difference becomes an opposition, a separation becomes a rigid split' and communication assumes the form of 'dramatisation' (i.e. words are not used so much to convey meaning as to conceal meaning or to project globs of bad feeling onto other group members).

The containing function of an organisation therefore refers to its capacity to contain human emotionality – fear, hatred, envy, love, resentment, hope, excitement – without being blown apart by the pressure of such feeling. Where this containing function is weak boundaries (the infinite number of lines of difference distinguishing people from each other) tend to become barriers rather than crossing places. In such situations difference no longer denotes variety, opportunity, possibility or excitement but danger or threat. Whereas boundaries invite transaction and exchange (of ideas, experiences and feelings) barriers signify exclusion, closed-ness, etc. In such situations communication is only possible with 'insiders' (hence the notion of 'insiderism' implicit in a number of aspects of contemporary social policy where it is assumed that 'it takes one to know one, parent one or treat one'), outsiders constitute a threat to be controlled and kept in their place (physically and psychologically).

Before ending this discussion of the notion of 'containment' I would like to add that this function probably operates in other settings beside the institutional or group one. In particular I would like to speculate that communities themselves, whether construed spatially or in terms of other collective identities, constitute social environments which vary in terms of their capacity to contain conflict and difference. As I have already noted, ethnically constructed communities built upon identities which are strongly projected into the past inevitably tend to produce an essentialised idea of a collective self which is relatively impermeable, brittle and therefore prone to fragmentation, and, if not timeless, then enjoying a quality in which the boundaries between past and present have become blurred and confused. Spatial communities such as neighbourhoods can also become closed, barrier-protected places and the existence of such defensive social dynamics does not require the presence of a group which perceives itself to be under threat. In north-west Leicester the Beaumont Leys area is a recently built mixed-tenure satellite estate but one with a high incidence of racial harassment. Here was a relatively newly formed neighbourhood with few established networks or forms of mechanical solidarity to protect which nevertheless presented itself as a closed and hostile white neighbourhood. It seemed that what white people were endeavouring to protect was a fragile illusion of collective advancement rather that the image of an abandoned and beleaguered minority as in the East End.

On the other hand, some spatially based communities do appear to have a greater capacity to contain conflict and difference, even within the East End. While some white activists on the Aberfeldy estate, one tucked alongside the river Lea on the very eastern fringe of Tower Hamlets, may have tended to turn a blind eye to the outrageous forms of racial harassment the other side of the Blackwall Tunnel approach road on the nearby Teviot Estate, within their own patch incidences of racial harassment were comparatively low. A number of factors contributed to this. There was the vital influence of the network of local white community leaders who had grown up together over a period of decades and retained many of the strongly egalitarian and tolerant values from their Labourist past. There was also the positive impact of the local Culloden School in promoting good race relations between children, in giving support to Bengali parents and in maintaining consistent links with the wider working class adult community (some of the key local white activists were also actively involved on the governing body of the school). The strong network of formal and informal organisations in places such as Easton and the Aberfeldy, many of which cross racial and ethnic boundaries, again suggest the importance of the sphere of 'the public' as a means through which differences can be articulated and worked through rather than left unspoken and suppressed.

Conclusion

Racism can be considered to be one of many inferiorising discourses which posit the existence of fixed biological or genetic differences. But while racisms may draw upon a common symbolic raw material they have many different histories and forms of local articulation. While the validity of the analytical distinction Anthias (1990) deploys between race and ethnicity should be preserved in practice, at a local and probably non-local level, it is sometimes hard to differentiate between racism and ethno-centrism. They are not exclusive phenomena, elements of both can be observed fused one upon the other. What was striking in all three areas studied was not the fixedness but the fluidity of ethnic and racial boundaries. Processes of muting and amplifying difference were highly heterogenous, quite different dynamics could be seen at work within the space of a few miles or less. These findings suggest that at the local level communities are not always to be found sheltering behind their defensive *'we-talks'* (Bauman, 1992). Irrespective of the actions of public policy makers sites facilitating dialogue are continually being constructed within local civil societies. These sites are no more locations for eternal misunderstanding than they are for *ideal speech.*

6
Finding Your Voice

Psychological empowerment

The concept of empowerment has enjoyed a brisk rise to fame over the last decade in diverse areas such as social policy and organisational development. As ever, popularisation has brought corruption and one finds the term being used today, for example, to disguise new forms of exploitation at work built upon Human Resource Management ideologies (Foster & Hoggett, 1999). Nevertheless, ambiguous as the term is for the time being it seems worth persevering with it, particularly because it highlights the way in which human emancipation and the exercise of power are inextricably mixed up.

Within social policy a great deal of attention has focused upon the formal mechanisms which, if in place, it is argued would facilitate the empowerment of citizens and service users. Long-standing models of citizen participation (Arnstein, 1971) have been supplemented by more recent 'rights-based' models (Coote & Pfeifer, 1991) and models of advocacy and self-organisation from the disability and mental health users movements (Lindow & Morris, 1995). Finally, in another possible sign of corruption (Barnes & Walker, 1996), the importation of market mechanisms into the public sphere has encouraged efforts to equate empowerment and consumerism.

But, while the existence of formal mechanisms may provide an important contribution to the process of citizen empowerment, such mechanisms in and of themselves do not empower unless there is a (individual or group) subject ready to use them. There is a danger within social policy that empowerment becomes something synonymous with 'user involvement' in service planning and delivery thus reducing a complex individual life to the simple status of a 'welfare service seeking being'. As Barnes and Walker (1996) note, as well as increasing influence over decisions effecting their care, 'empowerment should represent a process of personal growth' corresponding to an increase in the power of the individual and the group to exercise control over *all* aspects of their lives. Thus fundamentally, empowerment concerns the processes of human emancipation and development corresponding to the enhancement of freedom in its double sense as 'freedom from' and 'freedom to', that is, the realisation of our generative powers.

There is now a considerable body of literature on the theory of social movements which focuses upon what might be thought of as the 'external' factors which make for group empowerment. Although some of this work also considers some of the 'internal' factors relating to group identity (Kriesi et al., 1995; Melucci, 1989; Touraine, 1981), accounts which look at the individual and group psychology of empowerment are largely missing. The idea of this chapter is to make a contribution to this neglected dimension by looking at the link between the process of empowerment and the process of 'making conscious' as in 'becoming conscious of' or 'conscientisation' (Friere, 1970; Holland & Holland, 1984).

Central to this process is the ability to develop and articulate one's voice, i.e. one's experiences, needs and perceptions. Crucially, for most excluded and marginalised groups, this is not simply a question of finding spaces for dialogue within impervious government institutions, for this assumes that such groups have a voice in the first place which is simply waiting to be heard. In fact the problem is more complex. Many excluded groups must first find, develop or recover their voice. Indeed this is what becoming 'politically conscious' is primarily about.

The power to destroy thought

Previous chapters have focused on the way in which our capacity to make sense of and learn from experience is limited by our own fears. Sometimes facing up to things provokes too much anxiety. But while at times we may be our own worst enemies there is no shortage of real external enemies who may also have good reason to prevent us from becoming too thoughtful, that is, too aware of what is happening to us.

In Chapter 3 we considered the positive use of power by political leaders and others, that is, the use of power invested in one's person or role to enhance the capacities of others rather than to exploit or diminish them. This chapter will largely consider the negative use of power, that is, power as domination. The point is that the two forms of power relate to thought and other forms of symbolisation in different ways. Empowerment is intricately tied to the recovery, articulation and development of thought and feeling. But the use of power to oppress and dominate others is bound up with the refusal of thought, language and feeling, that is, their theft or corruption.

In democratic societies we are civilised enough to find the overt resort to domination repellent – particularly the use of violence in families and schools or in the care and control of young offenders, the mentally ill or the old and frail. However the use of rewards and sanctions such as favouritism, withdrawal of privileges, blocking of promotion opportunities, etc., remains a potent and culturally acceptable means of maintaining control of workers and welfare service users. In consent-based regimes domination is largely exercised through means which are much more covert and indirect. Rather than physical abuse here we often find regimes built upon subtle forms of emotional or psychic abuse.

I will begin an exploration of such covert means of exercising negative power with an examination of the theme of 'allusion'. The choice is deliberate for my belief is that allusion forms the link between a violence that is embarrassed or ashamed to speak about itself and the everyday life which proceeds in the shadow of this force. As such my analysis conforms to Gramsci's (1997) understanding of democracy as hegemony, a particular kind of relation between coercion and consent.

When someone alludes to something they may become more explicit if requested to do so. But what happens when clarity is not provided, when ambiguity is subtly maintained by denials, evasions, obscurantism, rationalisations and all the other arts that bureaucracies are so adept at? Many people working within the welfare state have recently experienced the scent of fear, that little unease which comes when one senses one's future is in doubt even though nothing has been said or will be said for some time. When something is alluded to the signified is made present but, in refusing to be made explicit, it also vanishes. An allusion is ringed by denial so that just at the very moment that it brushes against our consciousness it prompts the thought 'no, it could not be!'. Through allusion language is twisted, corrupted and foreclosed. The following example, partly biographical and partly imaginary, should illustrate the issue at point.

A child may assume that a neighbour's carefully and tastefully dec-orated rooms allude to the requirement that visitors, particularly young ones, must take care when using them. The child may seek to confirm this assumption either through verbal enquiry ('Is it all right if I play with my Power Rangers in your conservatory?') or through his behaviour (by massing them on the piano). In either case he may receive a reply which leaves him in no doubt about the rules governing behaviour in this context. However things may not always turn out like this. Some houses present themselves and their occupants to visitors in a more dis-turbing way. One may be greeted at the doorstep by an exclamation such as 'Oh, we didn't know you were bringing Harry with you!' Having been ushered into the front room Harry may be asked repeatedly if he would like to go out and play in the garden ('After all we're sure that there's little in here that could interest him'). The child may not take the hint, or it may attempt to put off going outside until it has stopped raining, in which case an attempt to mass the Power Rangers in any part of the room is likely to provoke the following kind of interaction. In response to the look of anxiety of Harry's parents the hosts smile at the boy and exclaim, 'Oh, we're sure Harry is sensible enough to know how to behave properly.' This in fact alludes to precisely the opposite, i.e. to the belief that Harry, being a child, cannot possibly be trusted. Sometimes, if the child is sharp enough, he may just be able to pick out a note of menace in the way in which such words are said. The point is that Harry, through his Power Rangers, requests an elaboration upon the rules which govern this situation. But no elaboration of the rules which are alluded to (by the style of the furnishings, the mannerisms and remarks of the hosts) is forthcoming. Instead the child receives a statement that he's a sensible boy and therefore must know how to act in a sensible way.

This kind of context is one of covert terror. Some writers, such as Perry Anderson (1977), have argued that this is indeed the character of democracy within capitalist society. In this classical analysis of Gramsci's account of the relationship between coercion and con-sent Anderson (p. 42) insists that the normal structure of capitalist power in bourgeois democracies is one dominated by culture and determined by coercion. The covert, silent and allusive nature of violence in such contexts is captured in the following extract which is worth citing in full:

The normal conditions of ideological subordination of the masses – the day-to-day routines of parliamentary democracy – are themselves constituted by a silent, absent force which gives them their currency: the monopoly of legitimate violence by the State. Deprived of this the system of cultural control would be instantly fragile, since the limits of possible actions against it would disappear. With it, it is immensely powerful – so powerful that it can, paradoxically, do 'without' it: in effect, violence may normally scarcely appear within the bounds of the system at all. In the most tranquil democracies today, the army may remain invisible in its barracks, the police may appear uncontentious on its beat (p. 43).

It may seem shocking to say this but in everyday life, in the normal transactions that occur in the family and the workplace, violence always exists in the background. Not violence directed toward the body but to the person and their feelings about self and others. At the level of appearances, of the verbally explicit, everything seems quite reasonable. In the example I gave above the hosts will in probability appear to be reasonable people – good citizens who pay their taxes without using an accountant, who profess to love animals (indeed they have a mastiff in the garden) and are kind to children ('they spoke reasonably to our Harry'). Because they appear in this way it would be the height of effrontery to suggest that perhaps they weren't as fond of children as they seemed. To accuse them of being child abusers would be inconceivable, but then again perhaps not too far from the truth, for their 'concern' for Harry may in fact mask a kind of hatred.

This drama is typically brought to a close either by Harry falling ill (with a vigorous tummy or headache) or when he inexplicably catches a piece of porcelain with his cuff thereby knocking it to the floor. In this way Harry signals that he has understood that his hosts see him as a despicable little boy who does despicable little things. His hosts have their convictions confirmed ('we love children – but the way some of them are turning out these days') and the satisfaction of Harry's father enacting the hatred that is really theirs. For them the most exquisite pleasure would arise if the father were to remain quiet save a menacing statement to the effect, 'just wait till we get home'. Through such a remark the child is brought to face a range of outcomes which are all equally unthinkable. By offering nothing tangible in the way of imminent punishment the child is left with nothing tangible to contain his anxiety. As others (Puget, 1988) have noted, political prisoners facing torture often find the experience of being tortured easier to cope with than the periods in between, periods in which there is no limit to one's imaginings because one cannot conceive of what they might do next. Real terror is always like this, its victory is achieved not through the act but the spaces in between.

The whole point about the house pictured above is not that it is the repository of beautiful objects (and therefore it doesn't matter if the odd one gets broken) but that it is designed to destroy any form of life within it (and in this it succeeds every time, even if a few things get broken as a result). Harry has been made to feel simultaneously admirable and despicable, he has been told that he is the kind of child who will act sensibly and senselessly, within the house he is arranged and disarranged like any of the ornaments.

The limits to reflexivity

The concept of reflexivity is central to much of contemporary social theory. In *The Constitution of Society* Giddens (1984) outlines a theory of social action which hinges upon the assumption that human agents 'have, as an inherent aspect of what they do, the capacity to understand what they do while they do it' (p. xxii). This capacity is what Giddens calls 'reflexivity'. Because he argues that human beings have this capacity Giddens is critical of any 'objectivist' social theory such as Marxism or Psychoanalysis which sees 'human behaviour as the result of forces that actors neither control nor comprehend' (p. xvi). Giddens tries to steer a course between structuralist inspired accounts of the subject such as Lacan's which, according to Giddens, reduce consciousness to a kind of 'froth' on the surface of an encompassing irrationality and purely rationalist accounts which give no space to the unconscious whatsoever. But in doing so Giddens is forced to disavow the possibility of an unconscious which can act *through* the subject, in other words he is forced to deny the possibility that at times visible or hidden forces really do connive to position individuals or groups as powerless objects.

The point I simply wish to make through the cameo in the previous section is that much of the vitality, tragedy and mystery of everyday life unfolds in a way that few, if any, of the participants are fully conscious of. We never fully understand what we do while we do it. Our capacity to be reflexive is constantly hemmed in by our own fear and others' violence – some ideas are just too dangerous to entertain either because they pose too much of a threat to one's own conception of self or because they pose too much of a threat to others. And where things cannot be thought about we are left with experience which we have no way of symbolising, feelings that cannot be given words. This, then, is a non-discursive world, in which the primary currency of human interaction is emotion rather than language, a world in which, if it exists at all, the symbolic often does assume the form either of flotsam or lies.

I hope the drama I portrayed is coherent enough to sustain the following hypotheses. Contrary to Giddens's account of reflexivity, a sequence of events may correspond little, if at all, to what participants were conscious of in either a discursive (i.e. capable of being articulated in words) or tacit sense. Harry's powerlessness arose as a consequence of what was left unsaid and unthought.

People interact at a number of levels. The statement 'Oh we're sure Harry is sensible enough to know how to behave properly' in fact operates at three levels:

1. the superficial content, one which in itself is tangential to Harry's request for an elaboration of the house rules;
2. the implied opposite – 'he's not to be trusted', etc.
3. at the deepest level, a paradoxical injunction.

Harry receives an injunction (Watzlawick et al., 1968) which directs him to resolve an unresolvable paradox (i.e. to be a sensible child). This puts the child in a no-win situation. Parents are very good at this; here are a few more from my own experience of parenting:

> sit still!
> oh do be a bit more grown up!
> stop fidgeting!
> behave!
> and (to a young infant) go to sleep!

The great thing about such injunctions is that because they guarantee failure the child is set up as a culpable object of the parent's legitimate wrath.

The third point to note from Harry's experience is that, whilst he is only conscious of the first level of communication, through his behaviour he shows that he has received and responded to communications at the other levels. Indeed the resort to a tummy ache is a desperate escape attempt, one that many children have a tacit understanding of. It follows that thought and language is simply one medium of communication. Unfortunately the unconscious, the affects and other media of communication are as yet little understood. What is clear is that we are all probably equally adept at unconscious communication, so we engage in struggle with each other even when unaware of it.

Symbolic abolition

How, then, is domination exercised where violence is concealed? By not making itself clear, by the use of ambiguity, by neither disclosing its intent nor its origins. In civilised societies it is not easy to admit one's own violent feelings – the contempt, hatred or envy one may feel towards colleagues, children, patients or clients. Cynics manage this in their own demoralised way but for the rest of us the exercise of domination, i.e. of power over others, is usually achieved at the expense of our capacity for reflexivity. To find pleasure in assuming authority over others, to be reminded of one's own capacity for cruelty, evokes guilt and anxiety. As a consequence domination, embarrassed about itself, operates by what is left unsaid, by the cultivation of ambiguity or through the destruction of thought and the foreclosure of dialogue (pestered by a child to give an account of the reasons for a decision the parent can always take refuge in the simple statement 'because').

Psychoanalysis has been preoccupied primarily with the unconscious as an endogenous production, as the product of our own internal anxieties. But the concept of foreclosure opens up an avenue for considering the way in which the unconscious is also a social production, something which arises from the effect of the power which other people exert over us. The dictionary defines foreclosure as 'the act of settling beforehand'. The child psychoanalyst Maud Mannoni (1973) gives an interesting example. She describes the familiar situation of the young child experiencing acute emotional tension upon the birth of a sibling. The child 'acts up', is aggressive and 'difficult', reverts to bed-wetting and so on. According to Mannoni such a child 'demands the right to understand the things happening to him in one or another aggressive reactions which make no sense.' The adult, on the other hand, rarely observes this, he or she 'blames an intention whereas the child offers a form of behaviour to be deciphered' (p. 24) but 'if replies are going to be foreclosed, the child will find it difficult to put its question, except in the form of behaviour disorders' (p. 27). In their discussion of 'foreclosure' Laplanche & Pontalis (1973) trace the relationship of this term to the concept of denial. They suggest 'foreclosure consists in not symbolising what ought to be symbolised ... it is a "symbolic abolition"' (p. 168).

In the following section I intend to shift the focus of attention to the voice of excluded communities in relation to the state. Here the argument reconnects with themes developed in Chapters 2 and 3. How do workers in the welfare state deprive people of their voice, perhaps not so much through conscious action as through forms of institutional disempowerment?

Some effects of power

As I mentioned at the beginning of this chapter models of citizen participation (e.g. Arnstein, 1971) have tended to focus upon the different kinds of participatory systems and mechanisms which have been devised to provide citizens with some direct form of voice within government, particularly at the grass roots level. The study of citizen participation however reveals that the exercise of voice is only partly influenced by the presence or absence of various formal mechanisms. The behaviour and assumptions of those with formal authority (e.g. public officials or elected representatives), which are themselves an outcome of the culture of government, has a crucial baring. Let us consider therefore the process of consultation at work in a hypothetical locality, a meeting in which local elected representatives and public officials are consulting 'the public' on a planning, housing or some other such issue. Let us make a further assumption that this is an urban area with relatively high levels of social and economic deprivation, one where many citizens are working class and a good minority are black.

Consider first that the meeting may be such that open argument and conflict is expressed, different values and priorities collide and rebound, 'the public' are given space both to speak and to be listened to. Decisions are taken, including decisions not to act on certain issues, and at the end of the meeting some views no doubt will have prevailed and some will have lost out. In all probability the decisions taken will reflect the views of those with formal authority, community representatives will feel that they 'lost' the argument but at least their views were made known in no uncertain terms.

In other words, they made their voice heard and, although they were defeated, they retained their own opinions, opinions which indeed may have been sharpened and strengthened as the result of argument. This then is the first effect of power, according to Bachrach and Baratz (1962) the capacity of one group of actors (in this case the local politicians and officials) to secure desired outcomes in interaction with others. In this situation those in government have got their way but the voice of opposition at least made itself heard.

Now consider a similar kind of meeting, but this time those with formal authority impose, wittingly or unwittingly, a set of 'game rules' on the situation which make it hard for community representatives to participate in a real way. This occurs so frequently one hardly needs to recite the details – a predetermined agenda, the constant use of technical jargon, volumes of reports and minutes to be waded through, an impervious chairman, seating arrangements which place politicians and officials at the front of meeting often on a raised platform, and so on. In other words the very form of the meeting itself excludes anyone who isn't white, professional, articulate or a political activist. As Young (1996) notes, in such situations a certain mode of speaking is privileged, one which often excludes the possibility that alternative voices might be heard. Typically community representatives leave such meetings feeling angry and frustrated, with a sense that no-one wanted to listen. They still know their own mind but they've been deprived of a voice, that is of a space in which to speak in their own tongue and be heard. Here then is the second effect of power, the power to exclude and silence through the 'mobilisation of bias' (Lukes, 1974).

Finally consider a similar meeting, convened in order to 'consult' the public about impending cuts in public services, in this case perhaps services for the elderly infirm. The cutbacks are 'explained' in terms of the need for rationalisation, that although certain residential establishments are to be closed this should be seen as a more effective use of existing resources. Constant assurances are given that no-one will suffer, residents of establishments which are to close will either be guaranteed alternative accommodation or provision will be made to provide more community-based and non-institutionalised forms of care. The meeting is handled 'sensitively', senior officers are at pains to explain the 'realities' of the situation they are in but opportunities are given for members of the public to express their anxieties. The meeting may well have a therapeutic feeling about it, those in authority behave in a caring manner, the layout of the meeting may express an assumed equality (chairs in a circle rather than an 'us and them' approach).

Again such meetings are familiar enough in Britain today. They often occur against a backdrop of demoralisation, a diffuse collective sentiment which accepts the 'inevitability' of deteriorating living standards for a growing proportion of the population (Joseph Rowntree, 1995). Typically local politicians and public officials are faced with having to implement policies over which they have no influence given the centralisation of control which has occurred within Britain since the early 1980s (Burns, Hambleton and Hoggett, 1994). In other words they are forced to collude with a greater power, they could act differently but the risks would be considerable. They console themselves with the thought that it is better that those with genuine concern for the least privileged manage a deteriorating situation rather than those with no concern.

Although in such meetings dissenting voices may still be heard, the essential tone of such meetings is one of reassurance in the face of public anxieties. Although unhappy, community representatives leave the meeting with a kind of begrudging acceptance that there seems to be no alternative and that those in positions of authority are doing their best. They may however feel anxious when contemplating having to explain this to their own members. In this meeting not only have the community representatives been deprived of their voice but in a way they no longer know their own mind. This then is the third effect of power, the power to define experience through the foreclosure of discourse. As I understand it this is what Lukes (1974) means by the third face of power, one encapsulated in this, by now famous, passage:

> Is not the supreme and most insidious exercise of power to prevent people, to whatever degree, from having grievances by shaping their perceptions, cognitions and preferences in such a way that they accept their role in the existing order of things, either because they can see it as natural and unchangeable, or because they value it as divinely ordained and beneficial? To assume that the absence of a grievance equals genuine consensus is simply to rule out the possibility of false or manipulated consensus by definitional fiat (p. 24).

In the first of the three interactions described above those without formal authority were nevertheless still able to speak their mind.

In the second interaction the community representatives still knew their own mind but had no opportunity to give voice to it in a way which could be heard. But in the third situation they were left with neither voice nor mind of their own. This gives us insight into the effect of power in all social interactions:

1. In some settings people are relatively free to think and speak as they wish;
2. In some settings, although they can think what they like, people are denied the means of giving voice to their experience;
3. In some settings people lose both their voice and their capacity to think for themselves.

Clearly the boundaries between these contexts are not hard and fast but what I have in mind here is the idea that any social group has a culture and a key attribute of this culture concerns the way in which power is exercised. The more oppressive the culture the less the internal life of the group that can be talked about and thought about. Conversely we might think of a democratic culture as one where this life is open to both thought and speech.

In the first setting personal or collective empowerment hinges upon the capacity to move from voice to action, i.e. the capacity to take the power to act as a transformative agent in the pursuit of one's own desired outcomes. In the second setting empowerment hinges upon the capacity to use one's own voice. But this voice does not have to assume the form of words. Sometimes groups speak much more powerfully through action – by withdrawing from a consultation exercise which has become meaningless, by direct action such as boycott, occupation or riot; as the phrase goes, 'actions speak louder than words'. In the third setting empowerment hinges upon the struggle to find one's own internal voice or, as Mannoni (1973) puts it, to gain access to 'the true word'.

In the following sections we will consider why certain things become difficult to speak of and think of. Finally we will consider a new possibility, that at a certain point we may even lose touch with our feelings about the predicament that we are in.

The suppression of voice

In the early 1990s I was privileged to work in Bulgaria in a workshop designed to explore group and intergroup behaviour. It was a time of great fear because of the possibility of Macedonia being drawn into a Balkan War. Sofia, where the workshop was held, was just 60 miles from the border. Themes of violence, uncertainty and chaos haunted the event which lasted for three days. In the final minutes I was working as consultant to a small group of Bulgarians who were among the youngest in the conference. Ruman, who had been very quiet throughout the three days but had watched and listened carefully to what was going on around returned to the issue of fear. The workshop had forced upon him the conclusion that the more we love the more we fear. He linked this to his own experience, to his fear of speaking of thoughts which were the most dear to him, of sharing an idea which was cherished. So he remained silent out of the fear that his gifts would be refused. His thoughts remained private, his longing to give suppressed by his fear of giving. It is only now, reflecting upon this experience, that I fully understand the idea that it may be better to love less in order to fear less, an idea which runs throughout Toni Morrisson's (1988) beautiful book *Beloved*.

Ruman's fear, that his gift would be refused, is a fear that we all share. As Marcel Mauss (1954) observed the exchange of gifts is an elemental form of social solidarity. Here I am concerned with language as a currency of exchange, with speech as a form of giving and receiving (Young, 1997) and with the exchange of private experience which is in some way dear to us, i.e. the 'full word' loaded with personal significance. Ruman's fear was that his gift would be refused. He felt passionately about something and longed to share it but he knew of the risk that we all take when giving.

How often in groups are voices just not listened to or the significance of their words denied? The vast majority of my students have been 'mature students', only a minority have been white middle class men, many have received no formal higher education before. Helping such students to speak in their own voice through their writing has been a vital pedagogic task. But, as bell hooks (1989) notes, the problem of speaking cannot be separated from the question of audience, to whom is one speaking. If the subject is to speak in her own voice then the audience must learn to hear in new ways. The 'academic community' is just one of the many 'expert systems' that Giddens (1991) sees as one of the hallmarks of modernity. He notes the de-skilling effect of such systems and the need for lay actors to reappropriate the knowledge and control that has to some extent been stolen from them by such systems. Many students experience the presence of this academic Other in terms of the theft of their capacity to speak and make sense of their own experience.

Academics, literary agents, editors and publishers form part of a broader 'expert system' which manages access to the publicly written word (Spender, 1981). Actors within such systems not only have the capacity to refuse, to deny significance to words which they see as having no value, they also have the capacity to appropriate them. Speaking of the experience of black women writers in the USA, bell hooks notes how they have faced a new danger, not that their voices will be refused but that they will be trivialised or romanticised through a process which 'turns the voices and beings of non-white women into commodity, spectacle'. (1989, p. 14)

Speaking truth to power

We may not speak out of fear that what we offer will be rejected or stolen. More usually we may not speak for fear of being attacked. As we shall see in Chapter 8, within any group some truths are potentially explosive particularly those which challenge the myths the group holds about itself. The most primitive of these probably correspond to Bion's (1961) group basic assumptions (Stokes, 1994). These are survival myths generated by collective fears of catastrophe (see Chapter 8). Bion's Basic Assumption Dependency corresponds to a culture of willed and willing subordination, a resourceless dependency regarding an accepted wisdom (a bible, elder, party leader, etc). Feelings other than love, gratitude and obedience towards this primal father will not be tolerated and voices questioning this accepted wisdom will be attacked. Basic Assumption Pairing corresponds to a culture of collusion in which pairings and alliances are formed to avoid truth rather than seek it. This is a culture in which a promised future is preferred to an unbearable present, an attitude of intense expectancy prevails but only so long as the saviour remains unborn. Feelings other than optimism and certainty about the 'future coming' will not be tolerated, voices questioning the inevitability or desirability of the coming transformation will be attacked. Basic Assumption Fight-flight corresponds to a culture of paranoia and aggressive solidarity in which the group mobilises to defeat an imagined internal or external enemy. Feelings other than fear, suspicion and contempt for the other will not be tolerated and voices questioning the actuality of threat or the necessity for offensive defence (i.e. deterrence) will be attacked.

In some situations strong group cultures will be reinforced by formal sanctions, in these situations dissidents may find that their life chances will be threatened. Until recently this was certainly the case in Britain's National Health Service (Hoggett, 1997). In such situations what is at stake may be not just one's emotional well-being but one's prospects, indeed one's job. Let me give an example to illustrate.

I once worked with a group of middle-ranking public managers in Northern Ireland. I, along with several colleagues, had been called in by the new top management – bright young things, many of them recently returned from training at Harvard Business School. The most senior executive was both charismatic and abrasive and had shown by his recent actions that he was quite capable of getting rid of colleagues who did not share the new thinking. This client had invited us to provide some management training for the middle tier and, he added, 'to sort out some of the Dodos'. At this time in my early career I didn't have the wit to refuse such an invitation. Working with the middle managers over a period of several weeks was a revelation. They provided a public service to a divided society in one of the most physically impoverished regions of Europe. On a daily basis they had to negotiate with members of para-military groups who organised squatting of public properties on a massive scale. We realised very quickly that they knew exactly how the new top management perceived them. They also had a far more realistic view of the strengths and weaknesses of the organisation than their seniors (a phenomenon not uncommon in organisational life). We soon began to realise that the main 'problem' within this organisation was the senior management itself. During the months that we worked with them the middle managers became increasingly confident that their experience of how things were was not only valid but probably essential to the future well-being of the organisation. Their hope was that senior management might be willing to learn from this experience of theirs, particularly if outsiders such as ourselves who were trusted by both parties could 'hold the ring'. We helped them to convene a meeting with senior management so that they could put their points. They were extremely anxious and fearful, it had taken them weeks to get the point where they felt strong enough to approach top management. As it happened just one member of senior management turned up. Even so when the meeting began the group collapsed into a state of confusion and anxiety, the task of putting their case was left to just a couple of individuals who slowly sank beneath the weight of their colleagues' hopes and expectations. Needless to say, no meaningful exchange occurred.

Speaking truth to power then is hard, particularly when the other has the formal authority to affect one's own life chances. The phrase captures both the difficulty but also the necessity of putting one's own question in one's own voice within institutional or communal settings which connive to create an uncontested reality. Within organisations disempowered individuals constantly seek out spaces, often the space of a supportive group, in which to rediscover their own sense of truth and the possibility that perhaps 'it's not just me who feels such things'. But rediscovering the truth of one's own experience is one thing, making public this truth to the loci of power is another. Returning to the theme of Chapter 3, we see how difficult it is to establish dialogue within 'power cultures'.

The unthinkable

The concept of 'voice' is central to democratic theory as it exemplifies the process of exerting pressure for change through argument and protest. Voice is 'political action par excellence' according to Hirschman (1970, p. 16). But to find one's voice is no easy matter. We have seen how through foreclosure one may be denied the words which would make sense of one's own experience. Such processes of 'symbolic abolition' are among the most penetrating forms of disempowerment. But how is it possible to have experience which cannot be thought about? How is it possible to be without voice and mind of one's own? Perhaps such questions provide us with a key to open up the vital issue concerning the way in which dominance is exercised in families, organisations and societies and specifically the way in which oppression is internalised, i.e. becomes a part of our subjectivity.

We can approach this issue by looking at the concept of human need. Doyal and Gough (1991) have argued that there are certain human needs which are universal. Specifically they argue that 'physical health/survival' and 'autonomy' are needs common to individuals in all cultures. By 'autonomy' they imply the capacity to 'initiate' or 'freedom of agency'. They see this capacity as dependent upon the level of understanding a person has about herself and her culture, her positive mental health ('the individual's cognitive and emotional capacity') and the objective opportunities to act. Doyal and Gough are highly critical of those on the left (e.g. Laclau & Mouffe, 1987) and the right (e.g. Gray, 1983) who see need as entirely relative, as something entirely constituted by cultural or discursive practices or by the play of power. But in adopting a universalist position which posits the existence of certain timeless needs Doyal & Gough are in danger of bending the stick too far the other way. For example, they provide no account of the relationship between need on the one hand and political action and consciousness on the other. In contrast I will argue that it is quite possible to adopt a universalist position and yet also insist that the *experience* of need is tied to the play of power and is therefore something which fluctuates according to historical circumstance.

There is a classic and, to my mind powerful saying which goes, 'what the eye doesn't see, the heart doesn't grieve for'. In other words the experience of need is inextricably linked to consciousness, and specifically the acquisition of political consciousness. Consider the struggle of black people for equality within western democracies over the last thirty years. Today black people feel the need for, and perceive the right to, many things that seemed inconceivable in the 1950s – not just equal rights but positive action to redress the structural disadvantage that black people experience in such societies. In other words, using Doyal and Gough's framework, the need for autonomy is experienced by different groups in a politically urgent manner at different historical moments. The paradox is that when people get off their knees and fight, their struggle is both prompted by need and yet at the same time corresponds to the expansion of experienced neediness. People become more needy as they experience their own powerfulness. Things that were once put up with no longer seem acceptable, people become demanding whereas before they were simply fatalistic. To put it another way: the more we know, the more frustrated we are, and the more we suffer.

Today, the balance of political forces may be changing once more, in countries like the USA and Britain. Many of the 'rights' which black people had barely established, for example to some form of positive action to address inequality, are now being withdrawn. As this occurs so black people's experience of their neediness becomes less secure – after all maybe there aren't the resources available, maybe positive action is a kind of paternalism which attacks the dignity of black people, etc. Imagine that this trend continued, imagine that in a further twenty years time the demand for race equality at work and in education was seen nostalgically as something that reached its apogee in the early 1980s but is now a thing of the past. Black people's experience of their own neediness would have slowly diminished, but this would not mean that their lack had become less. In fact quite the contrary, assuming processes of social polarisation in Britain and the USA continue, the sheer magnitude of human distress would undoubtedly increase. In other words as people's experience of the need for autonomy declines so they become less powerful. Their political consciousness enabled them to give words to what it was that they lacked but as this consciousness is undermined so people paradoxically become less demanding and therefore suffer less at a conscious level.

There is an important distinction to be made here between suffering and distress. Distress is the product of lack. But without consciousness of what it is that one lacks, this distress finds no translation into neediness and suffering. Lack therefore is a state of longing which cannot be named. For Lacan, lack has an existential status bound up with the insufficiency of language (Benvenuto & Kennedy, 1986). I do not wish to dispute this aspect of lack, here I am simply drawing attention to the fact that lack is also a historical and political phenomenon.

One is troubled but the words which are necessary to articulate this trouble, to provide the means to think about it, are absent. The only words available are the deadening and mystifying words that provide us with common sense (Lawrence, 1982) – a form of consciousness to be carefully distinguished from 'good sense' (Gramsci, 1977). Common sense makes the way things are self-evident; nothing else is possible, indeed nothing else becomes conceivable. Common sense is language robbery. To say that one lacks the true words to articulate distress is to say that one may experience it emotionally but not through language; it exists as a perturbation, as a disturbance, but one which remains incomprehensible:

> In fact, many people learn not to think their own thoughts, not to speak their own language, i.e. to 'unlearn' their own culture. People are in a sense being forced not to see the truth of their own reality any longer. (Fritze, 1982)

Once more we can see the process of 'symbolic abolition' at work but this time at the societal level rather than within the crucible of the family. This then is the primary level at which domination works, through the power to foreclose the possibility of thought, i.e. the possibility of constructing an internal voice. As bell hooks (1989) observes, 'for women within oppressed groups who have contained so many feelings – despair, rage, anguish – who do not speak, as poet Audre Lorde writes, "for fear our words will not be heard nor welcomed", coming to voice is an act of resistance' (p. 12).

The suppression of affect

In the passage above, bell hooks assumes the existence of a feeling which awaits a vehicle through which it can be thought about and given voice to publicly. It is possible however that processes of domination may impact upon the psyche at a still deeper level abolishing not just thought but feeling. But isn't the idea that emotion could be kept out of consciousness a contradiction in terms? How is it possible to have a feeling without being aware of it so that instead of rage one feels some kind of nameless perturbation?

The psychoanalyst Joyce McDougall (1986) provides a detailed examination of what Freud called 'the suppression of affect'. Freud noted how in normal experience a thought contained two elements, the idea and the affect. This is a vital discovery in itself, one that many of today's champions of 'discourse theory' tend to neglect, for what it means is that thought and language must be understood as both a cognitive *and* an emotional phenomenon. For words to have meanings they must carry emotional significance, otherwise they are simply facts. Indeed the 'withdrawal of significance' is itself a form of foreclosure where the affect is abolished rather than the idea. To give an example, many women experience organisational life in a way which differs dramatically to their male colleagues. Whilst men see themselves as being business-like, efficient and task-focused, women perceive rivalry, imperviousness and defensiveness but an appeal to the men to look at what they are doing to each other, no matter how diplomatically put, will normally be met with expressions of surprise or disbelief. Where men hold the power women who insist upon a degree of reflexivity about such interpersonal processes are often accused of imputing an unwarranted significance to events. In reality it may be the men who have colluded to 'withdraw significance' by draining events or actions of their emotional meaning. The academic community does this all the time. As bell hooks notes,

I see how many of the people who are writing about domination and oppression are distanced from the pain, the woundedness, the ugliness. That it's so much of the time just a subject – a 'discourse'.... I say remember the pain because I believe true resistance begins with people confronting pain, whether it's theirs or somebody else's, and wanting to do something to change it. (p. 215)

But what happens to affect if, through foreclosure, it becomes abolished, i.e. denied access to consciousness? McDougall notes how Freud spoke of 'the transformation of affect'. In other words, once suppressed and detached from the idea which makes it meaningful, affect becomes a free-standing internal phenomenon which is capable of assuming a variety of forms (Britton, 1992). It may become converted into hysterical symptoms. One of Freud's earliest cases was a young woman who had developed a paralysis of the throat – her experience of living in an oppressive 'Victorian' family was such that 'she couldn't swallow any more'. On the other hand the affect may be displaced and connected with ideas other than the one it was withdrawn from, as occurs with the various obsessions. The affect may also be externalised, here the rejected emotion is attributed to, or forced into, others. My pain becomes your pain. In this way various kinds of 'poisonous interaction' may be set up. Finally, and perhaps most commonly, the affect remains 'massive, anonymous, and detached from any specific ideational representation' (McDougall p. 152) as in anxiety states and hypochondria. In this instance affect obtains no psychic representation whatsoever, not even substitute or mystifying forms of representation. This leaves in its wake 'nothing but a mental blank' which runs the risk of continuing as a purely somatic event as the body itself becomes subject to attack. As McDougall notes, the individual is open to the danger 'that the soma may "think" its own solution to the event' (p. 154). Returning to Doyal & Gough's (1991) analysis we can therefore see how the destruction of a group's autonomy can not only lead to destroyed self-understanding but also to emotional distress and psychosomatic illness.

The hunger of the subject

The inseparability of thinking and feeling first understood by Freud was taken one step further by the psychoanalyst Wilfred Bion (1962, 1970). Bion sought to root human capacities such as thought and language firmly within the materiality of the body by asking us to entertain the hypothesis that the mind may in fact be modeled on the digestive system, but in this case a system for digesting experience. In everyday speech we talk of 'chewing things over', of some things being 'difficult to swallow', of not having 'properly taken something in', of 'digesting what has just been said', and so on. For Bion experience provides the nourishment for the mind, enriching our cognitive and emotional capacities, but only if it can be digested, processed and worked upon. If for some reason experience cannot be processed (as often happens to children who are sexually abused) then it will assume the form of indigestible psychical matter, that is as something potentially disturbing or poisonous to the system which may, as McDougall noted, eventually attack the psyche-soma itself.

Through this model of the mind Bion is suggesting that the need to be enriched by our experience is no less basic than the need to be enriched physically by the taking in of food. In this he builds upon Melanie Klein who had tentatively posited the existence of an 'epistemophilic instinct' as a way of developing Freud's observations upon infantile sexual curiosity (Meltzer, 1978). Bion takes this idea further, although curiosity may be at first bound to the desire for sexual knowledge – the knowledge of where babies come from and hence 'where do I come from?' – he acknowledges the thirst for knowledge as a motive in itself, 'seeking food for the mind' (Meltzer, p. 33). But let us be clear, Bion is speaking of 'emotional knowledge' not 'facts'. This is an embodied knowledge which enriches the moral, aesthetic and intellectual capacities of the person not disembodied knowledge, that is, 'head knowledge', acquired by virtue of the splitting asunder of reason and affect. Because of the existence of this need the child will continue to put its question, and if not through language then through behaviour, through dream-work or through the symptom. If Marx insisted that we are transformative beings then psychoanalysis also insists that we are truth-seeking beings. It is for this reason that the movement towards subjectivity, towards being a subject which can live in mind, voice and action of its own, can never be crushed. Despite the actuality of dominance the subject eternally returns.

7
Mobilising Fictions

Learning from experience

Illusions are having a hard time these days. European social democracy was already in crisis when the destruction of the Berlin Wall in 1989 seemed to symbolise the end of the illusion of socialism. Since then the status of ideology has nose-dived as writers rush to celebrate the so-called 'end of history'. Perhaps if we want a phrase to characterise this period then 'the end of illusion' would be as good as any. For the liberal middle classes at least this idea appears to have become part of a new Weltanschauung, a weary and survivalist realism tinged with cynicism. One that at times takes a somewhat masochistic pleasure in acceptance of 'the cold, hard facts' of life and the idea that only little changes are possible. At a cultural level the rise of postmodernism has also made us suspicious of anyone who appears to speak in a way that stresses what unites people. As I indicated in Chapter 2, there is now such an emphasis upon deconstruction and difference that any attempt to talk about what people experience in common runs the risk of being considered a 'homogenising disourse'. Reading the book *Postmodern Welfare* (Leonard, 1997) I was struck by the hesitant way in which even someone with a history of radicalism like Leonard broached the idea of common needs (p. 166).

Clearly, for those who still identify themselves as radicals the spread of this view of the world is troubling. Like many others of my age I have struggled to remain involved in politics over the decades while trying my best to have few illusions. And in attempting to stay in this position I have always found the phrase 'pessimisim of the intellect, optimism of the will' of Gramsci, the Italian Marxist, a tremendous comfort. This phrase, which the editors of the Prison Notebooks indicate was made by Gramsci into something of a programmatic slogan as early as 1919 in the pages of Ordine Nuovo (Gramsci, 1977, p. 175), struck me then and still strikes me today as being one of those rare keys towards furthering our understanding of political life. I have puzzled over this phrase for years and have offered at least one interpretation of it already (Hoggett, 1992). Note that the phrase assumes the form of a paradoxical juxtaposition between two sets of opposites – optimism and pessimism, intellect and will. And note therefore that its form is one through which opposites are contained (i.e. *both* pessimism *and* optimism) rather than split apart and separated (i.e. either pessimism *or* optimism). This is crucial, for what I want to explore in this chapter is what might be called *'the space that connects'* – inner to outer, subjective to objective, truth to untruth, fact to hallucination, and so on. This space, one that the psychoanalyst D.W. Winnicott calls 'the intermediate area between the subjective and that which is objectively perceived' (Winnicott, 1951, p. 3), is the space where contradiction and paradox can be maintained. It is exemplified by play and drama (we speak of going to see 'a play') but also by the psychoanalytic encounter itself, for all of these have the quality of being simultaneously real and unreal. It is a fundamentally illusory space, an absence which connects, but one which lies at the heart of human creativity and culture. Winnicott calls it *the transitional space* but we will speak much more of this later.

Let me return for now to the idea that radicalism needs to free itself of illusion. For while I held steadfastly to this view throughout the 1980s (and still do) I am now coming to appreciate the other side of illusion – illusion as the basis of play and creative transformation. I will represent these two aspects of illusion, the positive and the negative, through the terms 'fiction' and 'dogma'. Fictions are illusions which know about themselves. In today's parlance they are illusions which demonstrate reflexivity, something our children engage in every day when immersed in games of pretence. Dogmas, on the other hand, are illusions which believe themselves to be truths. They are an expression of our weakness rather than our strength. They derive from an attitude of compliance to the world rather than from an inner sense of ordinary hopefulness.

I wish to argue that what the left needs is the capacity and courage to enter willingly and deliberately into the world of illusion and to create its own 'mobilising fictions'. So, let us look at illusion, and what better place to start than Freud and his celebrated essay *The Future of an Illusion* (Freud, 1927).

Freud: the scourge of illusion

Anyone seeking an appreciation of both the positive and negative aspects of illusion in Freud's essay will be quickly disappointed. Freud is taking systems of religious thought as his target and his essay is a fairly merciless process of unmasking. While in the earlier parts of the essay Freud seeks to understand the power of religious thought over the ordinary individual he is quite unforgiving towards those responsible for perpetrating such ideas. For Freud (1927), religious thought is 'born from man's need to make his helplessness tolerable' (p. 25).

For Freud, it is the mother who is first experienced as God by the infant, who 'becomes its first love object and certainly also its first protection against all the undefined dangers which threaten it in the external world' (p. 34). One of these dangers is the father who, according to Freud, soon comes to replace the mother as the child's protector. Thus the child 'fears him no less than it longs for him and admires him' and, Freud adds, 'the indications of this ambivalence in the attitude to the father are deeply imprinted in every religion . . . (man) creates for himself the gods whom he dreads, whom he seeks to propitiate, and whom he nevertheless entrusts with his own protection' (pp. 34–5).

For Freud, the defining characteristic of an illusion such as a religious idea is that 'a wish-fulfilment is a prominent factor in its motivation'. Freud adds, thus 'we disregard its relations to reality, just as the illusion itself sets no store by verification' (p. 49). Interestingly enough Freud is unable to decide whether such illusions are also delusions. At one point he suggests that the boundary between the two is so slight that how one calls them comes down to 'one's personal attitude' (p. 49). Later he insists that some religious beliefs are so improbable that 'we may compare them . . . to delusions' (p. 50). Religion therefore is a form of self-repression, it is the creation of subjects who lack the maturity to live in a world without God the Father.

It is at this point, more than any other, that Freud puts himself forward as a knight of Enlightenment rationalism. For example we hear Freud saying that as 'the treasures of knowledge' become accessible so the more widespread will be the decline of religious belief, 'civilisation has little to fear from educated people and brain-workers' (p. 63). Regarding the victims of religious ideology he suggests, 'the time has probably come, as it does in an analytical treatment, for replacing the effects of repression by the results of the rational operation of the intellect' (p. 72). As a consequence those freed from the grip of religious belief 'will be in the same position as a child who has left the parental house where he was so warm and comfortable ... we may call this "education to reality"' (p. 81).

Let us reflect upon this for a moment. What is so striking about Freud's analysis (incidently one he pursued in exactly the same vein some five years later in the last section of *The New Introductory Lectures*)? While Freud can understand (immature) mankind's need for illusion he can see no positive value in it. Illusion is a sign of our weakness, it is defensive and protective, it borders on delusion. It turns away from reality, it is certainly not creative nor a vehicle through which human powers are developed. On the one hand there is illusion, on the other there is science; on the one hand there is the Pleasure Principle, on the other there is the Reality Principle; on the one hand there is solace and comfort, on the other there are the cold, hard facts of experience. Two separate worlds with no overlap, a striking dualism.

But what if an illusory idea was maintained even though it was known to be illusory? What if a story was able to retain its value and power even though the individual knew that it was just a story? What of the possibility that something might be considered both real and unreal, that a fiction might speak to fundamental human truths and that this paradox was tolerated and accepted by the believer rather than forced into some kind of resolution?

Just such a possibility had been propounded a few years before Freud wrote *The Future of an Illusion*, by the German philospoher Hans Vaihinger in his *The Philosophy of 'As if'* (Vaihinger, 1924). There is a fascinating section in *The Future of an Illusion* where Freud seeks to reject Vaihinger's philosophy of the 'As if' as grounds for preserving the status of religion in the modern world. According to Freud, Vaihinger's philosophy:

asserts that our thought-activity includes a great number of hypotheses whose groundlessness and even absurdity we fully realize. They are called 'fictions', but for a variety of practical reasons we have to behave 'as if' we believed in these fictions (pp. 43–4).

Freud is clearly impatient with this argument. The idea that something might be held to be simultaneously real and unreal, true and false, seems to be ridiculous to him. He adds,

> I am reminded of one of my children who was distinguished at an early age by a peculiarly marked matter-of-factness. When the children were being told a fairy story and were listening to it with rapt attention, he would come up and ask: 'is that a true story?' When he was told it was not, he would turn away with a look of disdain. We may soon expect that people will soon behave in the same way towards the fairy tales of religion, in spite of the advocacy of 'As if' (pp. 44–5).

On first reading this I must admit that I was stunned. I'd never realised before just how much of a 'rationalist' Freud was and what poverty of the imagination Freud's son, and possibly father, suffered from. Indeed, on reflection, we might wonder whether at times Freud was suffering from a surfeit of rationality. A kind of illness, one which Winnicott describes some fifty years later as the inverse of delusion, an illness related to 'being out of touch with the subjective world and with the creative approach to fact' (1971, p. 67). How strange that Freud, who perhaps more than any other figure in the last one hundred years revealed the realm of the irrational, was himself a supreme rationalist.

The philosophy of 'As if'

Freud admits that his own hopes are possibly illusory but 'my illusions are not, like religious ones, incapable of correction.... If experience should show – not to me, but to others after me, who think as I do – that we have been mistaken, we will give up our expectations' (p. 86). Secondly he points to a difference in the psychical quality or status of his own beliefs and those of his opponents. For his opponents belief systems are a way of staving off an immanent catastrophe,

> You have to defend the religious illusion with all your might. If it becomes discredited . . . then your world collapses. There is nothing left for you but despair of everything, of civilization and the future of mankind. From that bondage I am, we are, free. Since we are prepared to renounce a good part of our infantile

wishes, we can bear it if a few of our expectations turn out to be illusions. (p. 89)

With hindsight, knowing what we now know about the history of science, we can state that Freud is operating here with what Vaihinger already knew to be a naïve concept of science. Scientific world-views, what Kuhn (1970) much later called paradigms, are not so easily given up. For the scientist is also an emotional animal and the systems that are constructed are built upon the optimism which comes from the possibility of gaining some kind of understanding of a chaotic and mysterious world. Science itself can so easily become dogma. Vaihinger speaks of this as 'logical optimism' (p. 162):

> The logical infallibility of thought is adhered to by the logical optimist as though it were a Gospel in which he blindly believed; and with the same intolerance that accompanies religious superstition he regards the logical form in which he happens to think as better than any other.... The logical edifice...is so carefully protected from the fresh breezes of doubt.... Optimism here becomes conservative, reactionary and injurious like everything else that outlives its usefulness. (p. 162)

When Freud speaks of 'illusion' he is, for the most part, refering to what Vaihinger terms dogma. The exception is where Freud refers to 'illusions' which are nevertheless capable of correction, these Vaihinger speaks of as hypotheses, 'ideas as to whose objective validity there is doubt' (p. 125). For Vaihinger dogmas, 'ideas which are without hesitation regarded as the expression of reality' (p. 125), are to be contrasted both with hypotheses and fictions. For Vaihinger fictions are thought experiments, neither real nor unreal but devices for sense-making and the realisation of practical purposes. The whole philosophy of 'As if' is devoted to a celebration of fictions as perhaps the most crucial and creative element of intellectual and cultural life. For Vaihinger fictions are illusions which are upheld even though those upholding them know them to be illusions – the Atom, the Absolute, Infinity, Freedom. As we have seen, for Freud the rationalist, the idea of a fiction was ridiculous. Freud was only able to grasp the negative aspect of illusion, not its positive aspect.

So what then is a fiction? Vaihinger argues that 'the basic form of the fictive chain of thought is the following: A is to be regarded as if (as though) it were B or: *A is to be regarded as if it were B (although it is not B)'* (p. 260). Thus the atom is to be regarded as if it were matter and in law the individual is to be regarded as if he/ she were a free agent. Vaihinger adds, 'modern scientists, in so far, at least, as they have had some philosophical training, do not say that matter *is* composed of atoms' (p. 94). In contrast a hypotheti- cal chain of thought suggests that *A is perhaps B*, in other words hypotheses, unlike fictions, make claims (albeit tentatively) about reality. The power of a fiction lies in the way in which it facilitates our understanding of the world even though we know it to be unreal. The value of a fiction is not destroyed because of its unreality, something neither Freud nor his son were apparently able to appreci- ate. For although fictions are unreal they nevertheless draw upon reality and draw us back to reality. They are real and unreal, and hence more than any other form of thought have the character of being an illusion. Again, to cite Vaihinger, 'thought conducts us automatically to certain illusory concepts just as in vision there are certain unavoidable optical errors. If we recognise this logical illusion as necessary. . . and at the same time, see through them (e.g. God, Liberty, etc.) then we can cope with the logical resultant contradictions as necessary products of our thinking' (pp. 133–4).

The essence of a fiction is that it is self-contradictory. Consider, for example, the idea that the individual should be regarded as if he/she were a free agent. This very idea flies in the face of all that we know about the way in which human behaviour is influenced by biological, social and unconscious factors but, as Vaihinger notes, 'a careful psychologist and jurist does not say that man is a free agent, but that man, at any rate legally, and from a moral stand- point, be regarded and treated as if he were free' (p. 95). In treating A (the individual) as if it were B (a free agent) a judgement is performed with 'a simultaneous protest against the idea of its ob- jective validity, but with an express insistence upon its subjective significance' (p. 261). In other words the possibility of treating 'this non-valid judgement as nevertheless valid, is affirmed' (ibid.).

Whereas a fiction is a consciously held illusion, a dogma is an illusion which is unreflexively held. For instance, Vaihinger argues that when Christ taught 'God is our father in heaven' he probably meant 'treat God *as if* he were your father and as if he were a constant observor of your actions'. But for the followers of Christ this fiction became a dogma. Terrified believers experienced God *as* their heavenly father who was watching all of their actions. In other words, they took the fiction literally, not *as if it were true* but *as truth*. The *space between* the symbol (God) and the thing symbolised (watchful father) disappeared and the symbol became concrete, a thing-in-itself. As Segal puts it, the concrete symbol is used to deny loss, not to overcome it (Segal, 1986). In one of the most fascinating sections of *The Philosophy of 'As if'* Vaihinger propounds what he calls the 'Law of Ideational Shifts' a hypothesis which suggests that certain ideas, or systems of ideas, pass through a number of stages of development such as that from fiction, to hypothesis to dogma or vice versa.

For Vaihinger fictions lie at the heart of human development for they constitute the medium ('the light paper currency of thought' p. 160) between the internal and the external worlds. He speaks of them governing the point of 'exchange' between these worlds providing them with their 'intimate connnection' and 'intercourse'. It is almost as if we can think of fictions as the result of this intercourse, of this union between differences, the midwife which gives birth to meaning. Whereas the material of the external world is 'ponderous' ('hard and clumsy necessity' p. 161) through fictions it is changed 'into the light and evanescent thought which so little resembles it' (ibid.). Fictions are therefore the play materials of the mind. As Vaihinger notes, 'I recognised in play the "As if", as the driving force of aesthetic activity and intuition' (p. xxv). Thus he cites Nietzsche, 'why cannot we learn to look upon metaphysics and religion as the legitimate play of grown-ups?' (p. 346).

Fictions inhabit the space between the real and the unreal or, rather, the space where the real and the unreal overlap. Kermode (1967) suggests that fictions enable us to make sense of and 'to move' in the world. Kermode prefers to use the term 'myth' rather than dogma and, following Vaihinger, argues that fictions degenerate into myths whenever they are not consciously held to be fictive. Kermode notes how myths offer total and adequate explanations of things and as such are the 'agents of stability' whereas fictions are the agents of change (p. 39). But while we know that a literary fiction such as King Lear is not true, it is nevertheless not a falsehood in the sense of being a lie. Kermode takes Nietzsche to task for blurring this distinction between lies and fictions. It is not that any arbitrary system of beliefs can operate as a fiction. It is to be remembered that fictions are for making sense; lies on the other hand are for making no(n)sense. As Kermode puts it, fictions inescapably involve an encounter with oneself and with life. In Bion's (1962) terms they provide food for thought. Whereas lies are poisons, 'anti-Semitism is a fiction of escape which tells you nothing about death but projects it onto others' (Kermode, ibid.).

For Vaihinger the essence of the dogma is not so much that it misleads or misprepresents but that the space between the representation and the thing represented has been destroyed – God becomes the father rather than treated as if he were the father. Dogmas have lost their symbolic value and richness and become concrete (Segal, 1986). Barthes (1973) who also uses the term myth rather than dogma appears to make the same point when he argues, 'myth hides nothing and flaunts nothing' (p. 129) and later, 'what is characteristic of myth? To transform a meaning into a form. In other words myth is always language-robbery' (p. 131). Through dogma language loses its symbolic value, meanings become facts demanding compliance and the space within which the mind can play disappears. There is no in-between, and therefore there is no subject who can creatively weave meanings through this intermediate area of illusion, but one who is simply subject(ed) to dogma.

Playing and reality

D.W. Winnicott was a psychoanalyst and paediatrician who has had a tremendous impact upon clinical work with children, adults and families in Britain and North America. His ideas are just beginning to have an impact on social and political theory (Benjamin, 1988; Flax, 1990, 1993; Honneth, 1995; Giddens, 1991; Williams, 1998). If Vaihinger is the philosopher of *the space in between* then Winnicott is its psychologist.

Winnicott's book *Playing and Reality* (1971) is one that I have found myself returning to again and again. Through a series of studies it extends and develops some early ideas developed in two articles in particular – 'Transitional Objects and Transitional Phenomena,' written in 1951 and reproduced in *Through Paediatrics to Psychoanalysis* (1958) and 'The Capacity to be Alone,' written in 1958 and reproduced in *The Maturational Processes and the Facilitating Environment* (1965).

The central focus of all of this work concerns what Winnicott refers to as the third area of human living, 'one neither inside the individual nor outside in the world of shared reality' (1971, p. 110). In positing this third area Winnicott seeks to transcend the dualism of Freud's system built around the binary terms inner/outer, pleasure principle/reality principle, reason/unreason, etc. He adds, through a phrase which he returns to in his theory of play, that it is an area 'which is not challenged' for it performs a function vital to life, 'that of keeping inner and outer reality separate yet inter-related' (1958, p. 230). This area then is the area of transition, a transitional space filled by what Winnicott calls transitional ob-jects and phenonena, the first of which comprise that range of objects – teddy bears, bits of cloth or blanket – that infants de-velop a close attachment to if their development proceeds well enough, objects Winnicott describes as 'the first *not-me* possessions'. This first possession 'comes from without from our point of view, but not so from the point of view of the baby. Neither does it come from within; it is not an hallucination' (op. cit., p. 233).

The insightfulness of Winnicott's arguement cannot be exagger-ated. The transitional object is the first and most embryonic form of symbolisation developed long before the acquisition of language. As Winnicott puts it, 'we are witnessing both the child's first use of a symbol and the first experience of play' (1971, p. 96). There can be absolutely no doubt that this object is meaningful for the infant, its discovery is therefore equivalent to the birth of meaning in this one small life and thus the point of entry into culture. In a classic statement Winnicott adds,

> of the transitional object it can be said that it is a matter of agreement between us and the baby that we will never ask the question 'Did you conceive of this or was it presented to you from without?' The important point is that no decision on this point is expected. The question is not to be formulated (1958, pp. 239–40).

Winnicott returns to this paradox again and again. Against those who would insist that symbolic systems such as thought bear no correspondence to 'the real' and those, on the other hand, who would insist that thought approximates ever more closely to a real-ity which exists separately from our representation of it, Winnicott tirelessly reiterates that the first symbol is niether real nor unreal, 'we agree never to make the challenge to the baby: did you create this object, or did you find it conveniently lying around?' (1971, p. 96). Against those, probably including Freud, who would insist that a phenomenon must *either* be part of internal psychic life *or* external reality we have this third area, the space in between, *both* internal *and* external, real and unreal.

But there is at least one more paradox to master. Winnicott repeatedly describes this transitional space as a 'potential space' not an actual one. It is a space which initially 'both joins and separates the baby and the mother' (op. cit., p. 103); it is a full space, one filled up by playing and the use of symbols which draw upon material from both internal and external worlds (p. 51). It is a space of overlap, of both/and. Fuller (1980, p. 204) likens it to 'an imaginative denial of separation'. It should come as no suprise therefore that Winnicott refers to this space which cannot be a space as the area of illusion, that which both joins and separates. As he puts it, 'it is assumed here that the task of reality-acceptance is never completed, that no human being is free from the strain of relating inner and outer reality, and that relief from this strain is provided by an intermediate area of experience which is not challenged (arts, religion, etc.)' (1958, p. 240).

Let me take a step back to reflect upon this. Several years ago, when I first began writing this section, I could hear my eight-year-old daughter Jenny playing in the front room. Other than the dog asleep on the settee behind me there was no-one else in the house. Jenny had asked me to get her the zoo which had been put away in the cellar for over a year. She cleaned the base and then inspected the animals. Some, like the eagle, she recognised as old friends. I could hear her talking to them. Although she was physically alone she was surrounded by familiar others. I was also at play, though in my case I was playing with ideas. Any parent knows how fragile, how easily interrupted, such a play state is. But we agree not to break the spell. I would no more have dreamt of saying to Jenny (as I fear Freud's son might have done) 'don't be so silly, stop talking to those animals, don't you know that they are not real!' than a friend would have dreamt of telling me to stop kidding myself that I had something of use to say to the world. Because we allow ourselves our illusions we can allow others their's. Besides, as Winnicott notes, play is immensely exciting because of the precariousness of the relationship between the fluidity of dream-life and the actual recalcitrance of the objects of play, 'this is the precariousness of magic itself' (1971, p. 47). Remember what Vaihinger said about the lightness and evanescence of fictions, in play we are engaged with a plastic medium, one capable of being moulded, one pliant and supple.

The illusory self

Once we understand that illusions can be the basis for engagement with reality as well as a retreat from it, in other words once we have been able to distinguish illusion from delusion, then some traditional conundrums within social science might be resolved. Take the example of the self. It may be remembered that in the *Ego and the Id* Freud suggested that at first the ego was no more than the projection of a surface, i.e. a skin-boundary. As we saw in Chapter 2, one can see how for some, particularly those who follow Lacan in the conclusions he draws from the mirror-stage, this provides the basis for saying that identity is a delusion, an alienated construction. In contrast there are still some who continue to believe in the idea of a real self which stands at the centre of its own universe and has an essential and private core.

In contrast if we hold to the idea that identity, following the earliest ego, is an illusion then we are not thereby saying that it is in any necessary sense alienated or unreal. Indeed we might add that it is precisely those unfortunate enough not to be able to develop an adequate (i.e. fictional) illusion of self that are alienated from themselves. This may be either because their identity has lost its fictional quality and has become mythic or because, like Freud's son, they are incapable of generating illusion and condemned to matter-of-factness or what Bollas (1987) calls 'normotic illness'. To sustain a fiction of the self not only provides comfort when needed but it acts as the means whereby the not-yet of a life can come to be – through creative illusion we play with and shape the world, including our own future. In this sense identity is a generative phenomenon. The post-modern onslaught on the idea of the unitary self also requires reconsideration. Psychoanalysis from Freud onwards has challenged the idea of a unitary psychic structure but this in itself does not provide the grounds for concluding that the self is an essentially fragmented phenomenom. The motif which recurs throughout both Kleinian and post-Kleinian thought is the constant oscillation of the subject between disintegration and integration. The fiction of the self is a crucial element of the symbolic skin within which the subject is contained. As such it helps bind together and synthesise the objects, figures and fragments of the internal world. As Taylor (1998) puts it, 'there is something at the core of each individual which unifies the fragmentation of experience' (p. 335). We are one, and we are many.

The group illusion

Winnicott's theory of illusion does not seem to have been applied to the phenomenon of the human group, yet it would appear to have some important implications, not least because Bion's (1961) analysis of the non-pathological dimension of group life was largely underdeveloped.

At a certain point in time a number of people will have met often enough and the experience will have been good enough for the illusion of a group to emerge. One might think of this group illusion in terms of the existence of 'a group in the mind', something which enables each member to be alone and yet in the presence of the group. This group in the mind finds expression through stories that the group tells about itself, 'this is who we are' type stories. Following Winnicott we might add that we normally don't ask the group 'is this story true or did you make it up?' The key thing is that, in health, the group behaves 'as if' this is who they are.

Let me give an example. A few years ago I was invited to Norway to give a talk at a festival of Contemporary Arts on the theme of ecstasy. I was invited by a number of individuals who I subsequently discovered belonged to something called *Group K*. In its literature *Group K* stated that it 'explores and works within the areas between psycho-analysis, schizo-analysis, philosophy, literature and art.' Despite having fewer than ten members (including psychologists, architects and students) and being based in a medium-sized non-university town, *Group K* had organised a range of seminars and study groups over the previous four years. Here then was a group which not only had its own story but one which it had made explicit – it had a name and it could make statements about itself.

In my experience the naming of the group is a necessary part of the process of illusion formation. In the earliest stages when the group hardly exists beyond a seriality the giving of a name invites identification, 'we have a name therefore we exist.' If the illusion cannot be created or sustained then there is no group, simply a collection of individuals, Sartre's seriality. But once there is the illusion of a group, once there is faith in it, then it can project itself into the future. Meetings might be called, statements released, events organised and if there is commitment to the illusion it may begin to feel solid and durable. It develops a history. While members are alone they can be in its presence, that is, a group in the mind forms. There is talk about this group, others ask to join it, the first disagreement may be survived. Now the group exists in transitional space, the space of possibility between 'the given' and what might be dreamt of, the space of the not-yet.

The group illusion should be distinguished from another characteristic of the group, one with which it is often confused. I am referring to the existence of unconscious group phantasies – i.e. aspects of group life that cannot be thought about. The consultant to groups is constantly faced with such phantasies. For example, the group as a frightening persecutor before which all members are silenced; the group as an empty infertile space to which members have nothing to give and from which nothing can be received (see the next chapter for a detailed example of this kind of group phantasy). The question is, can the group use its own unconscious life, draw upon it creatively, or is it in thrall to this life?

But what if a group begins to take its illusions too seriously? In this situation the illusion loses its quality of play – 'the group' loses its symbolic quality and no longer acts *as if* it were innovator, saviour or prophet but operates according to an unreflexive assumption that it *is* these things. The illusion has lost its quality of being a fiction and has become dogma. The stories that it tells about itself are taken literally, as statements of fact and truth. To repeat what Vaihinger said of the fiction, a judgement is performed with a simultaneous protest against the idea of its objective validity but with an express insistence upon its subjective significance. It is not simply that the group retains the capacity to doubt its own story; rather the group accepts that viewed from one perspective its story is absurd, but insists upon taking pleasure in it nevertheless. In other words it insists upon the right to ambiguity, upon the right to inhabit the space in between truth and untruth, between cold, hard facts on the one hand and dreams and imagination on the other.

To reiterate, in Winnicott's terms, the creative group is a group at play. It can adopt a playful orientation towards the world that surrounds it but, perhaps more importantly, it can also adopt a playful attitude towards itself. It is able to laugh at itself, smile at its own earnestness, take pleasure in its inconsistency and yet, like any other group of children at play, insist upon an equal commitment to the serious task at hand. Moreover it is hopeful and therefore draws upon the phantasy of omniscience – it can dream of its own importance, of the things that it might do, of the creations that it might be capable of, of the enemies it might be able to slay.

In contrast there are some groups which cannot allow themselves to dream. In some groups cynicism is the overriding experience. Here one finds a hatred of anything living. Reason's purpose is to destroy, to strip bare, to reduce everything to the same level of useless equality, to find fault with everything. As Bion (1962, p. 98) notes, this orientation approaches any new development as a rival to be destroyed. Within the academic world the method of social criticism balances on the edge of pure cynicism, as if the task of the critic is merely to expose the naïveties or calumnies of others, as if the only meaning in life stems from the draining of meaning from life. The only development which can be tolerated is the development of criticism itself. Hence new genres of cynicism come and go until, like exhausted parasites on an emptied host, they die.

The development of cynicism as a diffuse late-twentieth-century phenomenon (Sloterdijk, 1984) is the downside of the development of more reflexive states of mind. The cynic sniffs out inauthenticity like a dog after a rabbit – pompousness, hubris, arrogance, naïvety, timidity, these are all fair game. But so is hopefulness, belief in others and trust. The cynic knows of these things precisely because of his self knowledge but the problem is that this reflexivity is coupled with a demoralised view of the world. When everything is subjected to deconstruction, criticism becomes an end in itself. And, when fetishised in this way it becomes an illusion in its own right, one which no doubt offers its own perverse form of consolation.

Mobilising fictions

Let me return to my starting point. The new *Weltanschauung* expresses its disdain for illusion from the perspective of one who is experienced in life, that is, 'wise before the years'. As one (male) ex-colleague of mine said to another (female) ex-colleague, 'welcome to the real world!' – i.e. stop complaining about excessive work loads and the lack of mutual support, this is how it is these days. Against this attitude let us remember Winnicott's view that no human being is ever free from the strain of relating inner and outer reality and that, if we are not to end up like Freud's son, we must live this tension between our dreams and reality in order to sustain a creative approach to fact. This is what I take Gramsci to mean when he speaks of 'pessimism of the intellect, optimism of the will – i.e. to know the cold, hard facts of the situation and yet sustain a creative orientation towards life.

Politics takes place in the space in between truth and untruth. It is not facts that move people but illusions. The failure to understand this has been one of the greatest weaknesses of the left and one of the most unfortunate legacies of the communist and reformist traditions of the early twentieth century. Throughout the twenty odd years I was involved in politics I was struck by the rationalism of the left, i.e. of the old Labour Party and beyond. By this I have in mind their belief in the power of reason, of fact, argument and persuasion in changing people's minds – to vote Labour, to take trade union action or to engage in a campaign. And yet I have also been struck by the way in which leftists, particularly when they grouped together, gave expression to beliefs and behaviour which were clearly non-rational – for example, their touching faith in the goodness of 'the class', their unshakeable conviction that if only the right policy or slogan could be found the spell which had been cast upon this slumbering giant would be broken, their tendency to reserve the most profound hatred for other groups whose values and ideas were closest to their own. It was as if unreason, having been banished or repressed from the collective consciousness of the left, re-emerged via the return of the repressed to haunt every thought and action of these would-be materialists.

As Freud's musings in *The Future of an Illusion* disclose, we cannot do without our illusions, just as we lay one to rest another comes in through the back door. And this is as it should be, for the problem is not illusion *per se*, the problem is illusion which is unaware of itself, i.e. fiction which has been confused with fact. Take the idea of 'community' as an example. Of course the very idea is an illusion. As Margaret Stacey (1969) discovered, scratch beneath the surface for the reality to which it refers and it evaporates into myriad inconsistent possibilities. So, our rationalist concludes, it follows that community does not exist, it is a mirage conjured up in order to offer the consolation of a warm fire in a cold world. But this is entirely to miss the point. Illusions are not logically consistent nor are they even approximations to truth, rather they are by nature ambiguous and paradoxical phenomena. But more importantly, in politics, the transitional space which illusions open up is also the space between the present and the future, between what is and what might be. Remember what Marx and Engels said in their celebrated *Theses on Feuerbach*:

> The question of whether objective truth can be attributed to human thinking is not a question of theory but is a practical question. Man must prove the truth, i.e. the reality and power, the this-sidedness of his thinking in practice. The dispute over the reality or nonreality of thinking that is isolated from practice is a purely scholastic question. (Marx & Engels, 1970, p. 121)

In politics then, the question is not whether community is true or not, the question is whether the idea of community has the power to effect a transition from what is to what might be. And, we might add as a set of crucial supplementary questions: what is the quality of this illusion? Which group is making use of it and for what purpose? The creative illusion, which I suggest we might think of in terms of a mobilising fiction, is perhaps the crucial tool in all liberatory struggles. It is in this sense that Jeffrey Weeks speaks of the gay and lesbian community:

> Lesbian and gay identities, and the communities which make them possible, and which in turn they sustain, are a precondition for a realistic sexual politics in the age of Aids. (Weeks, 1991, p. 95)

> In that sense, gay and lesbian identities are fictions, the necessary ways we mobilise our energies in order to change things. (Weeks, 1991, p. 98)

Of course the fictional element of identities is hard to sustain. In reality all group illusions will contain elements of dogma as well as fiction, and the greater the element of dogma the more that group will be driven to police its own boundaries. Where dogma dominates, the subversive must work towards deconstruction, i.e. towards exposure of the consolatory and life-denying elements of the group. Then it is possible to speak of 'the end of illusion'. But this is no 'end of history', simply a brief passage in the creative-destructive cycle of human and political life.

Welfare fictions

One of the unanticipated problems of the politics of difference is just how hard it has now become to speak about what people have in common. And yet despite our differences we still have much in common. We fall ill, we get old, we fall out with each other, we fall in love, we feel anxious about our future, we fight with our children, we struggle to make ends meet. For all but a tiny minority of the super rich, for whom the last situation is entirely novel, all of us encounter most of these life experiences irrespective of our gender, class or ethnicity. While the form that such experiences take may vary and while the kinds of support we seek to help us cope with such experiences may differ, the point remains that the experiences are nevertheless shared in common.

The danger with some post-modernist social theory is that the emphasis upon difference has become so fetishised that it is identity which has emerged as problematic, and hence also unity, solidarity and the common good. But there is no future for welfare unless people can fight together for some kind of shared vision, including a vision of a welfare society in which differences are respected. For some post-modernists such as Lyotard, talk about the need for an encompassing political vision is 'doomed to result in new oppressions under the banner of new metanarratives of liberation', as Leonard (1997, p. 146) puts it. It is as if the very search for a 'big picture', that is, some kind of alternative vision around which oppositional forces can mobilise, is a form of terrorism. And as a result, the danger is that we are disarmed.

In contrast I would suggest that the problem does not lie with the vision *per se* but with maintaining its fictional quality. Thus ideas such as 'the common good' and 'universalism' can be regarded as dogmas, hypotheses or fictions according to how they are used, by whom and for what purpose. As a dogma, universalism would constitute an idea which without hesitation could be regarded as an expression of reality. As a hypothesis it would be an idea whose objective validity remained in doubt. But as a fiction such an idea is a thought-experiment. The idea that there are universal needs or universal standards for making judgements about 'neediness' is both absurd *and* absolutely necessary. This was the idea of universalism that Simon Thompson and I had in mind when we pointed to the self-contradictoriness and incompleteness of the concepts of universalism and particularism and the resulting paradox that neither could be posited without calling upon the other (Thompson & Hoggett, 1996).

It is sometimes argued, for instance, that the universalistic principles which underlay the post-war welfare state were necessarily homogenising in their effect. I cannot accept this position. Traditional forms of universalism neccessarily created their own differences – between 'rough' and 'respectable', between deserving and undeserving poor, between 'proper' and 'improper' (e.g. single parent or non-heterosexual) families – while at the same time obscuring other differences such as those based upon gender. While the principle of universalism – from each according to her/his ability, to each according to her/his need – remains a laudable one it is nevertheless a fiction. Until utopia comes all societies, even global ones, will need to make allocative decisions which will lead them to use historically and culturally relative judgements about 'who gets what'. Even the eco-socialist policy of a guaranteed citizen's income, which as I suggest in Chapter 11 could be the basis for a new form of universalism, will create new social divisions while obscuring other differences. The point is that until such policies are implemented we can not be sure what their differentiating effects will be.

A universalist *ethic* is a normative thought-experiment, not just a device for sense-making but also a vehicle for the realisation of political purposes. In this sense it is a political fiction which can assist the mobilisation of groups in political struggle. Which fictions we might choose to give life to an alternative future vision of welfare is a question of debate. In the last two chapters of this book I make my own contribution to 'big picture' building. The point I am simply trying to establish here is that a political culture which is denied the capacity to develop new illusions is one which has been left without the imagination which could enable it to traverse the space between what is and what might be.

8

The Internal Establishment

In the previous chapter we examined some of the creative and imaginative dimensions of group life. In this chapter I will offer a particular way of thinking about the darker side of group life. Specifically I want to explore something that has been an almost constant feature of my experience of groups which start out with a radical political or cultural intent, that is, their underlying conservatism. I do not think that this is a particular feature of these kinds of groups but it is very ironic that even groups such as these, whose members are typically drawn to them because of their emancipatory values, are dogged by largely unconscious, reactionary impulses.

Two manifestations of this conservatism come to mind: first, the intolerance that one often finds in groups such as campaign groups or political parties – particularly I have in mind an intolerance towards thought (i.e. 'free' thinking). Second, and less obviously, the way in which groups become trapped within their own imagination. In connection with this I can remember a number of loose collectives that I have belonged to where idolatory of leadership or dependence on any kind of 'bible' was eschewed and yet where, after a brief flowering of experimentation, the life of the group became predictable and stultifying.

What I wish to explore therefore is that aspect of group life which stands opposed to its playful, experimental and life-giving qualities. I have found the ideas of Wilfred Bion (1961, 1970) helpful in thinking about this. We have encountered Bion in a number of previous chapters. Before developing a reputation as one of the most influential, perhaps the most influential, psychoanalytic figures of the second half of the twentieth century Bion had already undertaken highly innovative work with groups (Bleandonu, 1994).

Along with Kurt Lewin in the USA, Bion was one of the first to begin to understand the power of groups when used for educational and therapeutic purposes. Bion's initial thinking about groups, particularly about some of the powerful constellations of emotions and phantasies that can effect groups (the Basic Assumptions), was summarised in his book *Experiences in Groups* (1961). This chapter brings together some of these early ideas with some of his later work as a psychoanalyst (1970) to explore what I tend to think of as the anti-life forces at work within the human group.

Bion never ceased having the group in mind. His later explorations of psychosis and his theory of thinking have provided an avenue for examining the 'negative emotions' – i.e. those emotions which are antithetical to thought and life. Drawing upon the work of Bion, Rosenfeld, Meltzer and others this chapter develops the hypothesis that there exists in the life of the mind and the group an 'internal establishment' – a highly organised agency under whose protection a kind of life is allowed to continue. Within the group the establishment operates as an invisible, secretive and reactionary force which patrols the frontier of a section of the group's unconscious or what Bollas (1987) refers to as the 'unthought known'. In this case this is 'a known' which theatens the group illusion and therefore cannot be thought about. Later in the chapter I will provide a case study of the operation of the internal establishment within a purportedly egalitarian organisation. Finally I will consider some implications of this idea of an internal establishment for political and cultural practices.

Internal destruction

I wish to explore the hypothesis that an agency exists which operates as a reactionary force within the life of the mind and the group. I use the word 'reactionary' to convey the idea of something which is the locus of much of our destructiveness – destructive of our capacity to identify our feelings, 'to make sense', to give words to experience and to live truthfully. Perhaps the the term 'reactionary' understates what we may be dealing with here. When Rosenfeld (1987, p. 107) states, 'I believe that some deadly force inside the patient, resembling Freud's description of the death instinct, exists and can be clinically observed', he deploys the clarity that I am groping for.

Freud's concept of the death instinct has proved a discomforting legacy for psychoanalysis. It is primarily to those, including Bion, who were influenced by Klein that we must look for a sober account of our destructive possibilities. The starting point of this line of analysis lies in the notion that, from birth, the death drive exists as a force threatening to destroy us from within. As Rosenfeld put it, at the heart of human functioning lie primitive forms of anxiety which arise from 'the operation of the death instinct within the organism, which is experienced as fear of annihilation' (1971, p. 171). As we saw in Chapter 4, Klein (1958) had insisted that this destructive internal force is, in part, dealt with by being projected into figures in the outside world which are then experienced as bad and persecuting. That part of the death instinct which remains within the psyche is then turned upon these persecutory figures.

Put in ordinary language we might say that forces of life and death, creativity and destructiveness, lie within all of us. This is basic to the human condition. In other words, terror has an existential status. We cannot ask, 'what is this terror of?' It has no locus that can be pinpointed and at first it is attached to no object or structure. It is a self-reproducing, silent, deathly force. The process of projection that Klein speaks of is equivalent to the process of converting an internal terror into an external and identifiable threat. 'I fear' becomes 'I am frightened of' and 'I hate'. In other words, because of our terror we are capable of hate.

An agency that protects us from destruction

There is another primitive strategy for dealing with terror that Rosenfeld identifies. Rosenfeld suggests that a part of the death drive is used to create an internal agency which, through a perverted twist, offers to protect us from the terror of which it itself is a derivitave. Rosenfeld approaches an examination of this agency through a study of narcissism. From the perspective of the life force, narcissism can be considered as an over-valuation of self. This was Freud's starting point in his paper on narcissism, 'we say that a human being has originally two sexual objects – himself and the woman who nurses him – and in doing so we are postulating a primary narcissism in everyone' (Freud, 1914, p. 88). This self-idealisation can assume both the healthy form of feeling good about oneself and the more pathological form whereby one feels there is nothing good in the world but self. But, in a key passage, Rosenfeld suggests that a similar process may operate regarding the destructive part of the self:

> when considering narcissism from the destructive aspect, we find that again self-idealisation plays a central role, but now it is the idealisation of the omnipotent destructive parts of the self. They are directed both against any positive libidinal object relationship and any libidinal part of the self which experiences need for the object and desire to depend on it . . . they have a very powerful effect in preventing dependent object relations and in keeping external objects permanently devalued, which accounts for the apparent indifference of the narcissitic individual towards external objects and the world. (Rosenfeld, 1971, p. 173).

Thus we have an internal agency which stands opposed to the needy, desiring, life-seeking subject. Rosenfeld links this hostile life-destroying force to Klein's concept of envy. Envy is at the root of narcissism. To experience need is to experience dependence on the object which might satisfy that need, but dependence stimulates envy of that object. If we are to enter human relations – that is, if we are to become human subjects capable of engaging in any kind of exchange with others – then we must acknowledge our dependency both upon the natural and human environment. This is our dilemma, as Bion (1961) put it, we are group animals at war with our groupishness. Whilst the life force pushes us towards our human destiny the death drive rages against this possibility and offers the phantasy of living in our own self-sufficient universe. Envy attacks and spoils anything beyond self which is life-enhancing because it threatens this narcissistic phantasy by reminding us of our own lack. Indeed, envious attacks are directed not just at the external world but towards those loving, dependent parts of self which seek to establish symbiotic relationships with this world.

What, then, is the nature of this destructive agency? Again, it is worth citing Rosenfeld (1971) in full:

> The destructive narcissism of these patients appears often highly organised, as if one were dealing with a powerful gang dominated by a leader, who controls all the members of the gang to see that they support one another in making the criminal destructive work more effective and powerful. . . . The main aim seems to be to prevent the weakening of the organisation and

to control the members of the gang so that they will not desert the destructive organisation and join the positive parts of the self or betray the secrets of the gang to the police, the protecting superego, the analyst, who might be able to save the patient. (1971, p. 174)

Thus we have a highly organised internal agency operating as a kind of gang or Mafia. Meltzer (1968) noted the addictive relation of the self to this organisation is based on the offer of protection that the gang provides, 'where dread of loss of an addictive relation to the tyrant is found in psychic structures the problem of terror will be found at its core' (Meltzer, 1968, p. 400). Thus the fundamentally perverted character of this organisation for, as I noted earlier, it offers to protect us from the very terror for which it is an agent. As Steiner (1993, p. 8) notes, this pathological organisation 'contains' primitive anxiety by offering itself as protector but in a perverse sort of way, it feeds off our terror parasitically. Citing Segal (1972), Steiner adds that although this organisation is introduced to avoid catastrophe, it is the organisation itself which becomes a chronic catastrophe (Steiner, 1993, p. 49).

Before leaving this discussion two other characteristics of this organisation should be noted. First, Meltzer (1968) notes this organisation is versed in the art of slander and propaganda which is unleashed at the slightest sign that gang members might desert. Second, the stronger the grip of this organisation the more it resembles a delusional non-human world in which there is both complete painlessness and freedom to indulge in sadistic activity (Rosenfeld, 1971, p. 175).

Bion: the group in the mind

Reflecting on his patients' experience of being in the groups that he was conducting at the time Bion asks the question, when does the group begin? He adds that from one point of view it is perfectly clear that the group begins at 10.30 a.m, but then continues, 'but a shift of point of view, admittedly of some magnitude, on my part, means that I am viewing group phenomena that do not "begin",' (Bion, 1961, p. 88) – the point being that we are never not 'in the group' (p. 168). Bion is concerned to understand our 'inalienable inheritance as a group animal' (p. 91) and he traces this inheritance in a primitive grammar of group life, the emotional configurations of the 'basic group' (p. 90) – that is, the basic assumptions.

But Bion is saying more here than meets the eye. It is not just that we are never outside the group; the group is part of what we, as individuals, are. The group leaves an indelible imprint on the psyche or, as Bion puts it, 'there are characteristics in the individual whose real significance cannot be understood unless it is realised that they are part of his equipment as a herd animal' (p. 133). Bion's profound conjecture here, that in some way the mind is structured like a primitive society, remains a continuing thread running through all of his subsequent work. What is at stake is the survival of the mind and of society, as becomes clear when Bion examines the relationship between the 'basic group' and learning and development.

Hatred of a process of development is a characteristic of the basic group. Time, complexity, recalcitrance of the object to desire, all of these qualities of the world are hated in equal measure. There are no problems of membership or citizenship in the basic group such as would be entailed by a social contract based on reciprocity; rather belonging is automatic, 'a swift emotional response that comes of acquiescence in the emotions of the basic group' (p. 90). In contrast the sophisticated or work group represents a co-operative endeavour to pursue a common purpose in accordance to the requirements of the reality principle, that is, 'the need to develop rather than to rely upon the efficacy of magic' (p. 97). The three basic assumptions that Bion outlines correspond to different magical states of mind.

I find it useful to think of the basic assumptions as primitive survival myths whose source, according to Bion, can be traced to a pre-psychological, proto-mental level (Bion, 1961, p. 101ff.). As such they would seem to have the status of phylogenetic memory traces in a manner analogous to the earliest unconscious phantasies examined by Klein and her colleagues (Klein, 1952). The question is, survival from what? And the answer for the group/individual would seem to be the threat of dissolution or annihilation. It is striking how strong survival anxieties seem to be in the UK today. Several cultural factors seem to be at work – globalisation, ecological collapse and, in Britain's case, the penetration of market relations into the interstices of the welfare state. Bion's basic assumption phenomena are therefore 'defensive reactions to psychotic anxiety' (p. 189) – that is, ways of keeping anxiety about survival at bay.

What perhaps needs to be added is the later distinction Bion makes between catastrophic and persecutory anxiety – the basic fear is of the enemy within rather than of the enemy that comes from outside.

It is Meltzer (1986) who makes the link between Bion's concept of Basic Assumptions and the post-Bionic idea of an internal destructive agency. Meltzer notes how in one of his very last works, *A Memoir of a Future*, published in three volumes in the 1970s Bion returns explicitly to the theme of *Experiences in Groups*, his first major publication. Meltzer notes how in each work Bion evokes the picture 'of primitve, perhaps tribal, life in the depths of the mind' (Meltzer, 1986, p. 38). Meltzer (1986) conjectures that this proto-mental apparatus, organised as an establishment, operates on the borderline between mind and body and holds, or claims to hold, access to humoral and healing processes which ordinarily protect the body from noxious events which threaten it with attack. If, under certain circumstances, rebellion against this establishment occurs Meltzer asks 'might the thinking parts of the personality find that the privilege of immunological products had been cancelled and that everyday processes of defence against against bodily enemies . . . no longer operated' (p. 39).

Here then Meltzer asks us to consider the existence of an internal agency of oppression which invites us to live under its protection, indeed offers to save us from itself. At a psychological level the particular way in which this configuration finds expression will always be mediated by the biographical circumstance of the individual concerned. In other words the various internal agents will draw their character from the real others which have been involved in significant encounters with the individual during the course of his or her life – Meltzer's case study of 'Foxy' stands as one of the earliest and most vivid illustrations of this process (Meltzer, 1968). Whilst the struggle between the establishment and the life-seeking subject is present in all of us the manner in which it is enacted and resolved will always differ.

The group establishment

I have suggested that the concept of the internal establishment is derived from a psycho-social configuration which lies at the centre of the group-in-the-mind. Not suprisingly therefore it is in the life of actually existing groups (e.g. the family group, the work team, the social group, the political or cultural project) rather than more mediated social forms such as the organisation that we can see 'the establishment' at work most clearly. It seems odd however that, with the exception of Armstrong (1992), psychoanalytically informed analyses of group and organisational life (e.g. Obholzer and Roberts, 1994) have largely ignored the relevance of Bion's exploration of 'the negative emotions', that is, 'envious anti-linkage, anti-emotions, anti-knowledge and anti-life' (Meltzer, 1986, p. 26).

In what follows, therefore, I wish to make the case that in any social group there will exist an 'establishment'. The establishment relates to any area of the life of a group which cannot be thought about. But, whilst it cannot be thought about, in a peculiar way the group knows of its existence. In this respect it corresponds to what Bollas (1987) refers to as 'the unthought known'. For the time being I invite the reader to live with this paradox, that something can be known and yet not available to thought. I will illustrate what I mean by this phenomenom by providing a case study of a community project with which I was involved as a consultant.

The team consisted of 14 individuals, all but three of them professionals of one kind or another (e.g. planners, economic development workers, community workers, etc). There was a project Director and two senior managers/practitioners all of whom were themselves practising professionals. There were just two men in the team, one (perhaps not suprisingly) was the Director. Many of the women were strong feminists, three of the team were lesbians, two of the team were black, one of whom occupied one of the most junior positions in the team. The team took equal opportunities issues very seriously both in terms of the work that they did in the wider neighbourhood and in terms of the way in which they conducted themselves as a group. They saw themsleves operating in a democratic and egalitarian way, in other words as a group which expressed their objectives through the methods that they used.

An initial visit had convinced me that the basic issue confronting the project was the lack of a common sense of purpose – people were clear about their individual tasks but somehow they didn't add up to 'a whole'. This ambiguity was experienced by both the outside world and by the staff within the project. When I raised this issue with the whole team a number of comments were made, particularly by the two men, that while my impressions were interesting their relevance was not immediately apparent given that the project's objectives were quite clear having been prescribed by the politicians who first set up the project and continued to fund it. In one sense such comments were perfectly true, a clear state-ment of political objectives did exist. However it was also clear that the local politicians were now wavering in their own commitment to these objectives, so they weren't something 'set in stone' but something to be reaffirmed, renegotiated or fought for. But, there was a more crucial sense in which such comments were misleading for 'the objectives' appeared to have little meaning – they constituted facts that staff could refer to but not ideas that could be grasped and given meaning to. So I got off to a bad start, with the feeling that my initial impression was mistaken. A collective attitude prevailed that my obsession with purpose was a pecu-liar but harmless misconception that I could be forgiven for.

I then proceeded to ask participants to picture the team by drawing it. This technique is familiar enough to those who work with groups, its value lies in the use of imagery rather than words, a medium which enables people to represent that which otherwise might be difficult to explain verbally. The overwhelming impression from these pictures was of a group with a strong external boundary but with an unintegrated interior. Two people, quite independently, drew the organisation as a jigsaw but with wide open spaces between the pieces. Moreover there was a perception that the pieces were not firmly anchored – another picture drew the team as a set of buoys floating about on the surface, tied together like balloons. Although many of the pictures were quite startling, once more they were presented and talked about in a very matter-of-fact way. The group clearly didn't feel that my methods had revealed much so far. I decided to push the group more strongly over my perception of its lack of purpose but as the day proceeded I sensed a tremendous ebbing of energy and interest.

Over coffee in the afternoon I was approached by one of the two women managers. She was one of the newest members of the team, she had come from managing a women's unit in a London local authority and was clearly anxious that I seemed to be making little progress with a group which she herself was having a great deal of difficulty with. She hinted to me that the participants' apparent lack of interest in the pic-tures of the group was misleading, her sense was that it had in fact aroused a great deal of anxiety which was now hanging in the air. I resolved to challenge the group on this issue to bring the denial, if there was one, out into the open. When challenged in this way members of the group admitted that they did feel considerable anxiety, particularly about the existence of a number of differences within the group which the pictures had revealed. But, it was added almost immediately, what

point was there in exploring this for the differences which a few min-
utes ago appeared not to exist were now seen as huge and unresolvable.
My reply seemed a bit limp. I stated that all one could do about such
differences was talk about them. So the group talked about their differ-
ences but once more in the same energyless, matter-of-fact way which made
the topic seem boring and irrelevent. Once more I began to doubt my
judgement. I felt I was 'bobbing about' on the surface of things much in
the same way as others had described their experience of being in the
project.

As the conversation droned on I reflected upon something else the new
manager had mentioned. She had felt that the lack of common purpose
was a crucial element of the group but she represented this as an expression
of the group's internal dynamic, particularly the absence of any kind of
sharing by project staff, it was as if they were all isolates. She felt this
particularly as a manager, the workers she was responsible for refused to
share their activities with her except for in the most matter-of-fact way,
it was as if they did not want her to 'look in' on what they were doing.
As I was mulling this over another thought came to me. The group's
conversation which was circuitous and deadening kept returning to the
issue of 'diaries' – this was a feature of the weekly staff meeting which
the group both insisted upon and yet resented.

I adopted the posture of the naïve outsider, a privelege that anyone
new to a group can enjoy. I asked them to tell me what 'diaries' was all
about. They explained that it was the process by which the project team
members informed each other about meetings or events which were com-
ing up in the neighbourhood the following week. A piece of group history
was then revealed. One of the problems in the early days of the project
was that meetings in the local community were often attended by sev-
eral project members, each pursuing his or her own professional brief, at
the same time. It seemed as if no-one was trusted to represent the views
of the project as a whole, i.e. to act on the basis of authority delegated
by the others. Although this situation had been partly ameliorated, the
lack of trust was still manifest in the diary sessions which, it turned
out, were primarily used not to exchange information but 'to keep tabs
on each other'. Things now started to fall into place. The diaries filled
the one space during the week when everyone might meet. The space
was filled with information about facts (in this case facts about meet-
ings) rather than communication about experience. The possibility of
dialogue was thereby foreclosed.

It became clear that this was a group in which nobody had anything
to learn from anyone else (including myself). It professed its egalitarian-

ism and commitment to democratic values but practised distrust. It wasn't that group members were openly competitive with each other rather each had established a private territory which they proceeded to cultivate in glorious isolation from the others. The resulting individualism was not an aggressive, self-aggrandizing one, rather it was of a defensive form. Each person seemed to have erected barriers around 'his or her area of work' with a 'keep out' sign pasted on it (hence the spaces between the jigsaw pieces). But as a consequence each had to forego the possibility of obtaining validation and support from the others. The fake egalitarianism which had been sustained reminded me of Gufstafson's (1979) concept of pseudomutuality.

I doggedly persisted in dragging this picture of the group's values-in-use into the open. Interestingly enough the group never attacked me (as often happens in such situations) but appeared to go through a process of gradual admission of guilt. On reflection I think they may have got further if there had been an explosion and things had gone out of control.

The establishment guards an area in the life of the group which cannot be thought about. With regard to the group described above this area comprised an unconscious group contract which stated, 'no-one has anything to offer me' and, in return, 'I will not presume to offer anything to the others.' Fear and hatred of interdependence had triumphed over the need to give and be given to. The establishment epitomised the group's unconscious values-in-use which were profoundly anti-democratic and anti-collectivist. We can see, therefore, how the existence of the establishment relates to the unconscious life of the group, for neither the true nature of the establishment nor the truth which it represses can be thought about. It follows that the area of the life of the group which could be thought about and was therefore open to reflexive monitoring existed under the shadow of the lie.

As we saw in the previous chapter, every group has its own story. To say that such stories have an illusory quality is, following Winnicott, to draw due attention to the creative quality of all social life. Groups occupy potential space where nothing is simply 'real' nor simply 'hallucinated'. But this creative moment is so difficult to sustain. In Bion's terms, as soon as a new idea for containing experience is developed it tends to harden and atrophy, the imaginative fiction becomes a consolatory myth. To challenge the latter kind of story (one that is constantly reinforced by propaganda) is to persecute the group with intimations of shame. As Giddens (1991) points out, 'shame bears directly on self-identity because it is essentially anxiety about the adequacy of the narrative by means of which the individual sustains a coherent biography' (p. 65). At the level of the group, to the extent that the group's identity rests upon forms of organised self-deception, to that extent it will contain 'repressed fears that the narrative of self-identity cannot withstand engulfing pressures on its coherence or social acceptability' (ibid.). When one's story is destroyed then one's potency is also destroyed; one is exposed and one feels ashamed.

But feelings of adequacy and inadequacy are only part of the explanation. The story the group tells about itself is designed not only to mislead others, it is also designed to mislead the group itself. It is a self-deception. To destroy this is to blow apart the story that the group has told itself. When dissent breaks out, the new ideas threaten to inaugurate what Bion likens to a process of catastrophic change in which the group fears that it might fall apart.

In group life the step between illusion and delusion is short indeed. Steiner (1993, p. 65) reminds us of Freud's metaphor for the delusion – a patch over the place where originally a rent had appeared in the ego's relation to external reality. The establishment is a pathological organisation which patches over the rents and fissures in the group's illusion of itself. In the group described above the protection was provided quietly and diligently, primarily through a form of denial which dealt with potentially dangerous experience by draining it of significance, thus turning it into harmless fact. Instead of the mob, the establishment appeared to send round a team of accountants or bureaucrats whose task was to bore the opposition to death.

Passive and active consent

The internal society that Bion sketches lacks sophistication. But then this is only to be expected, for Bion is arguing, in a manner analogous to Freud through his myth of the 'primal horde', that a primordial society exists in the depths of the mind, one which operates on the boundary between psyche and soma, mind and body. From Bion's perspective the drama of the internal world is essentially a political one in which an internal establishment seeks to maintain its control by the use of lies and, ultimately, violence in the face of a constantly insurgent group of subjects who persist in asking too many questions. However, although the establishment is skilled in propaganda its real artistry seems to reside in its facility of being able to get its subjects lie to themselves; in this way its dominance can be maintained without having to resort too often to open terror. It may on occasions put out propaganda, but it relies on its subjects to believe in it.

All this leads me to ask whether the idea of the gang underestimates the sophistication of what we are sometimes dealing with here. The gang draws our attention to the coercive moment, to organised violence. The poet president Vaclav Havel dwelt on such issues during his time in jail. In his famous essay *The Power of the Powerless* Havel grapples with the complex relationship between truth and the lie in a way which is strikingly reminiscent of Bion. For Havel, collusion lies at the heart even of openly repressive regimes such as the one that imprisoned him. Speaking of the sullen acceptance of state propaganda that characterised Eastern Europe at that time, Havel insists:

> Individuals need not believe all these mystifications, but they must behave as though they did, or at least they must tolerate them in silence, or get along well with those who work with them. For this reason, however, they must live within a lie. They need not accept the lie. It is enough for them to have accepted their life within it. For by this very fact, individuals confirm the system, fulfil the system, make the system, are the system. (Havel, 1989, p. 45)

Paradoxically then, even the passive consent demanded by a coercive regime requires the active self-regulation of its citizens; the boundary between victim and oppressor is not so easily drawn. The kind of establishment Havel speaks of is one which does not need to hide its coercive nature, it is not ashamed of its lack of sophistication or subtleness. Those living under its 'protection' are under no illusion as to its nature.

But I have in mind a somewhat different kind of agency – one which still has a monopoly on terror but which operates primarily by drawing upon its subjects' willingness to be 'taken in'. Relying on a kind of innocence and gullibility, it leans upon their desire not to think too much. The citizen or group member under this regime is primarily self-regulating, actively consenting to his or her place in the order of things. Once more, therefore, we are drawn back to an examination of the nature of 'consent' in democratic societies, a theme we first began to explore in Chapter 6. Like Havel, Gramsci (1977) was also locked away inside prison when his mind turned to such issues. For Gramsci, the democratic state always has these two essential moments, of coercion and consent, violence and civilisation. He uses the term 'hegemony' to describe that particular form of domination in which consent is explicit and violence implicit.

Perhaps in contemporary consumer-based democracies we have become just too vulnerable to suggestion. We want to believe that we can have economic growth and social justice, continued material prosperity and an undamaged environment, economic freedom and social solidarity. Are these ideas true or false? Like all good illusions we have no way of knowing. What cannot be doubted however is that the illusionist we speak of here has such a willing audience, we so want to believe such things are possible.

And so it is with the group illusion: the members so want to believe in it. The corresponding collusion may, therefore, involve all of the group's membership. This poses new members with a problem. They may sense that something is afoot but will be denied any means of thinking about it. They will often offer a point of resistance to the establishment which will be both welcomed and resented by the other group members. The role of the external consultant is to identify those elements within the group which seek to resist or subvert the establishment, in order to develop an alliance for change with them. The consultant is not therefore neutral (i.e. simply a sounding board or facilitator) but an active partisan who appeals both to the 'better nature' of both 'the group' and the individuals within it. In undertaking this task it is important to avoid splitting the group into the good and the bad. Every group member, in differing proportions, is both a victim, a tyrant, a rebel and a collaborator – that is, part of the establishment and part of the opposition (Hoggett, 1997). The function of the establishment is to police this racket. I use the term 'establishment' as a way of referring to something which is:

1. deeply established – i.e. beneath the surface, not visible, more like a network than an institution;
2. a reactionary and secretive force;
3. capable of unleashing the utmost violence and terror to maintain its position if challenged but which will operate primarily through guile, propaganda and patronage during 'normal times';

4. skilled in drawing upon the worst qualities of its citizens, for example, their desire not to think too much, not to ask too many questions;
5. an area of silence in the life of the mind or the group where the body of the group is sensitive and should only be touched with the utmost care.

The hegemony exercised by the establishment is one based upon the organisation of the active consent of its citizens. But always, in the background, a more coercive approach is on hand if needed. As Perry Anderson, one of Gramsci's foremost British interpreters, put it:

> the day-to-day routines of a parliamentary democracy are themselves constituted by a silent, absent force which gives them their currency; the monopoly of legitimate violence by the state. Deprived of this, the system of cultural control would be instantly fragile, since the limits of possible action against it would disappear. (Anderson, 1976, p. 43)

Conclusion

Much earlier we noted how Klein's original account of the vagaries of the death drive described a movement from a state of internal terror to the projection of this state onto the external world so that 'I fear' becomes replaced by 'I am frightened of' and 'I hate'. There now exist a number of psychoanalytically inspired accounts of racism and ethnic hatred which seek to link social forms of exclusion with such psychological processes of projective identification (Rustin, 1991; Young, 1994). In this essay I have tried to trace another path that our destructiveness follows. Specifically I have sought to illuminate the way in which both the individual and the group seek to protect themselves from a truth which is catastrophic by turning away from life itself.

This struggle between development and destruction lies at the heart of the internal society that Bion suggests is part of our social nature. He transcends our habit of thinking in a binary fashion so that something must be either 'inside' or 'outside', psychological or social. The dynamic configuration he invites us to examine is both psychological and social, that is, psycho-social. This configuration exists as an immanent phenomenon providing a deep structure both for the life of the mind and the life of society. In other words, all societies, in their different ways, are set to work and get to work upon this structure. At a gut, emotional and pre-symbolic level we have all experienced terror, tyranny, collusion, retaliation and dissent before we first encounter them externally in the family and society. Each baby which arrives in this world brings with it a nascent appreciation of the politics of group life.

9
Hatred of Dependency

Care and justice

In the mid-1970s, before entering academic life, I worked in a fairly unique community mental health project. The project was the inspiration of Sue Holland who had been trained at the Tavistock Clinic as an adult psychotherapist and who was a long-time Maoist. The project, the Battersea Action and Counselling Centre, combined community action and various forms of therapeutic interventions, particularly brief psychotherapy with individuals in distress, and work with couples referred to us by the local Women's Aid organisation. At that time Battersea was a depressed working-class community in London. The project ran a day nursery, a food co-op and a welfare rights service. With local community activists gathered around a community newspaper called *Pavement* we were involved in a variety of campaigns including anti-fascist work on the local estates and a fight to save a local maternity hospital (Hoggett & Lousada, 1985). Our belief was that you couldn't address the emotional distress of people living in the area without tackling the social deprivation which was a part of their everyday lives. But we also believed that political action to fight injustice needed to be informed by a vision of human frailties and possibilities. Politics needed to take psychology seriously otherwise it became dehumanised.

Then as now such ideas struggled against the tide. Those who worked within welfare with a political action perspective tended to see talk of the need for care for the individual as something reactionary and oppressive. Those who worked therapeutically with individuals in social services and the NHS might acknowledge the importance of the environment but action tended to follow resources into treatment rather than prevention. Looking back on those times and with hindsight I can now see how, in our own small way, those of us involved in the project were trying to develop *a form of practice which was inspired both by an ethic of care and an ethic of justice.* Now I would say that both of these ethics must be combined if a one-eyed approach to the pursuit of human well-being is to be avoided.

Over twenty years on we can see how the ethic of justice within the welfare state has been under sustained attack since the early 1980s, an attack which seems to have continued no less strongly since the arrival of a new Labour government. But in this chapter I will argue that whereas social justice has always been at least an element of the explicit rhetoric of British welfarism, an ethic of care has never been securely developed within this body. It therefore seems to me to be no coincidence that the primary vehicle for recent attacks on welfarism has been the concept of 'the dependency culture'. It is as if our continued deprecation of the language of care has returned to haunt us as social justice is undermined by the use of a term which is intimately bound to this lost and disparaged vocabulary.

The 'dependency culture'

The concept of the 'dependency culture' was first introduced into British political life by Charles Moore, one of Thatcher's 'Golden Boys', who came briefly to prominence as Minister for Social Security in the mid-eighties before sinking, like so many of his comrades, in a mire of scandal. Unlike its originator the concept has proved enduring. Indeed one cannot but be struck by the fact that the arrival of a new Labour administration, far from sounding its death knell has given it a new lease of life. While pressure from activists and Labour MPs in late 1997 forced Blair's cabinet to reconsider their attack on single-parent benefits few of these critics questioned the principle of 'welfare to work' to which the concept of the 'dependency culture' was intimately linked. Criticism of 'welfare to work' was made more difficult once it became hitched perversely to the idea of empowerment couched in terms of the need to help (indeed 'wean') mothers and other claimants off benefits and into the labour market. Political opposition crystallised around the style of policy implementation not around the deeper and more fundamental issue, that is, what kind of society was it that could so scornfully attack the idea of dependency in its clamour to make everyone fit and available for labour?

Let me briefly summarise the case made against the dogma of the 'dependency culture' by social policy experts in the UK. The concept has obtained its gravitas from the work of the American, Charles Murray (1984), who, using the earlier idea of 'cycles of deprivation', became the leading exponent of the idea that in the USA and Britain an underclass of the permanently excluded was forming which included a growing army of the feckless, the workshy, the helpless and the dependent. The key point was, and this is what distinguishes Murray's work from some of those on the left who have also adopted the term underclass, that this social layer was self-excluding as much as it was excluded. This was allegedly a culture where the work ethic was weak, where social expectations were low and where individuals' heightened awareness of their rights was complemented by a weakened sense of their responsibilities – thus, according to proponents of this dogma, the high proportion of children born out of marriage, the vandalisation of the physical environment of the public housing projects where many of these people lived, the high rates of crime and so on.

Critics of the underclass thesis have developed their argument along a number of fronts. Attitudinal research conducted in the UK suggests that those claiming benefits subscribe to precisely the same norms, values and lifeways as the wider society (Dean & Taylor-Gooby, 1992) – this is precisely why being out of work is so hard, indeed the unemployed show a stronger work motivation than the employed (Gallie & Vogler, 1990). Recent research has also revealed the way in which different cultural assumptions lead different groups of lone mothers to attach different weights to the identities of mother and worker. Again, in a way which cuts across conventional stereotypes, black lone mothers appear to express a greater desire to integrate the identity of worker with that of mother than their white working-class contemporaries for whom the identity of mother is more primary (Edwards & Duncan, 1997).

A more fundamental criticism of 'dependency culture' however is that it is a concept which seeks to blame victims for their own circumstances. Far from being the makers of their own poverty the new mass of 'have-nots', which may or may not be construed in terms of an underclass, are a manifestation of the heightened social inequalities produced by the New Right restructuring of the last two decades (Joseph Rowntree, 1995). They are the victims of regressive modernisation (Hall, 1988) not addicts to a 'nanny state'.

There are a number of pieces of evidence to suggest that Blair and company also believe that the poor are partially responsible for their own circumstances. Thus the controversy surrounding the attacks on lone mother benefits in the autumn of 1997, for lurking in the background here was the idea that those on benefits needed both sticks and carrots to get off their habit. Indeed the controversy tended to obscure the fact that the need for the stick had already been happily ensconced in other pieces of welfare legislation such as the Job Seekers Allowance introduced in the last years of the Major administration. As Novak (1997) notes, in May 1996 Michael Meacher, the Shadow Employment Spokesman, was forced by the Labour leadership to retract a claim that Labour would abolish the JSA. Needless to say it has now been adopted without protest by the new administration.

The acceptance of the stick can be traced in part to Blair's adoption of Clinton's rhetoric of 'tough love' which mutated into his own philosophy of 'compassion with a hard edge'. 'Tough love' was a gift to Clinton from Dick Morris, the former Republican who became Clinton's adviser before the last Presidential election (and someone whose appetite for Washington's prostitutes was alledgedly even more gargantuan and unself-consciously public than the Kennedy brothers' thirty years earlier). As early as 1993 journalists such as Sarah Baxter had noted that the young shadow Home Secretary (i.e Blair) was using the rhetoric of tough-love to extend his crime brief to family matters. While few could complain, as Blair insisted, that parents had a responsibility for the behaviour of their children, journalists like Baxter could already see where this Republican implant might lead the opposition party. As she put it, 'there is a risk . . . that single mothers on benefits will end up paying for this right to air the argument. . . . The Conservatives are convinced that the Labour party has given the go-ahead to attack the welfare state. . . . Ministers are accusing women of being 'married to the state'' (*Guardian*, 9 July 1993).

In a way which few could have predicted beforehand the issue of welfare reform came to dominate the first year of the new Labour government. How can we understand this, why did it become Labour's foremost priority? There are a number of possible answers. One suggests that Labour had already become afflicted by the same perceptual impairment as its predescessors, i.e of confusing consequence and cause. The escalating social security bill, rather than being seen as a manifestation of the social polarisation which has accompanied the Anglo-American post-Fordist modernisation trajectory, was construed primarily in terms of the burden it placed upon our renewed competitiveness. Instead of a radical attack on the real causes of Britain's continued relative economic decline (the role of the city and finance capital, the dysfunctional effects of the pension funds, etc.) – some of which had already been outlined by Will Hutton before Labour came to power (Hutton, 1995) – we got a Labour government which appeared to locate the problem in the most powerless members of society.

But we are still scratching the surface here. At a deeper level 'welfare to work' links up with an economic ideology which has nothing to do with the Keynesianism which accompanied the founding of the British welfare state. Again, Labour here is simply following a path already being prepared in the 1980s when the relationship between employment policies and social policies began to be reversed. Social policies across a range of fronts, particularly education and social security, have been reshaped to make people fit for participation in an increasingly unregulated and competitive labour market (Dean & Taylor-Gooby, p. 54). Presumably this is where supply-side economics takes us, i.e towards what some have called 'the Schumpetarian Workfare State' (Jessop, 1994). But the human costs of an enterprise culture are worth pointing out, as Hugo Young recently put it, 'a greater contribution from every available citizen to improving GNP is the vision New Labour is determined on, although one that does not yet quite dare speak its sound-bite. This is a tough doctrine. Sympathy with underdogs and no-hopers is no longer a prime, or even a relevant, policy stimulant for senior Labour politicians' (*Guardian*, 9 December 1997). Let's be clear, what we have here is not socialism, nor (witness Roy Hattersley's fulminations) even social democracy, but a kind of social (or Christian) Darwinism.

Material and emotional dependency

I will come back to the new social policy with its focus on making people fit to labour at a later point but now I would like to reconsider the notion of the 'dependency culture' from another perspective. Rather than continue the argument about whether such a culture actually exists or what its effects may be I want to consider the term itself, for the very phrase has accrued to itself a deeply negative set of feelings. Even within social policy one finds the phrase being used unproblematically, as if the obloquy which, by implication, is now being heaped upon the idea of dependency should cause us no pause for reflection. But if dependency has become unquestionably bad what does this say about our culture and the conceptions of the human condition that presently permeate it?

The answer to this question will take us into progressively new terrain. But first I wish examine the meaning of dependency and its relationship to need. Let me use an example. Imagine someone, male and middle-aged, who has just been taken into hospital with pneumonia. He may not have been eating properly for over two months because of a very sore throat, which turns out to be the consequence of thrush. We would be saying nothing very surprising if we suggest that at this point he has become very dependent upon the medical staff to meet his physical needs. Physical need can be considered as a form of material need; money, time, distance, these are also material needs that force us to depend upon others for their satisfaction. But the patient does not just depend materially on the other to assess and treat his condition. The patient also has a need to do something with his fear of dying, his worries for his family, his feelings of shame about the child-like helplessness that he now finds himself temporarily reduced to. In other words he has emotional as well as material needs but these needs are not so easily admitted, even in a so-called post-Diana culture.

It seems odd that we should have to make the case for the existence of emotional needs and, by implication, for the idea that the human being is a fundamentally emotional being. But our culture is so dominated by certain kinds of rationalist assumptions, particularly regarding the interest-maximising autonomous individual, that the importance of emotion, affect and passion has to be continually restated. Because we are emotional beings we are also vulnerable beings. The patient in the hospital feels this no less than the child on her first day at school, or the seventy-year-old facing life alone for the first time on the death of her partner, or the frail elderly person who goes into residential care. In all such situations and countless others we struggle not to be overwhelmed by feelings and, to the extent that we cannot find the inner resources to contain and give meaning to what we experience, we depend upon others. We depend on them for reassurance and empathy, to show the strength and confidence in the future that we ourselves cannot at that moment find or just, simply, to be there, reliably and attentively, with us. We call this care, something all of us give and receive. Yet one of the great mysteries of the twentieth century is that until recently, outside psycho-dynamically informed disciplines, so little thought has been given to it. I say 'until recently' because of the way in which 'care' has now become something of a preoccupation within feminist political philosophy, but more of this later.

If we now look at the evolution of the welfare state it is clear that it was established primarily to address peoples' material needs. Its origins lie in the mutualism of the Friendly Societies and the municipalism of the old 'gas and water' socialists such as William Morris. Current attacks on the 'dependency culture' are clearly aimed at the universalist principle which inspired many past and present advocates of welfarism. This principle insists that social protection is a right which requires no reciprocation because the benefits and services, in Titmuss's immortal phrase, 'are part of the price we pay to some people for bearing part of the costs of other people's progress' (Titmuss, 1976, p. 133).

That the welfare state has made a major contribution to the material well-being of all members of our society cannot be doubted but, and this is crucial to my argument, in terms of its ability to provide for the emotional needs of its citizens, particularly the most vulnerable, its record is more one of failure than success. Wherever we look – residential care for the old and frail, the effect of asylums on those with mental illness, the hidden archipeligos of abuse within children's homes or the dominance of industrial models of nursing within the NHS – the welfare state's record of caring for the vulnerable leaves little to be proud of. Instead of providing care it stands accused of infantilising elderly people (Hockey & James, 1993), depersonalising patients (Menzies, 1960) and subjecting children at risk to regimes of intrusion and brutality. Far from encouraging dependency, these services have demonstrated an institutional inability to care *for* the emotionally needy. From the perspective of the emotional needs of its citizens the welfare state has failed to care, it has been dehumanising and it has dehumanised. And it has to be said that as citizens we have colluded with this, we have not cared enough about this failure to care.

Interestingly enough social democratic and socialist advocates of the welfare state have been sceptical, if not hostile, towards the idea of emotional dependency. In the article cited earlier Sarah Baxter reported how, in 1993, David Blunkett worried his female colleagues on the Labour front bench by his scornful references to Virginia Bottomley as the 'Florence Nightingale' of Major's cabinet. Looked at from the left the very mention of care brings in the room the baggage of altruism, do-goodism and paternalism. To give a recent example, Jenny Morris, herself a disabled person, argues that 'the only way to empower disabled people is to throw off the ideology of caring which is a form of oppression and an expression of prejudice' (Morris, 1997, p. 54). Morris both hits and misses the point here. She is right to observe the way in which dependency has become an axis along which the technology of power has been exercised – a point demonstrated for most of us by a visit to our GP. Dean and Taylor-Gooby (1992) refer to the 'socially constituted relations of dependency that furnish the levers for the power to which individuals are subject' (p. 150). But it is a short step from here (incidently, a step that Dean & Taylor-Gooby do not take) to the denial of dependency, and therefore interdependency, as a fundamental aspect of the human condition. The problem of empowerment is not resolved by wishing away the actuality of dependency, no more than the problem of human political emancipation is resolved by denying the actuality of human aggression and destructiveness. There is a deep-seated hatred of dependency within our culture which needs to be understood; I fear that otherwise it will leave an irredeemable scar upon the project of creating a better world.

I wish to suggest that the idea of dependency, both in its material and emotional forms, jars with a more powerful voice of the late twentieth century – the active voice. In contrast, dependency connects to two repressed voices within contemporary culture, the passive and tragic voices. It is to these that I will now turn.

The passive voice

Nature's shadow

Ours is a culture which disavows the continuing shadow that nature casts upon all of our lives: one which manifests itself in illness, disability, ageing and the prolonged period of helplessness that the infant human being, almost alone among the animal world, undergoes. Even Richard Titmuss saw dependency as an abnormal condition, albeit one brought about by the negative consequences of social change. As Dean & Taylor-Gooby note, Titmuss saw it as 'a departure from some natural and desirable state of independence' (p. 157). As Hockey and James (p. 107) note, 'if the pursuit of individual freedom is the hallmark of personhood then all those unable, through dependency, to hold to this aim are cast in less than fully social roles'. That dreadful phrase, 'the pram in the hall is the death of ambition' expresses the contempt for dependency which has marked our culture for too long. This position can only behold dependency as a constraint, 'only those without need, or without obligation to those with need, are able to achieve full human independence' (Hockey & James, p. 110). Cultures in which obligation is seen as an honour, as a source of one's social reputation, can scarcely be comprehended except as quaint anachronisms from the social anthropologist's rucksack.

It is at this point that I find my memory recalling an old friend. In the heady days of class struggle in the mid 1970s, along with a group of friends from the Trotskyite sectlet that we all happened to be in at that time, I came across the Italian Marxist, and ex-Maoist, Sebastiano Timpanaro. He produced two very interesting books, *The Freudian Slip*, and *On Materialism*. The latter was a brave attempt to forge the link between materialism and pessimism, particularly brave considering that at that time the revolutionary left carried the standard of voluntarism that today has been taken over by the very people they would have put up against the wall. In contrast, with more than a little sarcasm, Timpanaro urged his comrades to reflect upon their 'tranquil faith in historical progress' and insisted upon a 'pessimism with respect to nature's oppression of man, which would continue to be a cause of unhappiness even in communist society' (Timpanaro, 1975, p. 11). Drawing upon the work of the early 19th century poet Leopardi, Timpanaro draws our attention to our 'first nature', to a body that lives and dies, desires and suffers. Speaking of illness and weakness I feel he adopts a particularly perceptive turn of phrase when he suggests that such experiences may better aid our understanding of 'the passive aspect' of relations between man and nature' (p. 51). He speaks of nature, including our first nature, as the subsoil of society.

It is incredible to think of how times have changed. Twenty years ago those who supported even a glimpse of nature in the nature/nurture debate were regarded as irredeemably reactionary. It's the environment we said, that makes us what we are and, what's more, we contemplate ourselves in a world of our own creation. How radical we felt then, as if the people, united, could change anything; freedom was the overcoming of necessity. And who says this now? The biotechnologists, cyberfuturists, cosmopolitan intellectuals, the management consultants. This is the new hegemony, a massively idealistic and voluntaristic modernising movement where our freinds Tony and Peter can be found with their heads held high – not education, education but modernisation, modernisation! To para-phrase Guy Debord (1983), everything that changes is good, everything is good that changes. Suddenly to be champion of the unchanging, immutable, inert, stable, inflexible, incurable, untreatable, bloody minded, stubborn, constant and chronic is to be a subversive. The bourgeoisie have stolen our clothes.

In speaking of the passive voice it is important to differentiate this from the active/passive dimension of emotional life. Passivity, as I am using it here, is not to be confused with 'being done to' or taking the self as object in relations with others as might occur in masochism; rather it is about the force of fate, chance and nature. Peta Bowden (1997) puts it thus,

> Illness presents us with explicit and indisputable evidence of the pervasiveness of chance and vulnerability as inherent structures of our lives. As the sufferers of assualts of happenstance, we ex-perience the inescapable 'objectness' of our bodies. . . . The defenceless, thing-like fragility of body or mind is experienced in opposition to our purposes and values. (p. 112)

I am tempted to say that a society which cannot come to terms with the shadow nature casts upon the private lives of its citizens will also be one which can only spoil or take for granted the natu-ral physical environment upon which its continued material well-being depends. Denial of dependence affects our relations with nature no less than our relations with each other. As Lasch noted some time ago, late capitalism has developed a deeply narcissistic culture, one which is profoundly discomforted by the idea of lim-its and constraints (Lasch, 1978).

The denial of dependence also severely undermines the solidaristic ties upon which the idea of common welfare rests. The commit-ment to welfarism, particularly by the middle classes, is partly built upon a recognition of the fragility of well-being. An individual who recognises that she, her family or close friends could at any time experience an incapacitating accident, a stroke, a breakdown or the first promptings of Alzheimer's realises the imminence of vulner-ability. Except for the super-rich we all potentially depend heavily upon a framework of common care. And yet a narcissistic culture is one which, perhaps particularly in men, supports omniscient feelings of invulnerability, that fate will show its hand to others but not to me.

But we can go further. Vulnerability and dependency are not just things which are imminent, i.e. potentially waiting around the corner for us all. These things are also immanent, i.e. indwelling within each of us. Inside each one of us there is a small child which is open to wonder and yet so easily hurt. Inside each one of us there is a drifter and nomad, a failure, a non-survivor and all the other personas that the passive internal voice can assume. A good society would be one which could provide a place for such selves to be, without always seeking to empower them or thrust cures upon them. Sometimes people just want to rest and be taken care of, sometimes people just want to drift along without having to think too much. It follows that there is something seriously wrong with a society in which the bestowal of full citizenship is contingent upon fitness to join a labour market which increasingly has the feel of a jungle.

The unchanging

Andrew Scull, the historian of the asylum movement, reflecting upon the way in which the very idea of asylum, 'a place of shelter, refuge, retreat and sanctuary', has been degraded during the last century, suggests that 'there is little place . . . within such (an individualistic) world view for those who are excluded from the race for material wellbeing by chronic disabilities' (Scull, 1996, p. 14). In so saying Scull introduces another concept that is worth reflecting upon: 'Chronic: persisiting for a long time (usually of an illness or a personal or social problem)' (Concise Oxford Dictionary). Within the welfare state we know of this issue through cute little technical terms – 'the revolving door', recidivism – the patient who just doesn't get any better, who, even after the most thoughtfully (tastefully) designed care plan, is readmitted to the acute ward or is abandoned to what James Glass called the psychiatric proletariat (Glass, 1989).

Chronicity is something which fits poorly with a culture which is so enamoured with change. We expect medicine to cure. As John Stokes notes, 'since care is a slow process and does not provide the dramatic result desired, it is denigrated as being ineffective, whereas 'cure', which is exciting and offers a defence of omnipotent denial of the chronic nature of problems, is idealised' (Stokes, 1994, p. 122). If a group proves unable to benefit from treatment our interest wavers, interventions should lead to outcomes. Scull notes that many mental patients do not collaborate to seek recovery and this violates norms governing access to the sick role. Outside of medicine the same issue often characterises relations between professionals and other people who are deemed to be vulnerable or in need – elderly people, substance abusers, young offenders – very often members of such groups either also explicitly or implicitly reject the invitation to change or recovery.

Chronicity reminds us of the sheer persistence of behavioural patterns and the entrenchedness of feeling states, particularly feelings about self. To enable an individual to unravel the tens of thousands of hours of a life, to release the hold of the past, usually takes more than a handful of interviews with a harassed professional. Viewed from here, caring for the vulnerable is often not so much about change but being-with their unchangedness.

Tragedy and agency

In a thoughtful essay on the ethics of care Susan Mendus (1993) analyses recent feminist appeals to women's special or 'different' voice. In rejecting this proposition for an essentialism which disguises the possibility that this different voice is in reality a domestic and domesticated one she nevertheless retains the element of good sense in this appeal, the way in which it rejects the liberal emphasis on the activity of moral life and draws attention to the extent to which the roles women occupy are often multiple, unchosen and in conflict. She argues that women are frequently victims of their circumstances, rather than creators of their lives, in a way which men often find difficult to understand (p. 24). Mendus draws attention to the unchosen nature of much of moral life. The unresolvable dilemmas it often poses contribute much to the tragic dimension in human affairs.

Martha Nussbaum, in her book *The Fragility of Goodness* pictures tragedy thus:

> That I am an agent, but also a plant: that much that I did not make goes towards making whatever I shall be praised or blamed for being; that I must constantly choose between competing and apparently incommeasurable goods and that circumstances may force me into a position in which I cannot help being false to something or doing some wrong; that an event that simply happens to me may, without my consent, alter my life; that it is

equally problemmatic to entrust one's good to friends, lovers, or country and to try and have a good life without them – all of these I take to be not just the material of tragedy, but everyday facts of lived practical reason (Nussbaum, 1986, p. 5).

Understanding the passive voice therefore invites us to reconsider the question of agency. One of the most influential British researchers on family obligations and responsibilities is Janet Finch. In a recent book, *Negotiating Family Responsibilities*, Finch & Mason (1993) theorise the nature of the caring role in a way which contrasts sharply with Mendus. They insist that the responsibilities that people accept in the context of the family are negotiated rather than 'the consequence of following rules of obligation'. They are 'created commitments', typically the outcome of consciously chosen and strategic action. Finch & Mason return to Giddens's formulation of the relationship between agency and structure. Here structure is posited as 'constraint' or 'limit' to an agency which is still nevertheless supreme. But the problem with the agency/structure distinction lies in the way in which it tends to map these two terms onto an adjacent binary opposition, internal/external. Thus structure tends to be construed as something which acts upon us from outside rather than as something which acts through us, from the inside (Craib, 1992, p. 166ff.).

There are two senses in which the psyche has its own internal structure. As I illustrated in Chapter 1, each personal history leaves behind a precipitate of unconscious phantasies and internal object relations which give character to our inner life and to our relationships with other people. Temperley (1984) puts it thus,

> All of us, in our social relationships, seek partners who will join us in enacting the style of object relations which prevails within us. We subtly nudge and coerce each other with a myriad of often subliminal clues into dramas and unconscious games which are variously fulfilling for us. (Temperley, 1984, p. 101)

More radically, our first nature expresses itself through a number of universal human processes – splitting, projection, introjection, etc. – which provide the grain of humanity, our limits and our possibilities (Whitebook, 1995). Paradoxically Finch & Mason provide a vivid illustration of some of these internal processes at work in a case study of the relationship between Sarah, a woman in her late forties, and her mother (Finch & Mason, pp. 37–40). Sarah had spent most of her life under the shadow of her dominant mother who only now, with a senile husband, was reaching out towards Sarah for help. Finch & Mason examine the renegotiation of the relationship between Sarah and her mother which corresponds to the shifting balance of dependence and independence. Speaking of Sarah they note, 'she wants them to accept her help in a way that would make them more dependent on her than they have ever been in the past – a redefinition which clearly her mother is resisting' (p. 38). This kind of drama must be very familiar to many of us but, more often than not, what makes such dramas tragic is the blindness of the actors both to their own motives and to their feelings about the other. In other words, mapped onto relations of autonomy and dependence are struggles for recognition, confusions of personal boundaries, enduring circuits of identification and projection between parent and child, and so on.

The problem with many current models of human agency in the social sciences lies not just with the implicit idealisation of the concept but also with the baggage of the unitary self that goes with it. Rationalist models of agency such as Finch's presuppose a unitary self which chooses, acts and judges. But what Freud's investigations of the subject revealed was a house divided upon itself (Craib, 1992, p. 173). Which of our many selves acts or speaks at any point in time is always open to question and while some of these personas are familiar enough to us others wander like ghosts in the family home. It is for this reason that we sometimes appear to be our own worst enemy. Rationalist models of agency simply cannot comprehend how the subject gets stuck, fixed or fixes itself, how it procrastinates, flees from decisions, gets stuck in recurring patterns, falls back, repeats itself first time as tragedy later as farce, is entrapped and traps itself, acts in ways which are destructive to its own interests, destroys sense rather than makes sense and engages earnestly in projects for reasons which it entirely misunderstands. In short what we require are non-rationalist models of agency in which action, thought and affect are held simultaneously in mind without splitting one from the other.

To bring in the human dimension in this way, particularly the darker internal forces which affect our lives, is to further recognise the tragic dimension in life. There is a tremendous temptation to wish away all this complexity and messiness, but to do so would leave us, for example, with an idea of human agency which, while being easy to grasp, would lack depth and value. In the following sections therefore I will explore the implications of dependency and our ambivalence towards it for two issues within social policy – the concept of empowerment and the nature of the caring relationship.

Dependency and social policy

Empowerment

A friend of mine was once working with a voluntary organisation for children with disabilities in the Asian community. She met a man who refused to send his children to a good specialist school for children with severe disabilities. One of his main objections was that the school seemed to focus all of its attention on getting children to do things for themselves. He reasoned that this was stupid because if others (including himself) did these things for his children – e.g. tied their shoelaces, washed them, etc. – then they could spend their time being massaged, listening to music and enjoying other experiences which would maximise their quality of life. A second friend of mine working with the same Asian community was involved in running a club for elderly Asian people. She spent over a year trying to get the group to make its own choices about the things it wanted to do and using its own skills and resources to provide for itself. Eventually she gave up and reflected on the possibility that she hadn't taken cultural differences sufficiently into consideration. It seemed to her that the elderly people in her group expected someone to do these things for them. They had spent their lives caring for and supporting others and now they expected others to do this for them. I cite these examples because niether seems to fit easily wih the logic of empowerment which dominates so much of our thinking about social care these days.

In a provocative and thoughtful essay, Diane Gibson (1995) looks at empowerment in the context of care services for the frail elderly. Gibson notes how talk of 'rights' in the classical liberal tradition is central to contemporary concepts of empowerment. These rights emphasise self-assertion, self-determination, freedom of choice and independence of thought and action. The fact that many groups in western democracies still lack these rights tells us much about the way in which phenomena such as disability, age and psychological distress are still feared and devalued within such societies. Gibson insists that the power of 'rights talk' for changing social attitudes and expectations is as important as its practical and immediate value in changing power relations in the here-and-now of the social relations of welfare.

But Gibson also notes a number of real difficulties in implementing a rights perspective for some groups. In the context of residential care for frail elderly people who may experience dementia or other forms of physical or mental incapacity Gibson notes that talk of rights (e.g. to manage your own finances) runs up against a number of problems, problems which are 'relevant wherever a highly vulnerable population is involved' (p. 8). First of all, some individuals in severe confusional states may temporarily or permanently lack the capacity to make choices. Secondly, some individuals (perhaps particularly those with severe learning disabilities) may lack the means of articulating their choices in an immediately intelligible way. The role of independent advocacy may clearly be important in such instances but even this cannot resolve some of the following ethical dilemmas. Gibson, for example, describes an elderly resident suffering from dementia who had an intense dislike of restraint but who also had a balance problem which had resulted in a series of falls. Gibson asks, 'who is in a position to decide what the dominant interest of the resident is so that it may be protected?' (p. 8). The choices that people may wish to make may also have an impact upon the wellbeing of others, residents or staff. Individuals may lack, temporarily or permanently, the capacity to engage in moral reasoning in such a way that they can take the position of the other. Is it disempowering of staff to refuse the right of individuals to make such choices; and how are such decisions to be made? Thirdly, people may wish to make choices which are directly destructive to themselves. Joan Riviere (1936), in a powerful description of suicide, reflects on the feelings of despair and worthlessness that accompany acute depression. She illustrates how some individuals become gripped by the idea that everything they touch turns bad. They are so convinced of the actuality of their own overwhelming destructiveness that they choose death in a desperate attempt to protect those that they love and care for from themselves. This is the most extreme example of self-harm, but at what point does a passionate commitment to individual liberty give way to an equally passionate commitment to an ethic of care?

I raise all of these questions by way of a warning. A single-minded embrace of the rhetoric of empowerment can easily end up as yet another of those tyrannical totalising discourses that the post-modernists have told us about. It is not a question of either/or. You can be passionate in your pursuit of social justice and equally passionate in your belief in the virtues of compassion and concern if you are prepared to struggle with the contradictions that life in all its complexity inevitably brings. For social policy a central contradiction lies in the tension between respect for universal principles on the one hand and a realisation of the actual particularities of social relations on the other. Gibson (1995), for example, points out that while residents may in theory be empowered by the existence of a set of formal rights (enshrined in a Residents' Charter or suchlike) they are nevertheless often concerned that they will be targeted by staff if they complain. The existence of formal rights cannot overcome the asymmetries of power which are a part of the social relations of residential care in which they are embedded. Ultimately they are reliant upon the goodwill of others, particularly staff. Mendus (1993) usefully cites Kittay & Meyers (1987) to draw out this contrast between the universalism of social justice and the particularism of care:

> A morality of rights and abstract reason begins with a moral agent who is separate from others, and who independently elects moral principles to obey. In conrast, a morality of responsibility and care begins with a self who is enmeshed in a network of relations with others, and whose moral deliberation aims to maintain these relations (Kittay & Meyers, p. 10).

The ethic of care continually draws our attention to the particularities of relationships and the 'emotions and commitments which sustain them' (Mendus, p. 24).

There is a line of argument within the current empowerment debate which insists that calls for a radical renewal of professional practice miss the point. Genuinely empowering forms of social provision would do away with the necessity of dependency upon professional carers altogether. Demands for more reflexive forms of practice are simply another example of the 'myopia of therapeutic good intention' (Jack, 1995, p. 22). In contrast I suggest that such an argument is in danger of impoverishing the debate through an unwillingness to address the social relations of welfare in their institutionalised form – i.e. what actually goes on in schools, universities, prisons, hospitals, residential establishments, day centres, and so on.

Part of the problem lies in the way in which the debate about empowerment originated in social care, particularly through the experiences of what has become the 'disability movement'. This movement has been quite right to point to the socially disabling effects of professional practices and the way in which asymmetries of power have been socially constructed and maintained. Increasingly we can look forward to a future in which disabled people have the resources to control their own lives free from reliance on public services. But not all forms of dependency are socially constructed in the way in which some forms of disability have been and, moreover, many of the dependent relations we enter into within the welfare state are engaged in willingly in the knowledge that we will benefit from so doing. While it may be comparatively easy for the disability movement to 'solve' the problem of professionalisation by fighting for the anti-discrimination legislation and comprehensive disability income which would enable them to do without professionals altogether (Jack, 1995, p. 17) the problem of the professionalised welfare state apparatus nevertheless remains for all citizens, including disabled ones, who seek education, need health care or look for advice on a planning problem and so on. The nature of professional practices and cultures is critical to the social relations of welfare. The need to change such practices cannot simply be avoided, as some of those involved in the empowerment debate seem to wish to do.

Dependency, care and human development

I have tried to draw attention to the passive dimension of human life and in doing so have argued that human vulnerability is not just something which we all experience at certain moments in our life, when young or sick for example, but is something which is essential to our nature as human beings. Human development involves the journey from absolute to relative dependency and thereby to interdependence (Honneth, 1995, pp. 95–107). Even within organisations such as self-help organisations, which embody the principle of interdependency in its purest form, individuals depend on others in the process of give and take. Self-help organisations are no utopia. Even here the power that some members have acquired from their experience, skills or personal qualities can become the basis for corruption, for a tyranny of structurelessness. Just as human development involves learning how to combine autonomy with the capacity for concern it also involves the ability to learn how to depend upon others. Just as we need to learn how to use our own authority responsibly we also need to learn how to use and benefit from that authority of others which is derived from skill, knowledge and experience which we do not have.

To mention the word 'authority' is to rouse a thousand hackles but it is an issue that radicals have ducked for too long. Too often the desire to maintain a critical attitude towards all sources of power has slipped into a hatred of the very notion of authority *per se*. This has led to enormous difficulties surrounding leadership within political and social movements themselves, an oscillation between blind idolatory on the one hand and unswerving distrust on the other. Yet if we are to learn from each other and develop together we have to be able to accept each other's authority. Recognition of the other's authority goes hand in hand with recognition of our own lack. There are some people who go through life thinking that they have nothing to learn from their parents, that their teachers can't tell them anything that they don't already know, that all the knowledge of their senior colleagues is suspect, and so on.

Recognition of one's own lack implies an injury to one's narcissism which some people simply cannot endure. It is for this reason that Bion (1961) talks about the pain of development, for all development involves some degree of dependency on others and a part of us rages at this necessity. To contain this hatred involves learning how not to bite all the hands that would feed us, it involves learning how to receive and how to experience gratitude towards others' generosity. Only in this way can the life-force within us all flourish. It is only in this way that our destructiveness can be sublimated so that it contributes to a critical and inquiring attitude towards life, a critical stance which is not simply cynical or begrudging in its intent.

Trust in the authority of our fellows is therefore vital to our development but it is also one we have mixed feelings about. This ambivalence is likely to be most intense where the asymmetry of social relationships is most pronounced, i.e. where the impact of chance or fate is such that dependency becomes a temporary or permanent condition rather than a mode of relating which one freely enters into. Much of the recent feminist exploration of care is concerned with these forms of dependency, that is, those involved in looking after children or elderly relatives, the nursing of the sick, and so on.

Peta Bowden's (1997) analysis of nursing provides a rich account both of the dynamics of a caring relationship caught up in a world of 'wounds and decay' and of the historical subordination of nursing work and the profession that has arisen from it. Yet while Bowden is well aware of the inequality of the relationship between patient and nurse, reading Bowden I nevertherless had a growing suspicion that her account of nursing work remained in some respects an idealised one. There is no sense of the way in which the negative emotions inevitably intrude into such relationships – the patient's sense of shame and humiliation, the anger and hostility which is so often projected onto nurses by anxious and frightened patients, the 'back of stage' banter between staff on the wards which so often mixes humour, compassion and contempt for those in their care. The point is that hatred of dependency is not just a cultural phenomenon 'out there', as it were, it is also carried within carers and the cared for. Hatred and destructiveness are not absent from caring but central to it. Many women who have looked after elderly mothers will be familiar with the way in which periods of brittle civility alternate with bouts of aggression, spite and ingratitude. And this is by no means all one way, i.e. directed towards the carer, for the carer will also experience mixed feelings towards the one for whom she has had to give up so many life chances. At least the professional carer can use her role to survive the other's aggression. When the patient shouts at and abuses a nurse the latter can contain this hatred in a role that she can distance from herself whereas the daughter cannot fail to take her mother's abuse personally. To be effective, the one that cares needs to be emotionally tough and strong, capable of accepting and surviving the other's necessary attacks on them. Care is not just about gentleness and compassion; kindness can require cruelty, empathy can only be given where there is also the possibility of aggressive distance and detachment. In my experience women know about all of these things, probably better than men, yet many feminist considerations of the ethic of care are silent upon such matters.

In praise of dependency

In conclusion let us return to that scornful phrase 'the dependency culture'. The consistency of its use across the political spectrum suggests to me not just a veiled attack on the principle of social justice but also a society in which the passive and tragic dimensions of life are being pushed further from public consciousness into the private sphere. The dogma of 'private (or, more euphemistically, 'community') is best' when turned from the emptying of bins to the care of your old mum pushes the problem of dependency back onto families and particularly onto women. Moreover, although we have seen that institutional provision for the most vulnerable has left us with little to be proud of we also know that the most abusive relationships involving violence and murder occur in the home. Tolerable family relations can often be destroyed when the sudden pressures of acute financial or emotional dependency are loaded upon the delicate fabric of interdependency, the normal give and take of family life. Public can be, and often is, best not just because it has the capacity for transparency and openness to regulation in ways that the family does not but also because the intimate relation between carer and cared for is mediated by role and contract in ways which are absent in families.

In the language of Humphrey Littleton, to be a citizen of a western democracy does not amount to being no more than a hapless chicken trussed upon the endless conveyor belt of globalisation. We still have the capacity to shape the kind of society we want. This does not have to be a world where only the fit and the flexible can count as full human citizens. It is possible to imagine a world in which the most vulnerable were the most valued members of society, given the respect due to those who are facing or who have faced the most elemental boundaries of life – sickness, madness, death, despair. It is possible to imagine a society where dependency was not just begrudgingly accepted but recognised as a vital element of human development. But our's often seems to be a society in flight from these very things, a culture of counter-dependency, of invulnerability and one, without doubt, also haunted by the return of its own repressed.

A society with a genuine commitment to the care and development of its citizens, unlike ours, would have to put its money where its mouth was. The wages and conditions of many professional carers are an indication of the abusive intent society has towards them. Institutional innovation in public and not-for-profit organisations could be promoted rather than discouraged – sanctuaries and community asylums, small schools, primary nursing, therapeutic communities, hospices, holistic cancer clinics, community residential homes – these and many other developments of the last few decades could be brought in from the margins to the mainstream. Finally, the task of developing new forms of professional practice which struggled with the contradiction of being both empowering and caring could begin. We must learn to see the ethics of justice and care as complements rather than rivals. The challenge is to integrate the project of human emancipation, the search for a society which can give expression to the fullness of human powers, with the passive and tragic dimensions of human life. Anything else will sell us all short.

10
Ethical Foundations of Welfare Universalism

Welfare universalism at the crossroads

As we struggle to get some sense of the contradictory messages emanating from the new Labour government regarding the future of welfare it seems that at least we can say with relief that the days when the very idea of 'the social' was under attack are now over. But while Labour may have embraced communitarianism principles it is also clear that many of the tenets of neo-liberalism and moral-authoritarianism that Thatcherism was built upon also inform its policies. As Dean (1998) notes, Labour draws upon a complex mixture of moral repertoires. Thus it is salutory to remember that the fundamental steps in the neo-liberal transformation of the welfare state – the introduction of markets and competition, centralised decentralisation, the installation of workfare, the subordination of social to economic policy – have been largely taken in the 1990s after the last Thatcher administration.

They say that history repeats itself first time as tragedy. In this chapter I will illustrate how the ideal of unconditional mutuality outlined in the work of Richard Titmuss constituted one of the central ethical principles underlying the development of the post-war British welfare state. One cannot help being struck by the irony that the idea of mutuality is now used by a Labour government precisely as a means of reneging upon the commitment of government to the concept of welfare universalism. This chapter will examine mutuality in terms of those interlinked values – generosity, trust, interdependence, solidarity – which have often operated tacitily as the submerged foundation of welfare universalism in the UK. I will examine the character of such values, epitomised by the notion of the gift and the gift relationship, and their influence upon post-war social policy. Using Titmuss's writings (1968, 1971) I will seek to demonstrate the enduring significance of this ethical foundation. But I will also examine the way in which an unreflexive modernism led Titmuss and others to embrace a highly institutionalised realisation of this universalist ethic.

I will argue that the new era of globalised capitalism opens up new sources of vulnerability which provide the material basis for a new cross-class commitment to welfare universalism. What is required now is the development of a post-modern universalism, one which I argue could find expression in the idea of a welfare society rather than a welfare state. Fiona Williams (1989, 1992) has done much to initiate debate concerning one of the key parameters of a renewed universalism, i.e. the way in which such a commitment must be combined with an equally unwavering commitment to social diversity. More recently (Williams, 1998) she has begun the task of sketching a new set of principles for welfare based upon what she calls the 'politics of recognition'; principles, she argues, which are perhaps vital for the renewal of a radical vision of welfare given the exhaustion of social democracy. Returning to the theme of previous chapters I will argue that 'the quality of social relations' should be central to any project for the renewal of welfare. Seen as a complement to the equitable distribution of material resources we could think of these two principles as the twin pillars of a radical vision of a welfare society.

The gift relationship

Co-operative individualism

Reciprocity, give and take, is the cornerstone of convivial social relations. As Giddens (1971) notes the idea of reciprocity was anticipated by Durkheim (1893) who was at pains to repudiate the economic individualism which had become the orthodoxy of late-nineteenth-century political economy. As with the neo-liberalism of today, this was an orthodoxy which insisted that the collective interest was only a disguised form of personal interest and that altruism was merely concealed egoism. In contrast, according to Durkheim,

> even where society relies most completely upon the division of labour, it does not become a jumble of juxtaposed atoms, be-

tween which it can establish only external, transient contacts. Rather the members are united by ties which extend deeper and far beyond the short moments during which exchange is made ... we are involved in a complex of obligations from which we have no right to free ourselves. (p. 227)

Despite Durkheim's focus upon social relations and his critique of economic individualism the embrace of methodological individualism by the social sciences this century has run deep. As a consequence many of our ways of thinking about co-operative forms of human exchange are themselves cast in a methodologically individualist mode. I have in mind here a variety of theories which seek to explain social behaviour from what might be called a predominantly undersocialised (Wrong, 1961) perspective – for instance, the social behaviourism of Homans (1950) and other exchange theorists, game theoretical approaches to the study of co-operativeness (Axelrod, 1984), rational choice theory (Elster, 1978) and even some recent manifestations of associationism (Hirst, 1994). These theories are useful to the extent that they illustrate how mutual interest can on occasions emerge from self interest. But I wish to demonstrate, by outlining a number of other ways of thinking about these sentiments, how restricted these theories are both in terms of the picture of human nature they implicitly subscribe to and the vision of future societies that they deem possible.

When people are drawn, through the pursuit of their own self-interest, towards trusting others and co-operating with them then we have an interaction we could characterise in terms of 'co-operative individualism'. At the simplest level the practice of giving may be thought of as a learned pattern of behaviour acquired through the repeated experience that generosity to others normally brings about its own reward. In other words, given certain conditions (e.g. that I am not a person of bad reputation), the probability that another may do me a good turn is increased if I have in the past performed good turns for them. Crudely speaking, 'I give so that I might receive' – a rather calculating approach to generosity one might think.

So far we have focused on a situation where it is in my power to decide whether to give or take from another who is independent of me. But what of situations where one party's behaviour unavoidably has an impact upon the fortunes of another, in other words where there is some degree of interdependence?

Imagine a political or community group which has grown rapidly and needs to change the way in which it organises itself but is having difficulty in resolving a conflict between two sub-groups, one standing for the old ways and one standing for the new. A variety of solutions are possible. One group may triumph at the expense of another, a 'compromise' may be reached which suits no-one and where everyone is worse off, or a creative solution may be found where what each party gains outweighs what each has to give up. Within game theory the first kind of solution is often referred to as a win-lose solution, the second is a lose-lose solution, whereas the third is a win-win solution. We can see how the latter solution is equivalent to 'mutual gain'.

The problem with this way of seeing things however is that it decontextualises human action. Human agents, whether individuals or groups, are essentially seen as isolated monads engaging in a hypothetical game to which they arrive somehow shorn of culturally acquired expectations, the social networks to which they belong, the group and intergroup dynamics which have emerged through time in the history of the community group in question, and so on. For example, within some human communities, particularly those which historically have had to endure hardship and frustration, a particular kind of sub-culture emerges which combines elements of resignation and tolerance. In these settings loss can often be tolerated without immediate resort to retaliation (and hence the possibility of descent towards a lose-lose outcome) because of an expectation of some evening-out of losses and gains over time ('all life has its ups and downs'). Or, consider the unconscious dynamics which often operate in groups. In the kind of pseudo-mutual group (Gufstafson, 1979) that I examined in Chapter 9 a feigned equality masks intense feelings of envy and rivalry. Here it is vital that 'everyone remains the same'. The most intolerable idea is that some might gain advantage while others do not. In such groups it is preferable that everyone should lose rather than some obtain even the most temporary advantage compared to others.

The point is that human relations cannot be understood apart from the cultural, organisational and group settings in which they occur. As Granovetter (1985) notes, standard economic analysis 'neglects the identity and past relations of individual transactors' (p. 491). Human actions are always embedded in a social context, one which shapes the meanings we attach to the choices we perceive and the outcomes we envisage.

Particularistic reciprocity

If we take social relations rather than individuals as the object of social investigation then a number of new lines of enquiry open up before us. One approach is to link reciprocity to the cultural norms which are embedded in the many social networks of which we are a part – networks of kinship relations (Young & Willmott, 1957), friends and neighbours (Abrams *et al.*, 1989), religious and secular associations, work-based and professional solidarities and so on. As Watson (1980) notes, individuals are more or less integrated in a system of reciprocal obligations determined by their social identity.

This perspective, which has many similarities to the communitarian strand within political theory, suggests that the altruism demonstrated in the family by the mother for her child, or by the teenager for the elderly neighbour next door, or by the person who volunteers to help a disabled child to swim may be specific to the social identities and networks which define and sustain the immediate lifeworld within which that individual is immersed. Granovetter (1985), in his discussion of the concept of embeddedness, clearly has this idea in mind when he expresses scepticism about the value of the idea of a generalised morality. In contrast he states, 'the embeddedness argument stresses the role of concrete personal relations and structures (or "networks") of such relations in generalising trust and discouraging malfeasance' (p. 490). Thus the 'goodwill' which Ronald Dore (1983) discovered to be such an important lubricant of inter-organisational relations within families or communities of firms in the Japanese economy extended only to indigenous firms, as foreign firms have discovered to their cost. In other words the generosity exhibited may not be offered to *any other* but only to particular others – in *my* family, in *my* neighbourhood, of *my* ethnic background, in *my* workplace. This is a crucial paradox, the generosity of the volunteer cannot be doubted, yet at the same time there may be a conditional and particularistic character to it such that the same individual may be capable of acts of great kindness to some but may act indifferently or even callously to others. Indeed codes of honour and mutuality are sometimes strongest within communities of crime, 'honour among thieves' as Granovetter puts it.

It also follows that the strength of moral obligation will vary directly according to the strength and cohesion of the social networks which penetrate social life. In spatial or occupational communities where such networks are weak, where individuals lead an atomised and anomic existence, then we would expect the ties of reciprocal obligation also to be weak. Distrust would dominate over trust, every social transaction would be approached with an eye for personal gain. This is a de-moralised world in which human relations are indeed reduced to a rational calculus.

A universal norm of reciprocity?

The focus upon 'social relations' rather than decontextualised individual actors is an even stronger feature in third perspective on the nature of reciprocity, one which argues that there is a norm of reciprocity existing over and above the socially determined moral obligations characteristic of a particular culture existent in time and space. In other words, reciprocity is a moral universal.

The social function of the reciprocal exchange of gifts was first investigated thoroughly by the social anthropologist Marcel Mauss (1954). It was the work of Mauss which much later provided the foundation for the classical analysis of reciprocity provided by Gouldner (1960). Gouldner argues that while reciprocity may emerge from the experience of contingent patterns of interaction (i.e. through single or repeated encounters people may come to trust each other) the norm of reciprocity should also be viewed as a universal one without which (following Malinowski (1932) and others) any division of labour would be impossible to sustain. Gouldner is quite clear on this point, indeed he argues that reciprocity is 'no less universal and important an element of culture than the incest taboo' (Gouldner, p. 171). For Gouldner reciprocity is the essence of the social cement, the sentiment which binds social groups together, 'a kind of plastic filler, capable of being poured into the shifting crevices of social structures' (p. 175).

Gouldner suggests that reciprocity assumes the exchange of 'rough equivalents', that is, of gifts which are concretely different but roughly equivalent in value. Clearly the notion of equivalence will itself vary culturally – in traditional societies certain forms of dance or ritual ceremony would be judged a fair equivalent for the gift of certain goods, within many community organisations a club secretary may simply insist that her services are visibly appreciated by the organisation concerned via the ritual but genuine vote of thanks at the Annual General Meeting. The principle of 'rough equivalence' therefore provides the basis for tolerance within gift exchange and as such is antithetical to the idea of measurement. Drawing upon the distinction made by Blau (1964) between economic and social exchange Fox (1974) notes how economic exchange 'prescribes specifically the nature and extent of the favours exchanged' (p. 71). In contrast in social exchange, while there may be some generalised expectation of a future return, its exact nature is definitely not stipulated in advance. The idea of social exchange is central to the functioning of civil society. Not surprisingly the principle of rough equivalence has always been a core value within the community sector and recent attempts to impose the principle of economic exhange by the extension of managerialist methodologies to this sector cannot but lead to conflict or to the corruption of community organisations themselves (Taylor & Hoggett, 1994).

The concept of the gift exchange, as developed by Mauss, was also central to the analysis of another writer in the post-war period. Richard Titmuss is a crucial figure in the development of the philosophy of the modern British welfare state. Titmuss argues that the exchange of gifts is not primarily an economic transaction but 'an event which has significance that is at once social and religious, magic and economic, utilitarian and sentimental, jural and moral' (Titmuss, 1971, p. 210). Here Titmuss echoes the argument of Mauss who insists that the study of societies should adopt a morphological approach, i.e. one concerned with the whole rather than the parts. Thus, with regard to the exchange of gifts, the focus should be the relationship not the individual. From this perspective reciprocity is concerned not with the maximisation of outcomes of self-interested actors but with *the maintenance and reproduction of social relations themselves*. In other words social relations and social exchanges are an end in themselves, the essential embodiment of our 'species being'. Nowhere is this clearer than in the organisation of leisure activity. People will come together and form a club or association around the wildest and most obscure issue or for the most flimsy pretext. Take railway or military modelling as an example, it is astonishing to find the immense variety of clubs based around different scales, genres, traditions and so on. Concluding a short book a friend and I wrote some time ago which was based upon two years research on the social organisation of leisure we noted,

The clubs and associations described in this book are not merely settings in which people 'do' things; they were no mere means to an ends. . . . The groups are places to 'be' as much as to 'do', with their own histories, characters, dramas and meanings. (Bishop & Hoggett, 1986, p. 128)

It seems tiresome to have to continually point out to economists in particular that we are social beings and as social beings we do not require a motive to interact with each other. The problem requiring explanation is not why some people combine together to form groups and participate in social life but rather why some do not.

Subjectivity and the capacity for concern

So far we have observed how giving to others may be a tactic to obtain a return, a strategy for developing co-operation, a moral imperative forged through processes of acculturation or a universal expression of our basic sociability. I will now consider two further perspectives which suggest that generosity can also be unconditional.

Virtually all of the theories we have examined so far share one basic assumption; in giving I experience some kind of loss – a loss of time, money, energy, goods, etc. True, this loss may receive recompense in time, but the act of giving depletes me in some way. But entertain for a moment the converse idea, that the act of giving may be a way of overcoming an existing loss, making me more whole again in some way. Paradoxically it would follow that if I was unable to give I would feel lacking and unfulfilled.

Klein (1935, 1940, 1959) sees the capacity for concern as the cornerstone of our subjectivity. She suggests that the basis for moral concern lies in our primary ambivalence in relations to others (Butler, 1998). Ambivalence is stirred up particularly when we depend upon others. The more I need another the greater the potential to feel both intense love and intense hate towards this figure. Indeed for some people this hate is so strong that they can never admit to themselves that they need others. But the more intense my feelings the more difficult it is to express them overtly. If I can't hate the one I love to her face then at least I can attack her over and over again in my mind. Adults whose emotional development has proceeded well enough can preserve and enjoy relationships with the external other despite such attacks upon their internal counterpart. But this is a developmental achievement dependent upon the child's recognition that the real object has the ability to survive the destruction of its internal counterpart (Benjamin, 1994; Davis & Wallbridge, 1981, pp. 70–1).

It is only by the mobilisation of aggression that the infant can begin to test out the existence of an object which is separate from itself and move from dependence towards interdependence. As Axel Honneth (1995) notes it is only 'in the attempt to destroy his or her "mother" – that is, in the form of a struggle – that the child realises that he or she is dependent on the loving care of an independently existing person with claims of her own' (Honneth, p. 101). This then is the paradox of infancy and childhood as a consequence of which, according to Klein, as adults we are haunted by the real and imaginary injuries we inflict on others in our life, others who are still a part of our internal world and in that sense part of ourselves. The reparative drive is therefore ultimately a drive to make amends for our own hatred, to atone for our own violence. The attainment of subjectivity, that is the realisation of interdependence, ultimately depends upon our conviction that we have inside us something good enough to overcome our destructiveness. And while, according to Klein, this may in part be the outcome of constitutional factors it is also, crucially, contingent upon the impact of a benign environment. Thus in seeking to help others, in offering our concern, in endeavouring to make things better we are also seeking to repair our own internal world, to mend the rents and tears within the fabric of the self which are the inevitable outcome of the struggle to be our own person.

From this perspective the desire to preserve the environment from despoliation, the desire to help rebuild communities in Africa or in our own cities which have been crushed and demoralised, all of these can be considered expressions of the reparative drive. In this sense the nature of the other, the extent to which it objectively embodies strangeness or familiarity, is irrelevant for, considered internally, we know the other intimately. What is crucial is not so much the objective qualities of this other but its capacity to represent something internally for us. For this reason the reparative drive can be considered as *a generalised capacity to feel concern*. In this sense Rustin (1991, p. 22–3) is right to argue that Klein's position is far less pessimistic than Freud's given the way it stresses the existence of powerful positive emotions which are not mere sublimations of sexual aggression. In a world like ours which seems so full of rage and hate Kleinian theory suggests that these powerful forces are nevertheless capable of integration and resolution. Moreover, as Rustin notes, it is possible that the idea of 'the good society' itself or, as he has put it elsewhere, 'the social architecture of a more benign world' (Rustin & Rustin, 1984), may function as an almost universally shared internal representation.

Clearly the particular way in which this reparative drive finds expression will be socially constructed. It may be expressed in the philanthropism of the rich towards the poor, in the struggle to establish animal rights, to preserve the National Health Service or help out an elderly neighbour. It may also find expression in forms of service which are crudely patronising or disempowering to the one in receipt of such 'gifts'. As New (1996) notes, 'from the point of view of the person who feels remorse, the damage done to the internal objects must be repaired . . . but actions that fulfil that psychological function may be inappropriate' (p. 123). Because the reparative drive is always socially mediated it does not in itself give support to any particular social or political project – what is considered 'benign' as opposed to malign will vary according to cultural expectations and political values. What Klein provides is an account of some of the psychological underpinnings of the universal desire to give, a desire which can be mobilised equally through what Sorokin (1954, p. 459) calls 'tribal' or 'in-group' altruism as through 'universal' altruism. In other words, it is quite possible for the reparative drive of the individual to be harnessed by the paranoid mind of the group. To move beyond conditional forms of giving and reciprocity towards social practices which create solidarities across the boundaries of place, gender, culture and ethnicity it is therefore necessary to 'build societies which can contain hostility . . . and in which reparative principles are institutionalised' (New, 1996, p. 130). While agreeing entirely with the sentiment behind this statement I suggest that what we need is a society which can *embody* this impulse in a non-institutionalised way.

The gift that seeks no return

There is a final form of giving that must be considered, indeed for some such as Derrida (1992) it is the only true form of the gift. I have in mind here the gift which does not know of itself and the giver who is without self-consciousness as giver. According to Derrida, 'for there to be gift, it is necessary that the gift not even appear, that it not be perceived or received as gift' (1992, p. 173) and 'for there to be a gift, there must be no reciprocity, return, exchange, countergift or debt' (p. 170).

I do not wish to reproduce the somewhat tortuous path of Derrida's reasoning nor dismiss the value of anthropological understandings of the gift in the rather peremptory way that he chooses. But what we need to understand from Derrida is the way in which the gift is also essential to human freedom, 'that development of human energy which is an end in itself, the true realm of freedom, which, however, can blossom forth only with (the) realm of necessity as its basis. The shortening of the working day is its basic prerequisite' (Marx, 1974, p. 820). Marx draws our attention here to the two realms of freedom – 'freedom from (need)', on the one hand, and 'freedom to', on the other. The latter freedom is based on a human energy which flows out from us yet does not emerge from need. It is an inner propulsion which is not based on any sense of insufficiency but rather is the outcome of a fullness which overflows the self. This is desire: a sense of longing accompanies such experience, but it is a longing to give, to externalise an inner fullness (Hoggett, 1986). The person who gives in this way does so almost involuntarily. It is as if they are born along helplessly by a voluptuous force, an overflowing being, which seeks satisfaction through a real or imaginary other. They ask no return beyond the simple request that the other receive what they give so that this fullness of being can be made present (Derrida, pp. 168–9, reflects upon the coincidence that in both French and English a gift is called 'a present'). Is this not what human creativity is all about, the transmission of a vibrant, life-enhancing force from the one in whom at that point in time it can no longer be contained to others, any others, who happen to be at hand to receive it?

I think what I am saying is that there is an overlap between the expressive and reparative dimensions of life. Just as care can be seen as a creative act through which people seek to give expression to their inner being, so cultural production, perhaps particularly art and music, contains a strong reparative impulse (Tucker, 1992). To give two examples from my own city, Bristol, the expressive dimension plays a vital role in the healing work of the Music Space Trust and the Cancer Help Centre (Hoggett, 1999).

The ethical foundation of British welfarism

Gifts and strangers

There is clearly a huge difference between Gouldner's idea of a universal norm of reciprocity and the idea of a gift which seeks no return. Reflecting upon his study of the British Blood Transfusion Service, Titmuss (1971) noted that for most of the donors that were interviewed the prospect of personal benefit (even if in the longterm) weighed far less heavily than the idea of doing good. But crucially, 'for most of them the universe was not limited and confined to the family, the kinship, or to a defined social, ethnic or occupational group or class; it was the universal stranger' (p. 238). Indeed by prohibiting the donor from having the right to prescribe the group characteristic of the recipient the service 'presumes an unspoken shared belief in the universality of need' (ibid.). The enduring power of this belief is illustrated by the outrage which has accompanied recent attempts to introduce more commercial and managerialist principles to the organisation of the British Blood Transfusion Service.

The form of giving that Titmuss has in mind here is also clearly different from forms of particularistic reciprocity. For the other to whom I give is a stranger and not one necessarily familiar to my own group. Titmuss calls this 'anonymous helpfulness'. The recipient may in fact be a member of my own group, or even someone I know, but psychologically he is a stranger to me, just as the recipient has no way of knowing the donor, so the donor has no way of knowing the recipient. What I give to is a common pool from which others take according to their need. While in giving I seek no explicit return in cash or kind I nevertheless give in the expectation that I too can draw from this common pool when in need. Imagine a situation in which patients had to pay for all goods and services they consumed while in hospital, including blood; in such a situation all but a few saints or fools would immediately stop donating their own blood. So I am not totally disinterested, but in giving it is others' needs and an imagined common good that I have in mind most. For this reason Titmuss has good grounds to consider that such acts deserve to be called altruistic. Although such forms of giving are never totally disinterested (we hope that others may do unto us as we have done to them) our giving is not conditional upon this.

There can be little doubt that for Titmuss the British Blood Transfusion Service constituted an essential metaphor for the principle of collective welfare provision. Based upon a partnership between voluntary giving and state co-ordination the transfusion service also vividly represented the process by which each person freely gave to a common pool from which each drew according to his or her need. In its own small way the service was therefore redistributive.

We can see how the pool of blood symbolises the common pool of humanity which Titmuss pictured in somewhat idealised fashion in terms of a British people bound together in adversity during the Second World War. To this extent the idea of welfare that Titmuss and others had in mind drew attention to the integrative and consensual impulses in society and to a notion of community which transcended particularistic ties to embrace the needs of strangers. Indeed, as several commentators have noted (Baldwin, 1990), Titmuss's (1950) analysis of the transition of the British middle-classes from an ideology of self-reliance to one of solidaristic interdependence through the experience of the war has proved an enduring explanation of the coalition of social classes which enabled the brief flowering of the Beveridge era in the immediate post-war period.

Titmuss contrasted the sphere of collective welfare to that of the market place. In contrast to economics the discipline of social administration was therefore concerned with 'different types of moral transaction, embodying notions of gift exchange, of reciprocal obligations, which have developed in modern societies in institutional forms to bring about and maintain social and community relations' (1968, p. 20–1). In other words, for Titmuss, the institutionalisation of the collective good was not only a necessary expression of egalitarian values but it was also socially constructive in its own right – fostering integration and discouraging alienation, as Titmuss put it (1968, p. 22).

I will argue later that the post-war attempt to institutionalise the gift relationship was fundamentally misconceived. The enduring legacy of Titmuss lies not in the institutional forms of welfare which developed in the 1950s and 1960s but in the way in which his writings sought to develop an ethical ideal which could underpin the concept of a universalistic rather than particularistic (Spicker, 1993) model of welfare. The danger is that, given our experience of the last fifty years, the ideal of universalism is tied irrevocably to the institutional model of the welfare state (Thompson & Hoggett, 1996). In the concluding section to this essay I will argue that what we require, our mobilising fiction, is a non-institutional model of a welfare society.

What Titmuss represents in Britain therefore is the faded ideal of a universalistic welfare system in which each gives according to his or her ability and each receives, not just according to need but as of right. In societies based around the social organisation of scarcity the rhetoric of social rights and the extension of social citizenship (Marshall, 1949) is a crucial component of the strategy for equality. *As Titmuss (1976) constantly insisted, the poor and the structurally disadvantaged have a right to public goods and services because it is they who have been asked to bear the costs of others' progress.* In the absence of such social rights the recipient of services inevitably becomes construed as inadequate, blameworthy or undeserving, the target of 'means testing', surveillance and 'tough love'. In this sense Spicker (1993) usefully contrasts this 'thick' sense of universalism, linked historically with Titmuss's institutional model of welfare, to a 'thin' sense where provision is targeted primarily to those in need.

The corrupted gift: institutional welfare

A weakened redistribution

In contrast to the ethical ideal of collective welfare that Titmuss developed the actual reality of post-war welfarism in Britain was different in a number of respects. In reality the British welfare state never was particularly redistributive even from its inception. As Baldwin (1990, p. 121) notes, Beveridge's flat rate contributory system inevitably limited redistributive effects and was to be consistently opposed by the left-wing Bevanites within the British Labour Party. Nevertheless Esping-Anderson (1990, pp. 53–4) places the British welfare state in 1950 as the highest scoring system of that period in terms of his de-commodification index. Esping-Anderson accounts for the subsequent failure of the system to develop from this base in terms of the weakness of the British Labour Party after 1950. In a similar vein Deakin (1993) charts the watering down of Beveridge's proposals during their initial implementation in the 1940s and subsequently through the parsimony of Conservatism in the 1950s to a point where many facets of welfare provision became increasingly residual rather than universalistic in character. The weakened redistributive impact of the British welfare state, the failure to extend the universalistic principles of the National Health Service to the social services and other areas which lead to increasingly residualised forms of welfare provision by the 1970s can all be thought of as failures to implement a sound vision. But, perhaps more important for the political viability of welfarism, there were flaws within the post-war concept of universalism itself.

Universalism, consensualism and social homogeneity

Rather than use the vision of a welfare society as a mobilising fiction to transform existing social relationships the gradualist and consensualist Fabianism that Titmuss and others were immersed in led them to construe the idea of collective welfare simply as a means of modifying the excesses of a market-based society. His analysis of the common cause forged between the middle and working classes in wartime Britain provided a perceptive account of the conditions from which the British welfare state emerged. But he was unable to understand the contingent nature of the co-operation between social classes, which had occurred. In this context his desire for social integration required a blindness to the actual nature of power in class-based societies and the many ways in which the welfare state, if it were to be a viable and enduring institution within modern capitalism, would inevitably be called upon to contribute to the new regime of accumulation which emerged in the post-war period (Aglietta, 1987; Jessop, 1994). Titmuss's political ideology therefore obscured the way in which the welfare state would be required to reproduce existing relations of dominance and subordination and engage in explicit forms of social control and that these would become as important as its role in providing collective services and alleviating need (Offe, 1984).

Nor was class the only axis around which power relations were exercised, for in a sense the entire Beveridge system was based upon the assumption of a natural division of labour between male bread-winner and female houseworker and mother (Williams, 1989, pp. 123–4). To this extent women constituted an invisible population, one absent from the public sphere, the hidden hands by dint of which the male labour force could continue to engage in the world of real work. The very forms of provision of collective welfare were therefore ones which sustained and gave emphasis to this division of labour. Here, then, we see a possible danger in the language of the common good. Ideas of reciprocity and interdependence can so easily be harnessed to a political project which masks relation-ships of power across class, gender and other boundaries. Within the home what specific patterns of power are obscured by the idea of interdependence? Within the factory what actual power relations are masked by the sense of obligation felt by employees towards the 'good boss'? Titmuss's concept of universalism was not just blind to class and gender relations. Williams (1989) argues that, while his universalism was not based upon a nationalist notion of com-munity, in extending the concept of the stranger to include the poor and disadvantaged in other countries his vision was inhibited by an Imperialistic and paternalistic ideology which was common to the Fabianism of his time. The modern welfare state was seen as a civilising institution to be exported to Third World countries so that they might benefit from British wisdom and expertise.

An institutionalised universalism

Perhaps the most crucial way in which Titmuss's writing reflects the dominant assumptions of his time relates to the unreflexive modernism expressed in his uncritical support for the role of expert knowledge in the development of collective welfare provision. In this sense Titmuss gave expression to an emerging technocratic ideology, one which was to have a profound effect upon the particular character and form of all welfare states and not just Britain's. Pinker's introduction to one of the first books dedicated to the work of Titmuss captures this acutely:

> Titmuss's model is remarkable for its lack of active community involvement . . . and notable for its autocratic etatisme: the user is not consulted about his needs but is informed of them by politicians and bureaucrats acting, of course, on the basis of sound professional advice. (Pinker, 1977, p. 37)

Titmuss seemed blind to the dangers of professionalisation and to the possibility that the welfare state might itself become prone to capture by interest groups operating within it. I do not wish to recite all the arguments which have been made which draw attention to the way in which the welfare state became increasingly bureaucratised, unaccountable, paternalistic and impervious to the actual needs and requirements of service users and local communities. This critique of welfarism, from both the left and the right, now has a long and substantial pedigree (Hambleton & Hoggett, 1987, Hirst, 1994, Beresford & Croft, 1990, Lindow & Morris, 1995). Indeed the attenuation of democracy within the welfare state and its capture by internal interests (which would include political elites operating at both local and national levels) gives weight to those, such as Bookchin (1992), who have argued that the process of 'statification' should be seen as being as pernicious in corrupting forms of human conviviality and solidarity as the process of commodification.

From this perspective, far from having an integrative effect, the institutionalisation of the common good through the form of the welfare state constituted a new source of social alienation. Certainly the collapse of communist regimes in Eastern Europe in the late 1980s has revealed the tragic consequences of the tendency by many brands of socialism, from Fabianism to Leninism, to confuse social form with state form.

Given the origin of welfarism in the earlier forms of mutualism which provided the means of collective insurance against vulnerability in the 19th and early 20th centuries, and given the way in which our common welfare still rests upon the fabric of familial, neighbourhood and community-based networks of civil society, we might argue that the essential flaw of post-war collectivism lay in its substitution of rule-governed hierarchies for the self-organisation of welfare. In other words a professionalised welfare state apparatus grew parasitically upon the mutualism of civil society. Here, then, is the contradiction in Titmuss. On the one hand the ethical ideal he sketches draws our attention to the informal, associational, mutual and reciprocal – i.e. the pre-modern foundation of the common good. But in seeking to institutionalise that common good Titmuss also demonstrates a profoundly modernist enchantment with hierarchy and professional expertise.

Vagaries of the public service ethic

One of the paradoxes of the politics of welfare in the UK is that it was only after several years of cumulative Conservative attacks upon the welfare state in the late 1980s that the notion of 'a public service ethic' was rediscovered, or should we say, re-invented (Foster and Taylor, 1994). By the late 1960s an ethic of service had emerged within many of the professional groups which had grown within the welfare state during the preceding decades. It was an ethic which drew primarily upon altruistic individualism (Halmos, 1970) and while not philanthropic in character the concepts of professional responsibility it propounded were deeply paternalistic and its construction of 'the client' was often discriminatory and oppressive. In other words it was at root a conservative and deeply technocratic ethic which served the purpose of professional self-justification (Wilding, 1982) but in no way offered a mobilising vision through which the idea of a commitment to collective welfare could be sustained. Indeed by the early 1970s the welfare state in Britain assumed such a disfigured form that the new left tended to see the institutions of welfare as part of the problem of social emancipation rather than part of the solution. This critique was implicit in many of the community development projects which emerged at that time (Jones & Mayo, 1974) and in the new movement for women's liberation (Wilson, 1977). It probably found its sharpest articulation in the writings of *In and Against the State Collective* (London-Edinburgh Weekend Return Group, 1980) in the late 1970s.

Part of the cynicism that many welfare workers felt in the 1970s was fuelled by the sense that the idea of service had in any case become a con trick. I felt this acutely myself when I was a social worker on the Isle of Dogs long before its Thatcherite transformation. What could I do as a young middle-class, male graduate parachuted into a community I had no common experience with? Moreover I was single, without children, having never experienced the sadness of bereavement, the misery of poverty or the physical and emotional violence of demoralised families at war with one another. The situation was crazy and yet we were asked to believe that this was the first step upon a rewarding and legitimate career. The problem for me and many of my colleagues was to prevent an overwhelming cynicism from engulfing the humanistic and socialistic values that had drawn us to work outside the private sector. Tragically the rise of trade-union militancy within local government and the health service in the 1970s and early 1980s undermined the old and rather shallow values of public service without putting any new values in their place (Miller, 1996).

What is interesting about this period, one we might think of as the period of incipient crisis within the British welfare state, is the hegemony of technocratic and administrative rationality within the Labourism of that time (Hoggett & McGill, 1988). This was a welfarism which required no ethical foundation, as if the welfare state had become a self-evident end in itself. In this sense it seems remarkable that at the time of his death in 1973 the philosophical writings, as opposed to his more empirically based research, of a socialist humanist such as Titmuss actually had so little impact upon the Labour Party. It was only when the edifice of the welfare state began to crumble before the attacks of the new right in the 1980s and early 1990s that the tragic absence of a durable and mobilising ethical vision became apparent. For as market principles began to seep into the pores of the welfare state the realisation dawned that what had been hidden from view for many years was what was most valuable about this system – the ethic of trust and interdependence which still bound workers within the public sector together – and it is to this that we shall now turn.

The gift destroyed? The rise of the enterprise state

Farewell to goodwill

Reflecting upon developments within the UK welfare state since 1979 one can see with hindsight that it was as if at the heart of Conservative strategy lay a perverse desire to destroy the strands of trust and solidarity which had endured within the institutional fabric of welfare. Dore's (1983) analysis of the function of goodwill within Japanese capitalism is highly pertinent here. Dore's argument was that, unlike Anglo-Saxon forms of capitalism, the Japanese system was built upon networks of collaboration and trust between firms, 'networks of preferential, stable, obligated bilateral trading relationships, networks of relational contracting' (Dore, 1983, p. 467). Dore and others (Hofstede, 1991) linked this strongly collaborative inter-firm culture to the communitarian value system which dominates many Pacific-rim countries. In a similar fashion I would argue that although by the 1970s the British welfare state was a pale and disfigured example of an underlying ideal, the image it represented was still virtuous enough to retain the goodwill of the vast majority of its employees. Elsewhere (Hoggett, 1992, pp. 131–3) I have described the dilemma of commitment confronted by workers within the 'impaired body' of the welfare state. It was because of the existence of this continued goodwill that the welfare state was able to function effectively despite its hierarchical nature and despite the rigid divisions and boundaries spawned by professionalism, bureaucratic empire building and unimaginative trade unionism. There are countless examples that could be given where professional status, job description and organisational membership were ignored as nurses, auxiliaries, porters, social workers, health visitors, housing officers, clerks, teachers, accountants, personnel officers, and so on combined together to get on with the overriding task of producing public services. And it is precisely this, the networks of trust, interdependence and solidarity, which have been progressively destroyed over the last decade.

By shaping the new forms of production to their own political strategy the neo-liberals were able to fuse decentralisation with competitive individualism and thereby fragment the welfare state into a sea of tiny public enterprises (Hoggett, 1996) which, as they were drawn into the embrace of the market, were forced to go touting for customers. Training units in local authorities, educational psychologists in local education authorities, teams of secretaries within the

newly devolved executive agencies of the civil service, horticultur-
ists and sports centre managers, head-teachers in schools and general
managers in hospital trusts, all began to keep an eye out for the
main chance as compulsory competitive tendering, internal markets and other forms of internal trading spread inexorably across
the entire public sector.

The organisations of the welfare state became fragmented into
thousands of monadic units each drawn reluctantly into the pursuit of its own self-interest. Speaking of the education sector Ball
(1993) noted, 'for both parents, acting in the best interests of *their*
children, and senior teachers, acting in the best interests of *their*
school the market leaves little alternative but to engage in individualistic, competitive activity' (p. 109). In place of the ties of
goodwill and patterns of interdependence distrust spread like fire
across an arid scrubland exacerbating all the latent tensions and
rivalries – both in horizontal relations between schools, between
university departments, between hospitals and in vertical relations
between schools and Local Education Authorities, between service
departments and support services and between purchasers and providers. The dysfunctional effects of this spiral of distrust are massive.
Fox (1974) cites Zand (1972) instructively:

> One who does not trust others will conceal or distort relevant
> information ... will resist or deflect the attempts of others to
> exert influence... will be suspicious of their views, and not re-
> ceptive to their proposed goals... will try to minimise his
> dependence on others... will try to impose controls on their
> behaviour... but will be alarmed at their attempts to control
> his behaviour. (Zand, 1972, p. 230)

Fox adds that under these conditions there is no development of
the mutual bonds expressive of reciprocated trust, rather 'only the
calculated wariness and suspicion' expressive of reciprocated distrust.

The deepening of survivalist anxieties

The Balkanisation process enveloped those working within the former
welfare state more completely than those outside it. As flexibilisation
spread, providers of public services experienced increasing job and
career insecurity and as the demand to provide 'more for less' became louder so the accompanying intensification of labour left many
workers feeling as vulnerable and needy as the ill, the young, the

old and the marginalised that they sought to help (Cooper and Kelly, 1993; Rees and Cooper, 1992; Sutherland and Cooper, 1992). In these circumstances the temptation to seek salvation in one's own little enterprise was often difficult to resist. The loyalty that always existed to our school, our hospital or our department now took on a new character. The 'us' was no longer contained within a wider imagined community (*the* National Health Service, *the* Civil Service, *the* Local Education Authority) but became reconstituted as an isolated unit, at times almost a gang, pitched into a partly real and partly phantasised life and death struggle against other public enterprises who were equally paranoid. As one commentator put it, it was as if the new managerialism was paranoid-schizoid by choice (Obholzer, 1994).

While the concept of the common good was originally a political fiction used to mobilise a citenzenry drawn together through shared vulnerability now it was this self-same vulnerability, this time visited upon us by the image of a Britain in decline, which was used to divide worker against worker and citizen against citizen. In place of the idea of a community of strangers and a reciprocity which was not bound to the ties of my 'group' a new notion of welfare was forged, one based upon the fractured identities of 'our' school, 'our' housing estate, 'our' depressed city or region and indeed 'our' religion. As each group became drawn into the new market for public goods this identity was encouraged to obtain a defensive if not paranoid form. While I might give to *my* school or *my* community I may not be so inclined to give to another. And similarly for those who worked within the public services, the pressure to collude with management and colleagues in making sure that *we* survive was intense and, while workers might privately complain to each other, open resistance was seen to impair the chance of shared survival. According to Ball (1993, p. 111), 'it sets the dissenters against the interests of colleagues rather than against policies'. In place of broader sentiments of solidarity there was a gradual spread of neo-tribal loyalties. As Fox (1974) noted when speaking of the spiral of distrust, 'little can be expected, therefore, in the way of a community of values and sympathies; a shared universe of meanings, understandings and attitudes.'

From welfare state to welfare society?

A welfare state at the crossroads

I have argued that the post-war ideal of universalist welfare tacitly assumed the existence of a community of interdependent strangers sharing together an experience of actual or imminent vulnerability. Paradoxically, to the extent that modern welfare capitalism was successful in addressing such vulnerabilities it undermined its own mass psychological underpinning, i.e. an inclusive sense of social solidarity. Moreover, in the UK at least, this post-war ideal obtained a strongly institutionalised expression in which a fetishised respect for professional competence fused with a delight in economies of scale to produce the giant professionalised bureaucracies which we came to love and hate. But complex institutions do not simply collapse under the weight of their own contradictions, political action is required to destroy and to transform – this was the task of successive Conservative governments. By the time the new Labour government was elected in 1997 the British welfare state was close to disintegration.

In place of a community of vulnerable but interdependent strangers neo-Liberal policies were inspired by a new and powerful mobilising fiction. It was a fiction of the strong and autonomous individual motivated by a primary concern to maximise the welfare of self and family and whose efforts at self-improvement necessarily contributed to the well-being of others. There is no sense of social interdependence beyond the family here, indeed, as one famous slip revealed, no sense of society. Within this landscape the users of public services become recast as consumers whose only common identity derived from the simulated brand loyalty that marketing and quality assurance managers seek to generate towards the hospitals, schools and cities who hire them.

Today welfarism in Britain appears to stand very much at the crossroads. Despite the contradictory impulses within Labour's agenda some overall trends seem clear. First, as we noted in the previous chapter, social policy seems destined to become subordinated to economic policy, specifically to the imperatives of producing a fit and educated labour force ready to take its place in the newly deregulated and globalised markets (Jessop, 1994; Levitas, 1999). Secondly, and no doubt linked to the first, a rhetoric of mutualism and communitarianism appears to have been developed which, in stressing the importance of duty and obligation, seeks to undermine the discourse of rights and social citizenship developed by Marshall and Titmuss. It is in this way that Labour signals its abandonment of universalist principles in most areas of social policy.

New sources of vulnerability

The need for an alternative vision of common welfare is pressing. In what follows I will argue that the material conditions for an expanded rather than restricted concept of common welfare have now returned. But the existence of such conditions, in and of themselves, is insufficient to bring about a renewed commitment, it is also necessary for the left to recreate a mobilizing fiction that can transform latent support for a new kind of welfare society into an effective political force. First, let us consider the changed social conditions.

The concept of the common good implicit in Titmuss's ethical ideal is, as we have seen, grounded in analyses of the gift-relation provided by Mauss (1954) and others. But to provide a more secure foundation for welfare ethics it is necessary to go beyond what are essentially small-group models of unilateral transfer. In other words, we need to develop a model of what might be called 'collective altruism' which is not reducible simply to individual or group behaviour. Baldwin's (1990) analysis of 'social solidarity' seems crucial here. With Titmuss's analysis of the impact of the experience of war in mind he argues that *what fosters solidarity is the common experience of vulnerability*, 'a sense of community is encouraged, most simply, in the face of universally shared risk' (Baldwin, p. 34). Clearly this has traditionally been rooted in the experience of class but, as Baldwin demonstrates, even during the heyday of working class politics major social reforms could only be achieved when the working class was able to build a coalition with non-working-class interests. In other words the vision of universalistic welfare could only be sustained by a shared sense of a community of interdependent strangers rooted in a common experience of actual or incipient vulnerability.

Paradoxically, at the close of the twentieth century, we are witnessing the return of a widespread experience of acute and personalised vulnerability. First, the new structural conditions. The coherent labour market of the post-war consensus has been replaced by an increasingly fragmented one (Standing, 1992). Alongside the permanently excluded 'have nots' stand the newly insecure (Hutton, 1995) 'have somes' living on short-term contracts, part-time jobs, without career structures for themselves or their children, increasingly concerned about provision in their old age. Reporting on preliminary findings from recent research on people's beliefs concerning the nature, extent and risk of poverty and wealth in the UK, Dean (1998) finds that 'a fear of poverty extended up the income scale to respondents on middle and even high incomes' (p. 133). He also notes that the largest group of his respondents manifested a clearly 'survivalist' discourse. In other words as we approach the millennium it would seem that the material conditions are rapidly returning for the re-creation of that imagined community of interdependent strangers which was essential for the development of the early welfare state. But this time the nascent community is far more complex than that described by the coming together of two classes, each of which had suffered enormously from the experience of recession and world war. Social divisions within advanced capitalist societies are now much more complex than that which was contained by the simple idea of a working class and a middle class.

Vulnerability provoked by the spread of flexible and deregulated labour markets also overlaps with new, more globally systemic, sources of risk. The 'risk society' thesis (Beck, 1992) suggests a more diffuse experience of insecurity based upon a gnawing awareness of the dangers and problems generated by science and technology and the global interdependencies which bear upon the well-being of our natural environment. The two most contemporary examples of such risks – global warming and genetically modified foods – reveal the dangers that non-systemic ways of thinking and organising pose to our future well-being in a technologically sophisticated environment.

Beck (1992) offers a helpful distinction between scarcity societies and risk societies. Political struggle within the former is preoccupied with questions of equality whereas in the latter it is the question of safety which is paramount. Beck sees each society motivating different kinds of solidarity, the solidarity of need in scarcity societies and of anxiety in risk societies. Beck's thesis is that the conflicts endemic to scarcity societies were joined by those of risk societies in the 1970s. There is an ambiguity in Beck's analysis which I feel is important. On the one hand one gets the sense that he sees the vocabularies, practices, conflicts and power relations of risk and scarcity societies as irreducible to one another. On the other hand Beck recognises that the distribution of technological risk is linked to (if not determined by) social class, and ends up talking about 'poverty risks' and 'technological risks'. Furthermore Beck notes in passing (p. 230) the possibility of ecological variants of the welfare state.

A postmodern universalism

If a universalist commitment to common welfare were ever to grip the popular imagination again this would clearly need to be different to the social democratic version of the past. For one thing it would have to come to terms with the social diversity, the greatly more differentiated and particularised identities, which are such a characteristic of globalised capitalism. As I mentioned in the introduction, Fiona Williams has done much to open up this debate. For my own part I have suggested that the most appropriate method of combining universalism with a commitment to social heterogeneity is through the development of an associationist model of welfare (Hirst, 1994; Thompson & Hoggett, 1996; Hoggett & Thompson, 1998). A strategy such as this would have the added advantage of providing a non-institutionalised model of universalism. Accountability of professionals to actual and potential service users would be far more direct and unmediated, and the conditions for diffusion of co-operative, user-managed and stakeholder forms of welfare democracy would be provided. The role of government and local government would remain crucial, but as a funder and co-ordinator rather than provider. Only in this way could inequalities in power between contending particularisms be checked (Burns, Hambleton & Hoggett, 1994, Cochrane, 1998). In other words, the state's commitment to universalism would be manifest in fiscal and social policies rather than through the institutionalisation of service planning, management and delivery. Associationist models of welfare give primacy to the organisations and networks of civil society rather than to the institutions of the state and therefore, if realised, would replace the concept of the welfare state with that of the welfare society.

To these emerging lines of inquiry I would like to add another set of possibilities related to the idea of an ecological variant of the welfare state. In terms of fiscal policies the idea of a Basic Income has been central to this debate (Van Der Veen & Van Parijs, 1987; Van Parijs, 1993) and, more recently, the new forms of mutualism which have arisen around non-monetary systems of exchange (Offe & Heinze, 1992). Readers interested in the substance of such policies are referred to these and other writers who have a far more sophisticated grasp of political economy than myself. What I would like to do here is to examine the implications of a citizen's income in terms of our previous discussion of the gift relationship.

The key point about a citizen's income is that it is non-conditional. There is no means-testing nor any set of obligations attached to it. Van Parijs argues that as such it maximises the possibilities for 'real freedom', a society in which each individual has the greatest opportunity to do whatever she might want to do (p. 25) including, in his by now famous example, the opportunity to spend every day surfing if this is what she wished. In other words a citizen's income assumes the form of a gift that seeks no return. Would this not encourage selfishness and 'free riding', undermine the moral fabric of communities and discourage ambition? From the point of view of economic individualism and from certain variants of communitarianism this would certainly be the implication. I hope I have done enough to suggest that we are both more social and more benign beings than such perspectives give us credit for. The other problem with much communitarianism is a different one, it lies in the naturalistic idea of community that communitarians tend to harbour. The point about contemporary society is that most communities are 'constructed'. Surfers form communities with their own standards, mores and patterns of self-regulation no less than anybody else. Musicians, climbers, anglers, ornithologists, greens, LETS traders, pagans, travellers, 'festies' and vegans also construct their own communities. These are expressive communities (Purdue, Durrschmidt, Jowers & O'Doherty, 1998; Jowers, Durrschmidt, O'Doherty & Purdue, 1999) the emergence of which has been made possible by the gradual spread of conditions of 'weak abundance' (Van Parijs, 1993) in western-type democracies. Surfers are therefore just one example of many, these are all people in love with their activity, the pursuit of which contributes to their well-being (Bishop & Hoggett, 1986).

In Honneth's (1995) terms, these expressive communities are essential to people's sense of self-esteem. Indeed for many, particularly the young recruits to the burger-slinging and tele-sales economy, non-work has become the primary source of personal value. Far from promoting social policies which would assist in decoupling the sense of identity from work New Labour seems hellbent on making work the only source of value for everyone – devalorising all forms of non-waged productive activity (including child care) in the process (Levitas, 1998).

Perhaps most importantly the green movement has begun to develop a sustained critique of the productivist lifestyle for being both environmentally and humanly destructive. As Offe (1994) notes, when collective welfare is measured purely in terms of the quantity of resources available to meet need, we inevitably set off down a road which assumes that welfare can only be sustained by renewed economic growth, even at the expense of ecologically sound policies. Despite their perceptive criticisms of some of the new forms of insecurity the social democratic left in Britain (Borrie Commission, 1994; Hutton, 1995) continue to see the future of welfare as entirely dependent upon renewed economic growth. In other words, egalitarianism has been predicated upon productivist assumptions which have obscured questions of value. In contrast, as Titmuss (1974) noted, social policy should be concerned with 'social growth', that is with 'indicators that cannot be measured, cannot be quantified, but relate to the texture of relationships between human beings' (p. 150).

A moment's thought will suffice to demonstrate that in western capitalist societies there appears to be an inverse relationship between the performance of valuable work and remuneration. The kinds of activities that give value to life include caring, nurturing, protecting the physical and social environment, conflict resolution, community building, cultural production, educating, convivialising, etc. Such things as these, more than any others, are what contribute to the 'texture of human relationships'. Most of these activities are engaged in outside of work, many have been traditionally regarded as 'women's work'. They are what we do for and with our family and friends, in voluntary association with others, for fun and pleasure or out of a sense of concern. This is truly the welfare society, and the more impoverished this society the more we are driven to satisfy our emotional needs through forms which simulate the social.

I would suggest that in advanced capitalist societies we have striven to overcome material scarcity by generating a new form of poverty. In Britain and other European countries today there exists a barely repressed suspicion that the pursuit of material abundance has been achieved at the expense of the poverty of social relationships. The point is that productivist societies corrupt and undermine their own social fabrics while also destroying the fabric of the natural environment which surrounds them. Global inequalities, and the ecologically destructive lifestyles that sustain and reproduce such inequalities can only be addressed when the populations of advanced capitalist societies abandon their present commitment to unsustainable growth. But this cannot be done in the absence of an alternative and practically expressed vision of the good society.

Distribution, recognition and the realisation of human powers

Nancy Fraser argues that the struggle for justice in the twentieth century has evolved from one which hinged upon questions of redistribution, to one which now also focuses upon the struggle for recognition. This is a really helpful argument, my only criticism is that this way of thinking overlooks the importance of the generative impulse to both forms of politics. The realisation of latent human powers through new kinds of freedom and new forms of social relations lies at the heart of much Marxist, anarchist and green thinking, and has done for well over a century.

In contrast, British social democracy has been preoccupied with distributivist issues more or less since its inception. At times this has drawn the British left towards a narrow materialism, one which equates justice with the fair allocation of resources within the confines of the nation state. This preoccupation has eclipsed a broader view of the good society which focuses upon the quality of social relations between men and women, between generations, between and within families and communities, and between the users of welfare services and those who design and deliver them. When Titmuss talked of the 'texture of human relationships' he glimpsed the possibility that social policy might have something vital to say about the kind of world we want to live in. A quarter of a century later and we can see how this texture contributes enormously to an individual's sense of respect, esteem and self-confidence (Honneth, 1995).

In this book I have tried to do two things. I have tried to demonstrate how an understanding of the emotions can illuminate aspects of the struggle for justice as well as care. We cannot understand powerlessness without some sense of how domination gets internalised and becomes a part of our emotional make-up. Nor can we grasp the possibility of non-destructive relations between groups built around different sources of identity without appreciating the role that emotions such as fear and hate play in establishing relations of similarity and difference. I have also sought to illustrate something of the emotional foundation of understanding, dialogue, generosity and care; in other words, the way in which self can facilitate the development of other, that is, how we can make each other strong. But in exploring these issues I hope I have undertaken my second task, that is, to have revealed something about what contributes to the quality of human relations, the essential precondition for human recognition and development.

We have lived for too long in a society which pays lip service to our social, emotional and aesthetic needs and reduces welfare to a simple matter of consumption. In this last chapter I have tried to illuminate some of the best things we are capable of. The idea of the gift and the desire to give, the capacity for concern, the idea of the gift that seeks no return, the processes of gift exchange and the affirmation and celebration of social relationships as an end in themselves rather than a means to an end. All of these are central to the idea of society as an interdependent community of friends and strangers. I would argue that it is this that brings out the best in us.

References

Albrecht, L. & Brewer, R. (1990) *Bridges of Power: Women's Multicultural Initiatives*, Philadelphia: New Society.

Alford, C.F. (1994) *Group Psychology & Political Theory*, New Haven: Yale University Press.

Alford, D. (1975) *Health Care Politics: Ideological & Interest Group Barriers to Reform*. Chicago: University of Chicago Press.

Alperin, D. (1990) 'Social diversity and the necessity of alliances: a developing feminist perspective', in L. Albrecht & R. Brewer (eds) *Bridges of Power: Women's Multicultural Initiatives*, Philadelphia: New Society.

Anderson, B. (1983) *Imagined Communities: Reflections on the Origins and Spread of Nationalism*, London: Verso.

Anderson, P. (1977) *The Antinomies of Antonio Gramsci*, New Left Review, 100: 5–78.

Anderson, R. (ed.) (1992) *Clinical Lectures on Klein & Bion*, London: Tavistock/ Routledge.

Anthias, F. (1990) 'Race and class Revisited – conceptualising race and racisms', *Sociological Review*, 38, 1: 19–43.

Argyris, C. & Schon, D. (1974) *Organisational Learning*, Addison-Wesley.

Argyris, C. (1976) *Increasing Leadership Effectiveness*, New York: John Wiley & Sons.

Argyris, C. (1977) 'Double loop learning in organisations', *Harvard Business Review*, Sept/Oct: 115–125.

Armstrong, D. (1992) 'Names, thoughts and lies: the relevance of Bion's later writing for understanding experiences in groups', *Free Associations*, 26: 261–282.

Arnstein, S.(1971) 'A ladder of participation in the USA', *Journal of the Royal Town Planning Institute*, April, 176–182.

Arthur, C. (1970) 'Editor's introduction', K. Marx & F. Engels, *The German Ideology*, London: Lawrence & Wishart.

Axelrod, R. (1984) *The Evolution of Co-operation*, New York: Basic Books.

Bacharach, P. & Baratz, M.(1962) 'Two Faces of Power', *American Political Science Review*, 56: 947–52

Baldwin, P. (1990) *The Politics of Social Solidarity*, Cambridge University Press.

Ball, S. (1993) 'Education Policy, Power Relations & Teachers' Work', *British Journal of Educational Studies*, 41, 2: 106–121.

Barnes, M. & Walker, A. (1996) 'Consumerism versus empowerment: a principled approach to the involvement of older service users', *Policy & Politics* 24, 4: 375–392.

Barthes, R. (1973) *Mythologies*, St.Albans: Paladin.

Bateson, G. (1973) *Steps Towards an Ecology of Mind*, Paladin.

Baudrillard, J. (1983) 'The ecstacy of communication', in H. Foster (ed.) *The Anti-aesthetic*, Port Townsend, WA: Bay Press.

Bauman, S. (1992) 'Soil, blood and identity', *Sociological Review*, 40: 675–701.

Beck, U. (1992) *Risk Society: Towards a New Modernity*, London: Sage.

Benhabib, S. & Dallmayr, F. (1990) *The Communicative Ethics Controversy*, Cambridge Mass: MIT Press.

Benhabib, S. (1990) 'Afterword: Communicative Ethics and Contemporary Controversies in Practical Philosophy' in S. Benhabib & F. Dallmayr *The Communicative Ethics Controversy*, Cambridge Mass: MIT Press.

Benhabib, S. (1992) *Situating the Self: Gender, Community and Postmodernism in Contemporary Ethics*, Cambridge: Polity Press.

Benvenuto, B. & Kennedy, R. (1986) *The Works of Jacques Lacan*, London: Free Association Books.

Benjamin, J. (1988) *The Bonds of Love*, N.York: Pantheon.

Benjamin, J. (1994) 'The shadow of the other (subject): intersubjectivity and feminist theory', *Constellations*, 1, 2: 231–54.

Bick, E. (1968) 'Experience of the skin in early object relations', *International Journal of Psycho-Analysis*, 49: 484–6.

Bick, E. (1986) Further considerations on the function of the skin in early object relations', *British Journal of Psychotherapy*, 2, 4: 292–9.

Bion, W. (1957) 'Differentiation of the psychotic from the non-psychotic personalities', *International Journal of Psycho-Analysis*, 38: 266–75.

Bion, W. (1961) *Experiences in Groups*, London: Tavistock.

Bion, W. (1962) *Learning from Experience*, London: Heinemann.

Bion, W. (1967) *Second Thoughts*, London: Heinemann.

Bion, W. (1970) *Attention and Interpretation*, London: Tavistock.

Bishop, J. & Hoggett, P. (1986) *Organising Around Enthusiasms: Mutual Aid in Leisure*, London: Comedia.

Blau, P. (1964) *Exchange & Power in Social Life*, New York: Wiley & Sons.

Blauner, R. (1964) *Alienation & Freedom*, Chicago: University of Chicago Press.

Bleandonu, G. (1994) *Wilfred Bion: His Life & Works 1897–1979*, London: Free Association Books.

Bollas, C. (1987) *The Shadow of the Object: Psychoanalysis of the Unthought Known*, London: Free Association Books.

Bookchin, M. (1992) *Urbanization Without Cities: the Rise & Decline of Citizenship*, Montreal: Black Rose Books.

Bott Spillius, E. (1988a) *Melanie Klein Today: Developments in Theory & Practice. Vol 1: Mainly Theory*, London: Routledge.

Bott Spillius, E. (1988b) *Melanie Klein Today: Developments in Theory & Practice. Vol 2: Mainly Practice*, London: Routledge.

Bott Spillius, E. (1992) 'Clinical experiences of projective identification', in R. Anderson (ed.) *Clinical Lectures on Klein & Bion*, London: Tavistock/Routledge.

Bowden, P. (1997) *Caring: Gender-Sensitive Ethics*, London: Routledge.

Brass, E. & Koziell, S. (1999) *Gathering Force: DIY Culture, Radical Action for those Tired of Waiting*, London: The Big Issue Writers.

Britton, R. (1992) 'Keeping things in mind', in R. Anderson (ed.) *Clinical Lectures on Klein & Bion*, London: Tavistock/Routledge.

Burns, D. (1992) *Poll Tax Rebellion*, Stirling: AK Press.

Burns, D., Hambleton, R. & Hoggett, P. (1994) *The Politics of Decentralisation: Revitalising Local Democracy*, London: Macmillan.

Butler, J. (1990) *Gender Trouble*, New York: Routledge.

Butler, J. (1992) 'Contingent foundations: feminism and the question of modernism', in J. Butler & J. Scott (eds) *Feminists Theorise the Political*, New York: Routledge.

Butler, J. (1998) 'Moral sadism and doubting one's own love: Kleinian reflections on melancholia', in J. Phillips & L. Stonebridge (eds) *Reading Melanie Klein*, London: Routledge.

Carter, J. (ed.) (1998) *Postmodernity and the Fragmentation of Welfare*, London: Routledge.

Chisholm, M. (1990) 'Britain as a plural society', in M. Chisholm and D. Smith (eds) *Shared Space, Divided Space: Essays on Conflict and Territorial Organisation*, London: Unwin Hyman.

Clarke, J. & Newman, J. (1997) *The Managerial State*, London: Sage.

Clarke, W. (1999) *Activism & Participation: Roles, Relations & Dependencies*, Unpublished PhD thesis. University of Luton.

Clegg, S. (1989) *Frameworks of Power*, London: Sage.

Cochrane, A. (1998) 'Globalism, fragmentation & local welfare citizenship', in J. Carter (ed.) *Postmodernity & the Fragmentation of Welfare*, London: Routledge.

Cohen, S. (1985) *Visions of Social Control*, Cambridge: Polity Press.

Collier, A. (1977) *R.D. Laing: the Philosophy & Politics of Psychotherapy*, Sussex: Harvester.

Cooper, C. & Kelly, M. (1993) 'Occupational stress in Head Teachers: a national UK study', *British Journal of Educational Psychology*, 63: 130–43.

Coote, A. & Pfeffer, N. (1991) *Is Quality Good for You? A Critical Review of Quality Assurance in the Welfare Services*, London: Institute for Public Policy Research.

Davis, M. & Wallbridge, D. (1981) *Boundary & Space: an Introduction to the Work of D.W. Winnicott*, London: Karnac.

Day, G. & Murdoch, J. (1993) 'Locality and community: coming to terms with place', *Sociological Review*, 41, 1: 82–111.

Deakin, N. (1993) 'A Future for collectivism?', in R. Page & J. Baldock (eds) *Social Policy Review*, 5. University of Kent: Social Policy Association.

Dean, H. (1998) 'Popular paradigms & welfare values', *Critical Social Policy*, 55: 131–56.

Dean, H. & Taylor-Gooby, P. (1992) *Dependency Culture: the Explosion of a Myth*, Harvester Wheatsheaf.

Debord, G. (1983) *Society of the Spectacle*, Detroit: Black & Red.

Derrida, J. (1992) 'Given time: the time of the king', *Critical Inquiry*, 18: 161–87.

Dickens, P. (1990) *Society, Locality & Human Nature*, Hemel Hempstead: Harvester Press.

Dore, R. (1983) 'Goodwill & the Spirit of Market Capitalism', *British Journal of Sociology*, 34, 4: 459–82.

Dore, R. (1989) 'Where are we now: musings of an evolutionist', *Work, Employment & Society*, 3, 4: 425–6.

Doyal, L. & Gough, I. (1991) *A Theory of Human Need*, London: Macmillan.

Duncan, S. & Goodwin, M. (1988) *The Local State and Uneven Development*, Cambridge: Polity Press.

Durkheim, E. (1893) *The Division of Labour in Society*, trans. G. Simpson, The Free Press, 1964.

Eade, J. (1990) 'Nationalism and the quest for authenticity: the Bangladeshis in Tower Hamlets', *New Community*, 16, 4: 493–503.

Edwards, R. & Duncan, S. (1997) 'Supporting the family: lone mothers, paid work and the underclass debate', *Critical Social Policy*, 17, 4: 29–49.

Elster, J. (1978) *Logic & Society*, London: Wiley.

Esping-Anderson, G. (1990) *The Three Worlds of Welfare Capitalism*, Cambridge: Polity Press.

Etzioni, A. (1961) *A Comparative Analysis of Complex Organisations*, Glencoe: Free Press.

Fannon, F. (1967) *Black Skin, White Masks*, New York: Grove Press.

Finch, J. & Mason, J. (1993) *Negotiating Family Responsibilities*, London: Routledge.

Flax, J. (1990) *Thinking Fragments: Psychoanalysis, Feminism & Postmodernism in the Contemporary West*, Berkeley: University of California Press.

Flax, J. (1993) *Disputed Subjects: Essays on Psychoanalysis, Politics & Philosophy*, Routledge.

Foster, D. & Taylor, G.(1994) *Privatisation and Public Service Trade Unionism*, Occasional Papers in Sociology, Bristol: University of the West of England.

Foster, D. & Hoggett, P. (1999) 'Change in the Benefits Agency: empowering the exhausted worker?', *Work, Employment & Society*, 13, 1: 19–39.

Foucault, M. (1982) 'Afterword: the subject & power', in H. Dreyfus & P. Rabinow (eds) *Michel Foucault: Beyond Structuralism & Hermeneutics*, Brighton: Harvester.

Fox, A. (1974) *Beyond Contract: Work, Power & Trust Relations*, London: Faber.

Fraser, N. (1995) 'From redistribution to recognition? Dilemmas of justice in a "post-socialist" age', *New Left Review*, 212: 68–92.

Freidson, E. (1994) *Professionalism Reborn: Theory, Prophecy & Policy*, Cambridge: Polity Press.

French, W. & Bell, C. (1978) *Organisational Development: Behavioural Science Interventions for Organisational Improvement*. 4th ed. Prentice-Hall.

Freud, S. (1914) *On Narcissism: an Introduction*, S.E., 14, pp. 67–102.

Freud, S. (1917) *Mourning & Melancholia*, S.E., 14, pp. 237–58.

Freud, S. (1920) *Beyond the Pleasure Principle*, S.E., 18, pp. 3–64.

Freud, S. (1923) *The Ego & the Id*, S.E., 19, pp. 3–66.

Freud, S. (1927) *The Future of an Illusion*, S.E., 21, pp. 3–56.

Freud, S. (1933) *New Introductory Lectures on Psychoanalysis*, S.E., 22, pp. 1–182.

Friere, P.(1970) *Cultural Action for Freedom*, London: Penguin

Fritze, C.(1982) *Because I Speak Cockney They Think I'm Stupid*, London: Association of Community Workers.

Fuller, P. (1980) *Art & Psychoanalysis*, London: Readers & Writers Publishing Cooperative.

Gallie, D. & Vogler, C. (1990) 'Unemployment & attitudes to work', *Social Change and Economic Life Initiative: Working Paper 18*, Oxford: Nuffield College.

Gibson, D. (1995) 'User rights and the frail aged', *Journal of Applied Philosophy*, 12, 1: 1–11.

Giddens, A. (1971) *Capitalism & Modern Social Theory: an analysis of the writings of Marx, Durkheim and Max Weber*, Cambridge University Press.

Giddens, A. (1984) *The Constitution of Society*, Polity Press.

Giddens, A. (1991) *Modernity & Self-Identity: Self & Society in the Late Modern Age*, Cambridge: Polity Press.

Giddens, A. (1994) *Beyond Left & Right: The Future of Radical Politics*, Cambridge: Polity Press.

Glass, J. (1989) *Private Terror/Public Life*, New York: Cornell University Press.

Gorz, A. (1985) *Paths to Paradise: On the Liberation from Work*, London: Pluto Press.

Gouldner, A. (1960) 'The norm of reciprocity: a preliminary statement', *American Sociological Review*, 25, 2: 161–78.

Gramsci, A. (1977) *The Prison Notebooks*, London: Lawrence & Wishart.

Granovetter, M. (1985) 'Economic action & social structure: the problem of embeddeness', *American Journal of Sociology*, 91, 3: 481–510.

Gray, J. (1993) *Beyond the New Right: markets, government and the common environment*, London: Routledge.

Gray, J. (1983) 'Classical Liberalism, positional goals and the politicisation of poverty', in A. Ellis & K. Kumar (eds) *Dilemmas of Liberal Democracies*, London: Tavistock.

Gribbins, J. (1998) 'Postmodernism, post-structuralism and social policy', in J. Carter (ed.) *Postmodernity & the Fragmentation of Welfare*, London: Routledge.

Gufstafson, J. (1979) 'The pseudomutual small group or institution', in G. Lawrence (ed.) *Exploring Individual and Organisational Boundaries*. John Wiley & Sons.

Habermas, J. (1970) 'Toward a theory of communicative competence', *Inquiry*, 13: 360–75.

Habermas (1972) *Knowledge & Human Interests*, trans. J. Shapiro, London: Heinemann Educational.

Habermas, J. (1983) *The Theory of Communicative Action*, Oxford: Polity Press.

Habermas, J. (1984) *Reason and the Rationalization of Society*, London: Heinemann Educational.

Hall, S. (1988) *The Hard Road to Renewal*, London: Verso.

Hall, S. (1990) 'Cultural Identity and Diaspora', in Rutherford, J. (ed.) *Identity, Community, Culture, Difference*, London: Lawrence and Wishart.

Hamilton, A., McCourtney, C., Anderson, T. and Finn, A. (1990) *Polarised Communities*, Centre for the Study of Conflict: University of Ulster.

Halmos, P. (1970) *The Personal Service Society*, London: Constable.

Harre, R. (1979) *Social Being*, Oxford: Blackwell.

Havel, V. (1989) *Living in Truth*, London: Faber.

Havel, V. (1992) *Summer Meditations*, London: Faber.

Harrison, L., Hoggett, P. & Jeffers, S. (1995) 'Race, ethnicity and community development', *Community Development Journal*, 30, 2: 144–57.

Hilyard, P. & Watson, S. (1996) 'Postmodern social policy: a contradiction in terms?', *Journal of Social Policy*, 25, 3: 312–346.

Hinshelwood, D. (1987) *What Happens in Groups?*, London: Free Association Books.

Hinshelwood, R.D. (1989) 'Social possession of identity', in B. Richards (ed.) *Crises of the Self*, London: Free Association Books.

Hirschman, O. (1970) *Exit, Voice & Loyalty*, Cambridge, Mass: Harvard University Press.

Hirst, P. (1994) *Associative Democracy: New Forms of Economic and Social Governance*, Oxford: Polity Press.

Hockey, J. & James, A. (1993) *Growing Up & Growing Old: Aging & Dependency in the Life Course*, London: Sage.

Hofstede, G. (1991) *Cultures & Organisations: Software of the Mind*, McGraw-Hill.

Hoggett, P. (1984) 'Decentralisation, Labourism and the professionalised state apparatus', in R. Hambleton & P. Hoggett (eds) *The Politics of Decentralisation*, Bristol: SAUS Working Paper No. 46.

Hoggett, P., Lawrence, S. & Fudge, C. (1984) 'The politics of decentralisation in Hackney, in R. Hambleton & P. Hoggett (eds) *The Politics of Decentralisation*, Bristol: SAUS Working Paper No. 46.

Hoggett, P. & Lousada, J. (1985) 'Therapeutic intervention in working class communities', *Free Associations*, 1: 125–52.

Hoggett, P and Bishop, J. (1985) *The Social Organisation of Leisure: a Study of Groups in their Voluntary Sector Context*, Sports Council/ESRC.

Hoggett, P. & Hambleton, R. (1987) 'Decentralisation and Democracy', *Occasional Paper No. 26*, School for Advanced Urban Studies: University of Bristol.

Hoggett, P. & McGill, I. (1988) 'Labourism: means & ends', *Critical Social Policy*, 23: 22–33.

Hoggett, P. (1989) 'The labour of love' and 'a primary social medium': two problematics in contemporary psychoanalysis', Free Associations, 15: 87–107.

Hoggett, P. (1990) 'Modernisation, political strategy and the welfare state,' *Studies in Decentralisation and Quasi-Markets No.2*, Bristol:School for Advanced Urban Studies.

Hoggett, P. (1992) *Partisans in an Uncertain World: the Psychoanalysis of Engagement*, London: Free Association Books.

Hoggett, P. (1993) 'What is community mental health?', *Journal of Interprofessional Care*, 7, 3, 201–9.

Hoggett, P. (1996) 'New modes of control in the public service', *Public Administration*, 74: 9–32.

Hoggett, P. (1997) 'Human responses to destructive regimes', in E. Smith (ed.) *Mental Health in the Marketplace*, London: Routledge.

Hogget, P. & Thompson, S. (1998) 'The delivery of welfare: the associationist vision', in J. Carter (ed.) *Postmodernity and the Fragmentation of Welfare*, London: Routledge.

Hoggett, P. (1999) 'The city and the life force' in L. Nystrom (ed.) *City & Culture*, Stockholm: Swedish Urban Environment Council.

Homans, G. (1950) *The Human Group*, New York: Harcourt, Brace & Co.

Holland, S. & Holland, R. (1984) 'Depressed women: outposts of empire and castles of skin', in B. Richards (ed.) *Capitalism & Infancy*, London: Free Association Books.

Honneth, A. (1995) *The Struggle for Recognition: the Moral Grammar of Social Conflicts*, Cambridge: Polity Press.

bell hooks (1989) *Talking back: thinking feminist, thinking black*, Boston: South End Press.

Husbands, C. (1982) 'East End Racism 1900–1980', *London Journal*, 8, 1.

Hutton, W. (1995) *The State We're In*, London: Jonathan Cape.

Jack, R. (1995) 'Empowerment in community care', in R. Jack (ed.) *Empowerment in Community Care*, London: Chapman & Hall.

Jameson, F. (1983) 'Postmodernism and consumer society', in H. Foster (ed.) *The Anti-Aesthetic: Essays on Postmodern Culture*, Port Townsend, WA: Bay Press.

Jameson, F. (1984) 'Postmodernism, or the cultural logic of late capitalism', *New Left Review*, 146: 53–93.

Jeffers, S., Hoggett, P. & Harrison, L. (1996) 'Race, ethnicity and community in three localities', *New Community*, 22, 1: 111–26.

Jessop, B. (1994) 'The transition to Post-Fordism and the Schumpetarian Workfare State', in R. Burrows & B. Loader (eds) *Towards a Post-Fordist Welfare State?* London: Routledge.

Jones, D. & Mayo, M. (1974) *Community Work One*, London: Routledge & Kegan Paul.

Jordan, B. (1987) *Rethinking Welfare*, Oxford: Blackwell.

Jordan, B. (1989) *The Common Good: Citizenship, Morality & Self Interest*, Oxford: Blackwell.

Joseph Rowntree (1995) *The Joseph Rowntree Inquiry into Income & Wealth, Vol 2*, York: Joseph Rowntree Foundation.

Jowers, P., Dürrschmidt, J., O'Docherty, R. and Purdue, D. (1999) 'Affective & aesthetic dimensions of contemporary social movements in South West England', *Innovation*, 12, 1: 99–118.

Kakabadse, A. & Parker, C. (1984) *Power, Politics & Organisations*, John Wiley.

Kermode, F. (1967) *The Sense of an Ending*, London: Oxford University Press.

Khan, M. (1974) *The Privacy of the Self*, London: Hogarth.

Kikert, W. (1993) 'Autopoiesis and the science of (Public) Administration: essence, sense & nonsense', *Organisational Studies*, 14, 2: 261–78.

Kikert, W. (1995) 'Steering at a distance: a new paradigm of public governance in Dutch Higher Education', *Governance*, 8, 1: 135–215.

Kirkpatrick, T. (1996) 'Postmodernism, welfare and radical politics', *Journal of Social Policy*, 25, 3: 303–20.

Kittay, E. & Meyers, D. (eds) (1987) *Women & Moral Theory*, USA, Rowman & Littlefield.

Klein, M. (1935) 'A contribution to the psychogenesis of manic-depressive states', in Melanie Klein, *Contributions to Psycho-Analysis, 1921–1945*, London: Hogarth, 1948.

Klein, M. (1946) 'Notes on some schizoid mechanisms', in Melanie Klein, *The Writings of Melanie Klein, Vol. 3*, London: Hogarth Press, 1975.

Klein, M. (1952) 'Some theoretical conclusions on the emotional life of the infant', in M. Klein, P. Heimann, S. Isaacs & R. Riviere *Developments in Psychoanalysis*, London: Hogarth Press.

Klein, M. (1958) 'On the development of mental functioning', *International Journal of Psychoanalysis*, 39: 84–90. (Reprinted in: *Envy, Gratitude & Other Works*, London: Hogarth Press 1975).

Klein, M. (1964) 'Love Guilt & Reparation' in M. Klein & J. Riviere *Love, Hate & Reparation*, New York: W. W. Norton & Co.

Kohon, G. (1986) *The British School of Psychoanalysis: the Independent Tradition*, London: Free Association Books.

Kouzes, J. & Mico, P. (1979) 'Domain theory: an introduction to organisational behaviour in human service organisations', *Journal of Applied Behavioural Science*, 15, 4.

Kriese, H. Koopmans, R. Duyvendak, J. & Giugni, M. (1995) *New Social Movements in Western Europe*, London: UCL Press.

Kuhn, T. (1970) *The Structure of Scientific Revolutions*, 2nd ed. University Chicago Press.

Lacan, J. (1977) 'The Mirror Stage', in *Ecrits: a Selection*, trans. Alan Sheridan, New York: W. W. Norton & Co.

Lacan, J. (1988) *The Seminar of Jacques Lacan: Book II, The Ego in Freud's Theory and in the Technique of Psychoanalysis 1954–1955*, trans. Sylvana Tomaselli, New York: W.W. Norton & Co.

Laclau, E. & Mouffe, C. (1987) 'Post Marxism without apologies', *New Left Review*, 166: 79–106.

Laing, R.D. (1960) *The Divided Self*, London: Tavistock.

Laing, R.D. (1961) *Self & Others*, London: Tavistock.

Laing, R.D. (1962) 'Series & nexus in the family', *New Left Review*, 15, May/June.

Laing, R.D. (1970) *The Politics of Experience*, Harmondsworth: Penguin.

Laing, R.D. & Esterson, A. (1964) *Sanity, Madness & the Family*, London: Tavistock.

Laing, R.D., Phillipson, H. & Lee, A. (1966) *Interpersonal Perception: a Theory & Method of Research*, London: Tavistock.

Laplanche, J. & Pontalis, J.P. (1973) *The Language of Psycho Analysis*, London: Hogarth.

Lasch, C. (1978) *The Culture of Narcissism*, New York: Norton.

Lasch, C. (1985) *The Minimal Self: Psychic Survival in Troubled Times*, Pan Books.

Lawrence, E. (1982) 'Just Plain Common Sense: The roots of racism', in The Centre for Contemporary Cultural Studies: *The Empire Strikes Back*, Hutchinson.

Leonard, P. (1997) *Postmodern Welfare: Reconstructing an Emancipatory Project*, London: Sage.

R. Levitas (1998) *The Inclusive Society? Social Exclusion & New Labour*, London: Macmillan.

Lindow, V. & Morris, J. (1995) *Service User Involvement: Synthesis of Findings & Experience in the field of Community Care*, York: Joseph Rowntree Foundation.

London-Edinburgh Weekend Return Group (1980) *In and Against the State*, 2nd ed. London: Pluto.

Lowe, J. & Oliver, N. (1991) 'The high commitment workplace: two cases from a high-tec company, *Work, Employment & Society*, 5, 3: 437–50.

Lukes, S. (1974) *Power: a Radical View*, London: Macmillan.

Malinowski, B. (1932) *Crime & Custom in Savage Society*, London:Paul, Trench, Trubner.

Mannoni, M. (1973) *The Child, his 'Illness' & the others*, Penguin University Press.

Marshall, T.H. (1963) 'Citizenship & Social Class', in *Sociology at the Crossroads*, London: Heinemann.

Martin, L. (1994) 'A case study of user involvement and advocacy in "community care" in Wiltshire', in P. Hoggett & L. Martin, *Consumer-Oriented Action in the Public Services: National Report for the United Kingdom, Working*

Paper WP/94/23/EN, Dublin: European Foundation for the Improvement of Living and Working Conditions.

Marx, K. (1970) *The Economic & Philosophical Manuscripts*, London: Lawrence & Wishart.

Marx, K. (1970) *Capital*, Vol. I. London: Lawrence & Wishart.

Marx, K. (1974) *Capital*. Vol. 3, London: Lawrence & Wishart.

Marx, K. & Engels, F. (1970) *The German Ideology*, London: Lawrence & Wishart.

Mauss, M. (1954) *The Gift: Forms & Functions of Exchange in Archaic Societies*, trans I. Cunnison. London: Cohen & West.

McCarthy, T. (1991) *Ideals & Illusions: On Reconstruction and Deconstruction in Contemporary Political Theory*, Cambridge Mass: MIT Press.

McDougall, J. (1986) *Theatres of the Mind: Illusion & Truth on the Psychoanalytic Stage*, London: Free Association Books.

Meltzer, D. (1968) 'Terror, persecution and dread – a dissection of paranoid anxieties', *International Journal of Psychoanalysis*, 49: 396–401.

Meltzer, D. (1975) 'Dimensionality in mental functioning', in D. Meltzer, J. Bremmer, S. Hoxter, D. Weddel, I. Wittenberg (eds) *Explorations in Autism*, Perthshire: Clunie Press.

Meltzer, D. (1978) *The Kleinian Development: Part III, The Clinical Significance of the Work of Bion*, Perthshire: Clunie Press.

Meltzer, D. (1986) 'Family patterns and cultural educability', in D. Meltzer and others *Studies in Extended Metapsychology: Clinical Application of Bion's Ideas*, Perthshire: Clunie Press.

Melucci, A. (1989) *Nomads of the Present*, London: Radius.

Mendus, S. (1993) 'Different voices, still lives: problems in the ethics of care', *Journal Applied Philosophy*, 10, 1: 17–27.

Menzies, I. (1960) 'A case-study in the functioning of social systems as a defence against anxiety', *Human Relations*, 13: 95–121.

Menzies I. (1987) *Containing Anxiety in Institutions*, London: Free Association Books.

Meszaros, I. (1970) *Marx's Theory of Alienation*, London: Merlin Press.

Miller, C. (1996) *Public Service Trade Unionism & Radical Politics*, Aldershot: Dartmouth.

Mitchell, J. (ed.) (1986) *The Selected Melanie Klein*, Harmondsworth: Penguin.

Morley, D. & Robins, K. (1990) 'No place like Heimat: images of home(land) in european culture', *New Formations*, 12: 1–23.

Morris, J. (1997) 'Care or empowerment? a disability rights perspective', *Social Policy & Administration*, 31, 1: 54–60.

Morrison, T. (1988) *Beloved*, Pan Books.

New, C. (1996) *Agency, Health & Social Survival*, London: Taylor & Francis.

Norval, A. (1998) 'Memory, identity and the (im)possibility of reconciliation: the work of the Truth & Reconciliation Commission in South Africa', *Constellations*, 5, 2: 250–63.

Novak, T. (1997) 'Handling delinquents: the introduction of the Job Seekers Allowance', *Critical Social Policy*, 17, 1: 99–109.

Nussbaum, M. (1986) *The Fragility of Goodness, Luck & Ethics in Greek Tragedy & Philosophy*, Cambridge University Press.

Obholzer, A. (1994) 'Managing social anxieties in public sector organisations', in A. Obholzer & V.Z. Roberts *The Unconscious at Work: Individual & Organisational Stress in the Human Services*, London: Routledge.

Obholzer, A. & Roberts, V.Z. (1994) *The Unconscious at Work: Individual and Organisational Stress in the Human Services*, London: Routledge.

Offe, C. (1984) *Contradictions of the Welfare State*, London: Hutchinson.

Offe, C. (1992) 'A non-productivist design for social policies', in P. Van Parijs (ed.) *Arguing for Basic Income*, London: Verso.

Offe, C. (1994) *Disorganised Capitalism: Contemporary Transformations of Work & Politics*, Cambridge: Polity Press.

Offe, C. & Heinze, R. (1992) *Beyond Employment: Time, Work and the Informal Economy*, Cambridge: Polity Press.

Ogden, T. (1979) 'On projective identification', *International Journal of Psycho-Analysis*, 60: 357–73.

Ogden, T. (1986) *The Matrix of the Mind: Object Relations and the Psychoanalytic Dialogue*, Northvale, NJ: Jason Aronson.

Ogden, T. (1992) *The Primitive Edge of Experience*, London: Maresfield Library.

Ollman, B. (1971) *Alienation: Marx's Concept of Man in Capitalist Society*, London: Cambridge University Press.

Olsson, G. (1984) 'Towards a sermon on modernity', in D. Gregory (ed.) *Recollections of a Revolution*, London: Macmillan.

Omi, M & Winant, H. (1986) *Racial Formation in the United States from the 1960's to the 1980's*, N. York: Routledge & Kegan.

Palazzoli, M., Grillo, S., Selvini, M. & Sorrentino, A.M. (1989) *Family Games: General Models of Psychotic Processes in the Family*, London: Karnac Books.

Pedler, M., Burgoyne, J. & Boydell, T. (1991) *The Learning Company: a Strategy for Sustainable Development*, London: McGraw-Hill.

Peters, T. & Waterman, R. (1982) *In Search of Excellence*, New York: Harper & Row.

Pheterson, G. (1990) 'Alliances between women: overcoming internalised oppression and internalised domination', in L. Albrecht & R. Brewer (eds) *Bridges of Power: Women's Multicultural Initiatives*, Philadelphia: New Society.

Pinker, R. (1977) 'Preface', in D. Reisman, *Richard Titmuss: Welfare & Society*, London: Heinemann.

Puddephat, A. (1987) 'Local state and local community: the Hackney experience', in R. Hambleton & P. Hoggett (eds) *Decentralisation and Democracy*, SAUS Occasional Paper 28, Bristol: School for Advanced Urban Studies.

Puget, S. (1988) 'Social violence & psychoanalysis in Argentina: the unthinkable & the unthought', *Free Associations*, 13: 84–140.

Purdue, D., Dürrschmidt, J., Jowers, P. & O'Docherty, R. (1997) 'DIY Culture, Extended milieux: LETS, veggie boxes & festivals' *Sociological Review*, 45, 645–67.

Raz, D. (1986) *The Morality of Freedom*, Oxford University Press.

Reason, P. (1984) 'Is OD possible in power cultures?', in A. Kakabadse & D. Parker (eds) *Power, Politics & Organisations*, New York: John Wiley.

Rees, D. & Cooper, C. (1992) Occupational stress in health service workers in the UK', *Stress Medicine*, 8: 79–90.

Reich, W. (1972) *The Mass Psychology of Fascism*, Souvenir Press.

Riviere, J. (1936) 'A contribution to the analysis of the negative therapeutic reaction', *International Journal of Psycho-Analysis*, 17: 304–20.

Robinson, S. (1984) 'The parent to the child', in B. Richards (ed.) *Capitalism & Infancy*, London: Free Association Books.

Rodrigue, E. (1956) 'Notes on symbolism', *International Journal of Psycho-Analysis*, 37: 147–58.

Rosenfeld, H. (1971) 'A clinical approach to the psychoanalytic theory of the life and death instincts: an investigation into aggressive aspects of narcissism', *International Journal of Psycho-Analysis*, 52: 169–78.

Rosenfeld, H. (1987) *Impasse and Interpretation*, Andover: Tavistock Publications.

Rustin, M. (1988) 'Shifting paradigms in psychoanalysis since the 1940's', *History Workshop Journal*, 26: 133–42.

Rustin, M. (1991) *The Good Society & the Inner World: Psychoanalysis, Politics & Culture*, London: Verso.

Rustin, M. & Rustin, M. (1984) 'Relational preconditions of socialism', in B. Richards (ed.) *Capitalism & Infancy*, London: Free Association Books.

Sartre, J.P. (1994) *The Anti-Semite and the Jew*, Schocken Books.

Sartre, J.P. (1952) *Saint Genet, comédien et martyr*, Paris: Gallimard.

Sartre, J.P. (1966) *Being & Nothingness*, New York: Washington Square Press.

Sayers, J. (1991) *Mothering Psychoanalysis: Helene Deutsch, Karen Horney, Anna Freud & Melanie Klein*, Harmondsworth: Penguin.

Sedgwick, P. (1982) *Psycho Politics*, London: Pluto.

Segal, H. (1973) *Introduction to the Work of Melanie Klein*, London: Hogarth Press.

Segal, H. (1986) *The Work of Hanna Segal: a Kleinian Approach to Clinical Practice*, London: Free Association Books.

Schein, E. & Greiner, L. (1977) 'Can organisational development be fine tuned to bureaucracies?', *Organisational Dynamics*, 5, 3: 48–61.

Schlosberg, (1995) 'Communicative action in practice: intersubjectivity & new social movements', *Political Studies*, XLIII: 291–311.

Scull, A. (1996) 'Asylums: utopias & realities', in D. Tomlinson & J. Carrier (eds) *Asylum in the Community*, London: Routledge.

Segal, H. (1972) 'A delusional system as a defence against the re-emergence of a catastrophic situation', *International Journal of Psycho-Analysis*, 53: 393–401.

Sennett, R. (1998) *The Corrosion of Character*, N. York: W.W. Norton.

Shilling, C. (1997) 'The undersocialised conception of the embodied agent in modern sociology', *Sociology*, 31, 4: 737–54.

Shields, D. (1989) 'Social spatialization and the built environment: the West Edmonton Mall', *Environment & Planning D: Society & Space*, 7, 147–64.

Sibley, D. (1988) 'Purification of space', *Environment & Planning D: Society & Space*, 6: 409–21.

Sinason, V. (1989) 'The psycholinguistics of discrimination', in B. Richards (ed.) *Crises of the Self*, London: Free Association Books.

Sinason, V. (ed.) (1994) *Treating Survivors of Satanist Abuse*, London: Routledge.

Sivanandan (1990) 'All that melts into air is solid: the hokum of New Times', *Race & Class*, 31, 3: 1–30.

Sloterdijk, P. (1984) 'Cynicism – the twilight of false consciousness', *New German Critique*, 33: 190–206.

Soetters, J. (1986) 'Excellent companies as social movements', *Journal of Management Studies*, 23, 3: 299–312.

Sorokin, P. (1954) *The Ways of Power & Love*, Boston: Beacon Press.

Spender, D. (1981) 'The gatekeepers: a feminist critique of academic publishing', in H. Roberts (ed.) *Doing Feminist Research*, Routledge & Kegan Paul.

Spicker, P. (1993) 'Can European social policy be universalist?' in R. Page & J. Baldock (eds) *Social Policy Review: 5*, University of Kent: Social Policy Association.

Spicker, P. (1993) 'Understanding particularism', *Critical Social Policy*, 39: 5–20.

Stacey, M. (1969) 'The myth of community studies', *British Journal of Sociology*, 20, 2: 134–47.

Standing, G. (1992) 'The need for a new social consensus', in P. Van Parijs (ed.) *Arguing for Basic Income*, London: Verso.

Steiner, J. (1993) *Psychic Retreats*, London: Routledge.

Stokes, J. (1994) 'Institutional chaos & personal stress', in A. Obholzer & V.Z. Roberts (eds) *The Unconscious at Work*, London: Routledge.

Stokes, J. (1994) 'The unconscious at work in groups & teams: contributions from the work of Wilfred Bion', in A. Obholzer & V. Roberts (eds) *The Unconscious at Work*, London: Routledge.

Sutherland, V. & Cooper, C. (1992) 'Job stress, satisfaction and mental health', *British Medical Journal*, 30: 1545–8.

Suttles, G.D. (1972) *The Social Construction of Communities*, Chicago: University of Chicago Press.

Symington, N. (1986) *The Analytic Experience: Lectures from the Tavistock*, London: Free Association Books.

Szekacs, J. (1985) 'Impaired spatial structures', *International Journal of Psycho-Analysis*, 66: 193–9.

Taylor, D. (1998) 'Social identity & social policy: engagements with postmodern theory *Journal of Social Policy*, 27, 3: 329–50.

Taylor-Gooby, P. (1994) 'Postmodernism and social policy: a great leap backwards?', *Journal of Social Policy*, 23, 3: 385–404.

Taylor-Gooby, P. (1999) 'Bipolar bugbears', *Journal of Social Policy*, 28, 2: 299–303.

Temperley, J. (1984) 'Settings for psychotherapy', *British Journal of Psychotherapy*, 1, 2: 101–12.

Thompson, S. & Hoggett, P. (1996) 'Universalism, selectivism & particularism: towards a post-modern social policy', *Critical Social Policy*, 16, 1: 21–43.

Timpanaro, S. (1975) *On Materialism*, London: New Left Books.

Titmuss, R. (1950) *Problems of Social Policy*, London: HMSO/Longmans.

Titmuss, R. (1968) *Commitment to Welfare*, London: George Allen & Unwin.

Titmuss, R. (1976) *Commitment to Welfare*, 2nd ed. Allen & Unwin.

Titmuss, R. (1974) *Social Policy: an Introduction*, London, George Allen & Unwin.

Titmuss, R. (1971) *The Gift Relationship*, London: Pantheon Books.

Tonnies, F. (1887) *Community & Association*, trans. C. Loomis, Routledge & Kegan Paul, 1974.

Touraine, A. (1981) *The Voice & the Eye*, Cambridge: Cambridge University Press.

Tseelon, E. (1992) 'Is the presented self sincere? Goffman, impression management and the postmodern self', *Theory, Culture & Society*, 9, 2: 115–28.

Vaihinger, H. (1924) *The Philosophy of 'As if': a System of the Theoretical,*

Practical & Religious Fictions of Mankind, trans. C.K. Ogden, London: Kegan Paul, Trench, Trubner & Co.

Van Parijs, P. (1993) *Marxism Recycled*, Cambridge: Cambridge University Press.

Van der Veen, R. & Van Parijs, P. (1987) 'Universal grants versus socialism: reply to six critics', *Theory & Society*, 15: 723–757.

Wall, D. (1999) *Earth First! And the Anti-Roads Movement*, London: Routledge.

Wallman, S. (1984) *Eight London Households*, London: Tavistock.

Watson, D. (1980) *Caring for Strangers*, London: Routledge & Kegan Paul.

Watzlawick, P., Beavin, J. & Jackson, D. (1968) *The Pragmatics of Human Communication*, Faber.

Weber, M. (1922) 'The social psychology of world religions', in H. Girth & C.W. Mills (eds) *From Max Weber: Essays in Sociology*, Routledge & Kegan Paul, 1948.

Weeks, J. (1991) *Against Nature: Essays on History, Sexuality & Identity*, London: Rivers Oram Press.

Whitebook, J. (1994) 'Hypostatizing thanatos: Lacan's analysis of the ego', *Constellations*, 1, 2: 214–230.

Whitebook, J. (1995) *Perversion & Utopia: a Study in Psychoanalysis and Critical Theory*, MIT Press.

Wilden, A. (1972) *System & Structure: Essays on Communication & Exchange*, London: Tavistock.

Wilding, P. (1982) *Professional Power & Social Welfare*. Routledge & Kegan Paul.

Williams, F. (1989) *Social Policy: A Critical Introduction*. Polity Press.

Williams, F. (1998) 'Good-enough principles for welfare', paper to the Open University 'Rethinking Social Policy' Group, Open University: December.

Williams, F. (2000) *New Principles for Welfare*, Cambridge: Polity Press.

Winant, H. (1994) *Racial Conditions: Politics, Theory, Comparisons*, Minneapolis: University of Minneapolis Press.

Winnicott, D.W. (1947) 'Hate in the countertransference', in Winnicott, *Through Paediatrics to Psychoanalysis*, 1975. London: Hogarth Press.

Winnicott, D.W. (1950) 'Aggression in relation to emotional development', in Winnicott, *Through Paediatrics to Psychoanalysis*, 1958. London: Hogarth Press.

Winnicott, D.W. (1951) 'Transitional objects and transitional phenomena', in Winnicott, *Playing & Reality*. 1971. London: Tavistock.

Winnicott, D.W. (1958) 'The capacity to be alone', in *The Maturational Processes and the Facilitating Environment*, 1965, London: Hogarth Press.

Winnicott, D.W. (1971) *Playing & Reality*, London: Tavistock.

Wirth, L. (1964) *On Cities and Social Life: Selected Papers*, ed. A. Reiss. Chicago: Chicago University Press.

Wistow, G. & Barnes, M. (1993) 'User involvement in community care: origins, purposes & applications', *Public Administration*, 71: 279–99.

Wrong, D. (1961) 'The oversocialised conception of man in modern sociology', *American Sociological Review*, 26, 2: 183–93.

Young, I.M. (1996) 'Communication and the other: beyond deliberative democracy', in S. Benhabib (ed.) *Democracy & Difference*, Princeton: Princeton University Press.

Young, I.M. (1997) 'Asymmetrical reciprocity: on moral respect, wonder, and enlarged thought', *Constellations*, 3, 3: 340–363.

Young, R. (1994) *Mental Space*, London: Process Press.

Zand, D. (1972) 'Trust & managerial problem solving', *Administrative Science Quarterly*, 17, 2: 229–39.

Zizek, S. (1990) 'Eastern Europe's republics of Gilead', *New Left Review*, 183: 50–62.

Index